Polarized America

Polarized America

The Dance of Ideology and
Unequal Riches

Nolan McCarty, Keith T.
Poole, and Howard Rosenthal

The MIT Press
Cambridge, Massachusetts
London, England

MIT Press books may be purchased at special quantity discounts for business or sales promotional use. For information, please email special_sales@mitpress.mit.edu or write to Special Sales Department, The MIT Press, 55 Hayward Street, Cambridge, MA 02142.

This book was set in Palatino on 3B2 by Asco Typesetters, Hong Kong and was printed and bound in the United States of America.

Library of Congress Cataloging-in-Publication Data

McCarty, Nolan M.
Polarized America : the dance of ideology and unequal riches / Nolan McCarty, Keith T. Poole, and Howard Rosenthal.
    p.   cm. — (Walras-Pareto lectures)
Includes bibliographical references and index.
ISBN 0-262-13464-0 (alk. paper)
1. Equality—United States. 2. Polarization (Social sciences) 3. Income distribution—United States. 4. United States—Politics and government—2001– I. Poole, Keith T. II. Rosenthal, Howard. III. Title. IV. Series.

HN90.S6M37   2006
320.973—dc22   2005056753

10   9   8   7   6   5   4   3

From NMc to Janis, Lachlan, and Delaney
From KP to Janice
From HR to Illia, Manu, and Gil

Contents

Acknowledgments

Work on this book officially started almost a decade ago when Howard Rosenthal gave the Walras-Pareto lectures, based in part on our joint work, at the University of Lausanne. He is very grateful for the warm reception from his hosts, particularly Alberto Holly, Damien Neven, and Elu von Thadden, and for Alberto's persistence in insisting that the book be finished.

The intellectual origins of the book are even older. Our central obligation is to the analytical approach to politics that developed in the 1960s and 1970s at four universities, Carnegie Mellon, the University of Rochester, Washington University in St. Louis, and the California Institute of Technology. Rosenthal owes much to the stimulus of his early colleagues at Carnegie Tech—Otto Davis, Melvin Hinich, James Laing, and Peter Ordeshook—and to his later collaborators Thomas Romer, Thomas Palfrey, and Alberto Alesina.

Keith Poole was the most influenced by the Rochester school, as he was trained by the two central figures in the development of the analytical approach, William Riker and Richard McKelvey. McKelvey stopped at Carnegie Mellon on his way to Caltech. Most unfortunately, we have lost both Bill and Dick. We hope they are looking and reading from above.

Nolan McCarty began his research career as a graduate student in the Graduate School of Industrial Adminstration (GSIA) at Carnegie, his dissertation being supervised by Poole and Rosenthal. His interest in American politics was in no small part kindled by Larry Rothenberg, a visitor from Rochester. McCarty's early papers with Poole and with Rothenberg are the origins of the campaign contributions analysis in chapter 5, which also continues work that Poole and Rosenthal conducted with Romer.

Shortly after Poole and Rosenthal began their collaboration, Rosenthal spent a year as a Fairchild Scholar at Caltech. During this stay Poole and Rosenthal wrote their 1984 *Journal of Politics* piece "The Polarization of American Politics," the protoplasm of this book.

Poole's first gig at Carnegie was as one of the two inaugural fellows of the postdoctoral program in political economy at GSIA. This program and some of the research reflected in this book found financial support thanks to the efforts of Alan Meltzer. Many of the other postdoctoral fellows, especially Zeev Maoz, David Austen-Smith, Randy Calvert, Fritz Schneider, Guido Tabellini, Peter Van Doren, Alesina, Jim Snyder, and Rothenberg, were an integral part of our research environment.

As our joint work progressed, we benefited from a lot of release time and research assistance provided by think tanks. McCarty and Rosenthal were both National Fellows at the Hoover Institution. All three of us have been Fellows at the Center for Advanced Study in the Behavioral Sciences. If this book conveys a message successfully, the kudos go to Kathleen Much, the Center's editor *par excellence* (a.k.a. the "Book Doctor"). Rosenthal was also a Visiting Scholar at the Russell Sage Foundation, where sitting next to Frank Bean would lead to valuable contributions to chapter 4. He and McCarty also participated in the RSF-sponsored Princeton working group on inequality. The other members of that working group—Larry Bartels, Paul Dimaggio, Leslie McCall, and Bruce Western—have provided lots of feedback on much of this manuscript. The RSF support is reflected in the work reported in chapter 6. The broader inequality project of RSF also led to Rosenthal's collaboration with Christine Eibner, which is reflected in chapter 4.

Poole and Rosenthal have also benefited from multiple NSF grants from the political science program and the supercomputer program. Indeed, this project is very much technology-driven. The NSF supercomputer project gave us the capacity—today available in high-end PCs—for a dynamic analysis of the 11 million individual roll call votes that took place between 1789 and 1996. Without this support, chapter 2 of this book would not have been imaginable, and the rest of the book would not have followed.

Special thanks are owed to Robert Erikson and David Rhode, two superb editors of the *American Journal of Political Science* who encouraged this research at a time when the *APSR* had its head and somewhat more of its anatomy buried in the tar pits of traditional congressional scholarship.

Research on this project was both facilitated and hindered by the fact that the three of us accumulated eleven institutional affiliations, as visitors and regular faculty, during the gestation of this project: Brown, CASBS, Carnegie Mellon, Columbia, Free University of Brussels, Houston, Hoover, NYU, Princeton, USC, and UCSD. Our colleagues at these institutions provided insight and advice on this project that more than compensated for the lost productivity of moving around so much.

Rosenthal would especially like to thank his colleagues from ECARES at the Free University of Brussels—Erik Berglöf, Patrick Bolton, Mathias Dewatripont, and Gerard Roland—for the insights that came from eating lots of baguette sandwiches in the Canadian ambassador's residence. He also thanks his fellow MIT alums Sam Popkin and Susan Shirk. McCarty extends a special thanks to Doug Arnold, Larry Bartels, Chuck Cameron, Tom Gilligan, John Huber, Ira Katznelson, Keith Krehbiel, John Matsusaka, Bob Shapiro, and Greg Wawro, both for advice on this project and for support early in his career. He'd also like to thank his junior colleagues Josh Clinton, David Lewis, Adam Meirowitz, and Markus Prior for helping to keep his mental faculties perking during our daily Starbucks run. Poole would like to thank his former colleagues at the University of Houston—Ray Duch, Harrell Rogers, Bob Lineberry, Kent Tedin, Ernesto Calvo, Noah Kaplan, and Tim Nokken—who gave valuable feedback on portions of this book while he was the Kenneth L. Lay Professor of Political Science. Poole would also like to thank Gary Cox and Mat McCubbins for convincing him to live by the sea and the palm trees.

This book reflects a steady development of our research in the near-decade since the Walras-Pareto lectures. The lectures covered the topics found in chapters 2 and 5, but both of these chapters reflect substantial additional research. Much of the material in chapter 2 and a wisp of chapter 3 appeared in our AEI monograph *Income Redistribution and the Realignment of American Politics*. Chapter 2, however, reports substantial additional findings on the evaluation of competing hypotheses about polarization. Chapters 3, 4, and 5 reflect entirely unpublished material. Chapters 1 and 6 draw heavily on Rosenthal's essay in the RSF volume *Social Inequality*, gracefully edited by Kathy Neckerman, and an essay McCarty wrote for a volume edited by Paul Pierson and Theda Skocpol.

Last but not least, we are very grateful to Jim Alt, who organized a presentation of the first draft at the Eric Mindich Encounter with Authors at Harvard in January 2005. We would like to thank all the participants for their very useful comments, with special thanks to Mo Fiorina, who got stuck in one more East Coast blizzard. We thank the participants, too numerous to cite individually, who participated in the many seminars we have presented on the topics in this book, as well as our editor John Covell and the four anonymous reviewers who provided excellent feedback on earlier versions of the manuscript.

1   The Choreography of
       American Politics

We dance round in a ring and suppose, But the Secret sits in the middle and knows.
—Robert Frost

In the middle of the twentieth century, the Democrats and the Republicans danced almost cheek to cheek in their courtship of the political middle. Over the past thirty years, the parties have deserted the center of the floor in favor of the wings. In the parlance of punditry and campaign rhetoric circa 2004, American politics have "polarized." Scarcely a day went by without headlines such as the *San Francisco Chronicle*'s "Where did the middle go? How polarized politics and a radical GOP have put a chill on measured debate."[1] Story after story attempted to explain the seemingly unbridgeable divide between red and blue states. Was the country divided on moral issues, national security, or NASCAR? Even the First Lady offered her diagnosis, as the Associated Press reported: "First Lady Laura Bush thinks the news media is increasingly filled with opinions instead of facts, and suggested...that journalists are contributing to the polarization of the country."[2]

What public commentators missed, however, was that polarization was not a solo performer but part of a tight ensemble. Polarization's partners were other fundamental changes in the American society and economy. Most important, just as American politics became increasingly divisive, economic fortunes diverged. Middle- and high-income Americans have continued to benefit from the massive economic growth experienced since the Second World War. But material well-being for the lower-income classes has stagnated. For each story about successful people like Bill Gates and Sam Walton, there are contrasting stories about low-wage, no-benefit workers.

That Wal-Mart is the center of both the good news and the bad underscores how unequally America's economic growth has been allocated. To put some hard numbers on the disparities, in 1967 a household in the 95th percentile of the income distribution had six times the income of someone in the 25th percentile. By 2003 the disparity had increased to 8.6 times.[3] *Census*

It is important to note that inequality rose in a period of increasing prosperity, with the added riches going much more to the haves than to the have-nots. Households with an annual income of over $100,000 (year 2000 dollars) increased from under 3 percent in 1967 to over 12 percent in 2000. Even the middle of the income distribution was more prosperous. In year 2000 dollars, median income increased from $31,400 in 1967 to $42,200 in 2000. Inequality probably had a real (versus perceived) bite on consumption only at the very bottom of the income distribution. This increase in riches, albeit unequal, is likely, as we explain in chapters 2, 3, and 4, to have contributed to polarization.

Economists, sociologists, and others have identified a number of factors behind the shift to greater inequality. Returns to education have increased, labor union coverage has declined, trade exposure has increased, corporate executives have benefited from sharp increases in compensation and stock options, and family structure has changed through rising rates of divorce, late marriage, and two-income households. An additional factor helping tie our ensemble together is the massive wave of immigration, legal and illegal, since the 1960s.

The new immigrants are predominantly unskilled. They have contributed greatly to the economy by providing low-wage labor, especially in jobs that American citizens no longer find desirable. They also provide the domestic services that facilitate labor market participation by highly skilled people. On the other hand, immigrants have also increased inequality both directly, by occupying the lowest rungs of the economic ladder, and indirectly, through competition with citizens for low-wage jobs. Yet as noncitizens they lack the civic opportunities to secure the protections of the welfare state. Because these poor people cannot vote, there is less political support for policies that would lower inequality by redistribution.

In this book, we trace out how these major economic and social changes are related to the increased polarization of the U.S. party system. We characterize the relationships as a "dance"—that is, relationships with give and take and back and forth, where causality can run both ways. On the one hand, economic inequality might feed directly into political polarization. People at the top might devote time and resources to supporting a political party strongly opposed to redistribution. People at the bottom would have an opposite response. Polarized parties, on the other hand, might generate policies that increase inequality through at least two channels. If the Republicans move sharply to the right, they can use their majority (as has been argued for the tax bills of the first administrations of Ronald Reagan and George W. Bush) to reduce redistribution. If they are not the majority, they can use the power of the minority in American politics to block changes to the status quo. In other words, polarization in the context of American political institutions now means that the political process cannot be used to redress inequality that may arise from nonpolitical changes in technology, lifestyle, and compensation practices.

Measuring Political Polarization

Before laying the groundwork for our argument that political polarization is related to economic inequality, we need to discuss how we conceptualize and measure political polarization. What do we mean by "polarization"? Polarization is, for short, a separation of politics into liberal and conservative camps. We all recognize that members of Congress can be thought of as occupying a position on a liberal-conservative spectrum. Ted Kennedy is a liberal, Dianne Feinstein a more moderate Democrat, Joe Lieberman even more so; Olympia Snowe is a moderate Republican and Rick Santorum a conservative Republican. The perception of conservativeness is commonly shared. There is a common perception because a politician's behavior is predictable. If we know that Olympia Snowe will fight a large tax cut, we can be fairly certain that all or almost all the Democrats will support her position.

There are two complementary facets to the polarization story. First, at the level of individual members of Congress, moderates are vanishing. Second, the two parties have pulled apart. *Conservative* and *liberal* have become almost perfect synonyms for *Republican* and *Democrat*.

Because we are social scientists and not journalists or politicians, we need to nail these shared impressions with precise operational definitions. When two of us (the two not in high school at the time) published "The Polarization of American Politics" in 1984, we measured polarization with interest group ratings. Each year, a number of interest groups publish ratings of members of Congress. Among the many groups are the United Auto Workers (UAW), the Americans for Democratic Action (ADA), the National Taxpayers Union (NTU), the American Conservative Union (ACU), and the League of Conservation Voters (LCV). Each interest group selects a fairly small number of roll call votes, typically twenty to forty, from the hundreds taken each year. A senator or representative who always votes to support the interest group's position is rewarded with a score of 100. Those always on the "wrong" side get a score of 0. Those who support the group half the time get a score of 50, and so on.

To see that moderates had vanished by 2003, consider the ratings of the Americans for Democratic Action for that year. The possible ADA ratings rose in five-point steps from 0 to 100. Of the twenty-one possible ratings, nine were in the range 30 through 70. Yet only eleven of the hundred senators (McCain, AZ; Campbell, CO; Lieberman, CT; Breaux, LA; Landrieu, LA; Collins, ME; Snowe, ME; Nelson, NE; Reid, NV; Edwards, NC; and Chafee, RI) fell in one of the nine middle categories. In contrast, ten Democrats got high marks of 95 or 100 and fourteen Republicans got 5 or 0. That is, more than twice as many senators (24) fell in the four very extreme categories as fell in the nine middle categories (11).

Our 1984 article documented two findings about the scores of the ADA and other interest groups. First, the interest groups gave out basically the same set of ratings or the mirror image of that set. If a general-purpose liberal interest group like the ADA gave a rating of 100 to a representative, the representative would nearly always get a very high rating from another liberal interest group, such as the LCV, even when the interest group focused on a single policy area, like the environment. Similarly, a 100 ADA rating made a very low rating from a conservative group like ACU or NTU a foregone conclusion. This agreement across interest groups meant that interest groups were evaluating members of Congress along a single, liberal-conservative dimension. Individual issue areas, such as race, no longer had a distinctive existence. Second, the interest groups were giving out fewer and fewer scores in the moderate range in the 40s, 50s, and 60s. Moderates were giving way to more extreme liberals and conservatives. Put simply, the interest groups had little difficulty placing Ted Kennedy and Jesse Helms as ideological opposites, and they were finding fewer and fewer Jacob Javitses and Sam Nunns to put in the middle. The change we noted occurred in the last half of the 1970s; indeed, our data went only through 1980.

We summarized our findings by combining all the ratings to give a single liberal-conservative score to each member.[4] We then measured polarization in a variety of technical ways, which we explain more fully in chapter 2. One measure was simply how much the scores for members of the two political parties overlapped. If moderates were abundant in both parties, there would be substantial overlap, or low polarization. If the Democrats had only liberals and the Republicans only conservatives, there would be no overlap, or high polarization. We found that the overlap had shrunk.

Using interest group ratings only, however, has two limitations. First, interest groups select only a small number of roll call votes. The ADA, for example, uses just twenty per year. But each house of Congress conducts hundreds of roll calls each year. ADA's selections might be a biased sample of this richer universe.[5] Second, interest group ratings became common only in the second half of the twentieth century. We cannot do a long-run study of polarization, inequality, and immigration just on the basis of interest group ratings. So we developed NOMINATE, a quantitative procedure that would score politicians directly from their roll call voting records, using all of the recorded votes. To locate the politicians' positions, these techniques use information on who votes with whom and how often. For example, if Arlen Specter votes with both Hillary Clinton and Bill Frist much more frequently than Clinton and Frist vote together, then these techniques position Specter as moderate, in between those more extreme senators. Using this algorithm over millions of individual choices made by thousands of legislators on tens of thousands of roll calls allows us to develop quite precise measures of each member's position on the liberal-conservative spectrum. In chapter 2, we go into much more detail about how these measures are calculated. We also discuss the various ways we measure polarization from these scales. In the remainder of this chapter, we measure polarization by the average difference between Democratic and Republican legislators on the DW-NOMINATE scale. The acronym DW-NOMINATE denotes Dynamic Weighted Nominal Three-step Estimation. The procedure is described in McCarty, Poole, and Rosenthal (1997). Hereafter in this book, we abbreviate to NOMINATE. NOMINATE is based on all recorded roll call votes in American history and permits us to look at long-run changes in polarization.

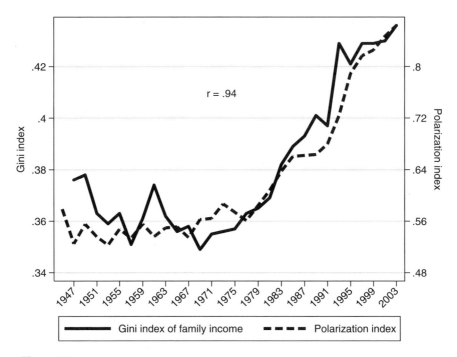

Figure 1.1
Income Inequality and House Polarization
Source: Gini index from the U.S. Census Bureau (2005)
Note: Polarization is measured as the difference between the Democratic and Republican
Party mean NOMINATE scores in the U.S. House. The Gini and polarization measures
correspond to the first year of each biennial congressional term.

The Common Trajectory of Polarization and Inequality

Our measure of political polarization closely parallels measures of economic inequality and of immigration for much of the twentieth century. We show this correlation with three plots of time series.

One measure of income inequality is the Gini coefficient of family income calculated by the Bureau of the Census. The Gini coefficient shows how the entire distribution of income deviates from equality. When every family has the same income, the Gini is zero. When one family has all the income, the Gini is one. In figure 1.1, we show the Gini and polarization in the post–World War II period.[6] Income inequality falls from 1947 through 1957 and then bounces up and down until 1969. After 1969, income inequality increases every two years, with a couple of slight interruptions. Polarization bounces at a low level until 1977, and thereafter follows an unbroken upward trajectory.

We stress an important aspect of the timing of the reversal in inequality and polarization. In some circles, both of these phenomena are viewed as the consequence of Ronald Reagan's victory in the 1980 elections. Both reversals, however, clearly predate Reagan and Reaganomics. Reagan conservatism was a product sitting on a shelf in the political supermarket. In 1980, customers switched brands, arguably the result of a preference shift marked by rising inequality and party polarization.[7]

When we relate polarization to citizen political preferences in chapter 3, we can look only at the period from the 1950s to the present. Our principal data source for the chapter, the National Election Study, first polled in 1952. When we look at citizenship and campaign contributions in chapters 4 and 5, we are further restricted to starting in the 1970s. The Census Bureau began asking questions on both citizenship and voter turnout in 1972, and the Federal Election Commission kept campaign finance data starting in 1974. Despite these data limitations, we should emphasize that polarization underwent a long decline in the first two-thirds of the twentieth century. We cannot relate the decline in polarization to the Gini or other Census Bureau measures of inequality, but we can see the larger picture thanks to an innovative study by Thomas Piketty and Emmanuel Saez (2003).

Piketty and Saez used income tax returns to compute the percentage share of income going to the richest of the rich. In figure 1.2, we plot the share going to the top one percent of the income distribution. This longer series matches up nicely with our polarization measure over the entire twentieth century.

The decline in polarization throughout the first seventy years of the twentieth century is echoed by much of the literature written toward the end of the decline or just after. During this period, Americans were seen as having grown closer together politically. In 1960, the sociologist Daniel Bell published *The End of Ideology: On the Exhaustion of Political Ideas in the Fifties*. A year later, the political scientist Robert Dahl pointed to a nation moving from oligarchy to pluralism (Dahl 1961). Similarly, the new "rational choice" school in political science emphasized Tweedle-dee/Tweedle-dum parties focused on the median voter (Downs 1957), members of Congress largely concerned with constituency service (Fiorina 1978), and universalism in pork-barrel politics

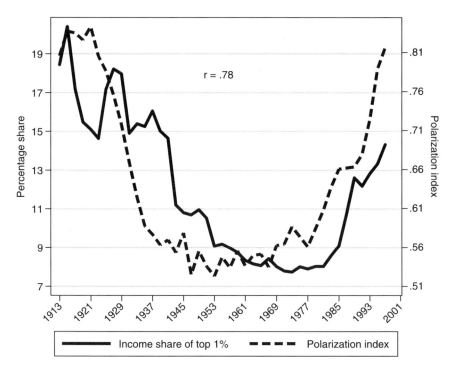

Figure 1.2
Top One Percent Income Share and House Polarization
Source: Income shares from Piketty and Saez (2003), table II.

(Weingast, Shepsle, and Johnsen 1981). What these authors were pointing to was echoed in analyses of roll call voting patterns in the House and Senate. Put simply, the fraction of moderates grew and the fraction of extreme liberals and extreme conservatives fell from 1900 to about 1975 (Poole and Rosenthal 1997; McCarty, Poole, and Rosenthal 1997). By the beginning of the twenty-first century, the extremes had come back.

The corresponding story for immigration is told by figure 1.3. Immigration is captured by looking at the percentage of the population that is foreign-born. (This is the only measure available before the Census Bureau began biennial collection of data on citizenship in 1972. From 1972 on, we will look, in chapter 4, at the percentage of the population represented by those who claim to be non-citizens.) For comparison, we have taken the polarization period back to 1880, the first census after the modern Democrat-Republican two-party system formed upon the end of Reconstruction following the elections of 1876.

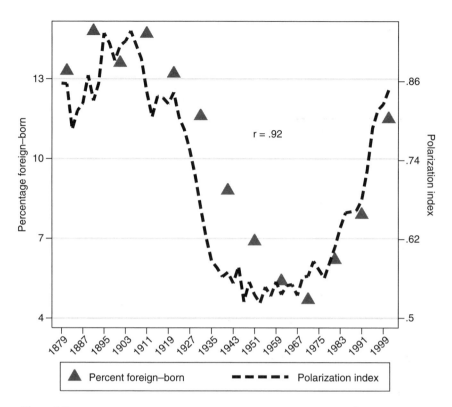

Figure 1.3
Percent Foreign-Born and House Polarization
Note: Each observation of foreign-born population corresponds to a U.S. decennial census.

Until World War I, the percentage of foreign-born living in the United States was very high, hovering in the 13–15 percent range. With the curtailing of immigration, first by the war and then by the restrictive immigration acts of the 1920s, the percentage of foreign-born falls continuously until the 1970 census, just after immigration was liberalized by the 1965 reforms. The percentage of foreign-born thereafter increases sharply, exceeding 11 percent in the census of 2000. In 1970, a majority of the foreign-born had become naturalized citizens. By 2000, a substantial majority of the foreign-born was formed by noncitizens. Parallel to the track of immigration, polarization hovers at a high level until 1912 and then declines until 1967, with the exception of the uptick in the 1940s. The immigration series, like the income series, largely parallels our polarization measure.[8]

When we ourselves first saw figures 1.1, 1.2, and 1.3, we realized that major indicators of the politics, the economics, and the demographics of the United States had followed very similar trajectories over many decades. We decided to investigate the political and economic mechanisms linking these three trajectories. This book reports the outcome of our investigation.

A Focus on Income

Throughout the book, we look at income and other components of economic well-being as an important variable in defining political ideology and voter preferences. We do not, however, discount the importance of such other factors as race and "moral values." We chose to emphasize economics partly because we seek to redress an imbalance in political science: income has been largely ignored, and race-ethnicity and class (as measured by occupation rather than income) receive more attention. We chose economics also because many public policies are defined largely in terms of income. Certainly the tax bills of 1993, 2001, and 2003 were among the most important domestic policy changes of the Clinton and George W. Bush administrations. Indeed, the overwhelming majority of congressional roll calls are over taxes, budgets, and economic policies, especially after the issue of *de jure* political rights for African-Americans left the congressional agenda at the end of the 1960s. Most importantly, income is closely related to how people vote, to whether they participate in politics by either voting or making campaign contributions, and to whether they are eligible to vote as United States citizens.

Race does appear to be related to the current absence of redistribution in the United States (Alesina and Glaeser 2004) and to the absence of public spending in local communities (Alesina, Baqir, and Easterly 1999; Alesina and La Ferrara 2000, 2002). The claim that welfare expenditures in the United States are low because of race has been made by many authors, including Myrdal (1960), Quadagno (1994), and Gilens (1999). The basic claim of this literature is that the correlation with poverty lowers the willingness of voters to favor public spending for redistribution. But it is hard to see racism as hardening in the last quarter of the twentieth century when inequality was increasing. Racism and racial tension seem to have been rife when inequality was falling: recall the lynchings and race riots in the first half of the century and the urban riots of the 1960s. (Similarly, with regard to occupation or class, unionization has been declining since the 1950s.) We do explicitly consider race when treating ideological polarization in Congress and income polarization in the mass public, but it does, in historical perspective, appear appropriate to make income and economics our primary focus.

The Dance Card

In our second chapter we document the polarization of politicians. Most of our evidence concerns the two houses of Congress; we also include brief discussions of the presidency and a number of state legislatures. Polarization has increased for two reasons. First, Republicans in the North and South have moved sharply to the right. Second, moderate Democrats in the South have been replaced by Republicans. The remaining, largely northern, Democrats are somewhat more liberal than the Democratic Party of the 1960s.

The movements we observe tell us only about the relative positioning of politicians. We say that Republicans have moved to the right because newly elected Republicans have, on the whole, voted in a more conservative manner than the Republicans who remain in Congress. Northern Democrats, in contrast, don't look sharply different from the Democrats of old.

At the same time, however, how policy issues map onto liberal-conservative preferences may have changed. The Republicans have moved sharply away from redistributive policies that would reduce economic inequality. The Democrats as analyzed by John Gerring (1998), a political scientist at Boston University, have moved their platforms away from general welfare issues to issues based on ascriptive characteristics (race, gender, and sexual preference) of individuals. For example, figure 1.4, drawn from Gerring, shows that the Democrats increased emphasis on general welfare through the 1960s but then deemphasized it in the 1970s. The turn in platforms thus matches the reversals in economic inequality and polarization. Parallel to Gerring's results, we show that race as an issue has been absorbed into the main redistributive dimension of liberal-conservative politics. Taxes, minimum wages, and other traditional redistributive policy areas continue to be liberal-conservative issues; they have been joined by issues related to ascription.

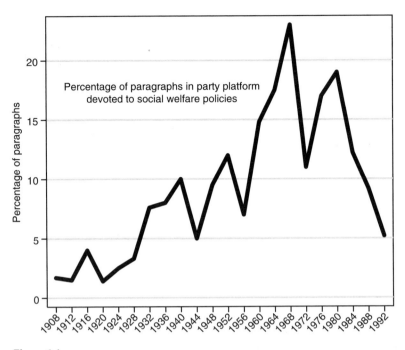

Figure 1.4
Attention to Social Welfare in Democratic Party Platform
Source: Author calculations based on Gerring (1998), figure 14, used by permission.

What explains the changes in polarization and the accompanying rhetoric? The changes, we argue, have no simple institutional explanations, such as primaries, reapportionment after censuses, and gerrymandering. We thus open the door for inequality and immigration to be the dance partners of polarization.

We proceed, in chapter 3, from politicians to the mass electorate. We use survey data to argue that both partisan identification (Democrat, Independent, or Republican) and presidential vote choice are increasingly linked to income. The relatively poor are increasingly Democratic and the rich Republican. We show that income is important in subgroups of the population that are frequently treated as homogeneous voting blocs based on racial conservatism or moral values. Indeed, the income effect is now stronger in the South than in the North and stronger among white "born-agains" or evangelicals than among other whites. We reconcile our findings with the observation that high per capita income states are now blue (Democratic) and low per capita income states are red (Republican). We also observe that real per capita income, equity ownership, and home ownership for average Americans has dramatically increased as polarization has increased. These increases, we argue, are largely consistent with the hypothesis that the main cause of polarization has been a move to the right by Republicans.

In chapter 4 we show that movement to the right, away from redistribution, has been facilitated by immigration. Over the past thirty years, noncitizens have become not only a far larger share of the population but also disproportionately poorer. Because noncitizens are ineligible to vote, less pressure to redistribute comes from the bottom of the income distribution. For example, the Council on Medical Service of the American Medical Association reports that in 1999 immigrants represented about 10 percent of the overall population but 22 percent of those without health insurance.[9] The association of voting rights with citizenship thus diminishes support for federal health insurance. Indeed, Congress, in recent years, has restricted access to Medicaid for immigrants.[10]

In chapter 5 we argue that polarization in Congress is echoed by patterns of campaign contributions. Contributions are increasingly concentrated on ideological extremes. The strongest evidence that campaign contributions have had a polarizing effect are the soft money contributions to political parties. We show that contributors with extreme liberal and extreme conservative preferences gave a disproportionately large share of soft money. This polarized giving, most likely accentuated by the 527 loophole to the recent McCain-Feingold legislation, has reinforced the ideological extremism of political parties and elected officials.

We use chapter 6 to study the impact of polarization on public policy. We show that changes in such policies as taxes and minimum wages have mirrored the historical trends we found in polarization. As polarization has increased in the past thirty years, real minimum wages have fallen; top marginal tax rates and estate tax rates have been reduced. In addition, we discuss how, in the American system of "checks and balances," polarization reduces the possibilities for policy changes that would reduce inequality.

Because legislation in the United States cannot be produced by a simple parliamentary majority, a minority of liberals or a minority of conservatives is frequently able to block policy change.[11] The veto powers of political minorities are particularly important when status quo policies are not indexed for inflation. Federal minimum wages are fixed in nominal dollars. A conservative minority has been able to block substantial increases in the minimum wage, even when the Democrats had unified control of Congress under Jimmy Carter and in the early Clinton administration. Therefore, the real minimum wage has fallen. David Lee (1999), an economist at the University of California at Berkeley, has argued that failures to increase the minimum wage are responsible for about half the increase in the disparity between the wages of the median worker (50th percentile) and those of the worker in the 10th percentile of the wage distribution. Lee's work ties the absence of policy change to increased inequality. We, in turn, argue that polarization favors the policy status quo.

Immigration policy aptly illustrates how sticky status quos can affect inequality. Goldin (1994) documents how presidential vetoes withheld restrictive immigration legislation until the 1920s even though congressional majorities had favored it for several decades. During the period before World War I, polarization rose and income inequality was extremely high. The logjam was finally broken by the restrictive immigration laws of the 1920s. The new status quo also proved to be sticky. Reform came only after forty years, with legislation in 1965. As long as the status quo of the 1920s held, immigration, inequality, and polarization all fell. Subsequent to 1965, the new policy has prevailed despite an increase in popular support for restricting immigration.

Before we can analyze the policy consequences of polarization, we need to establish when and how polarization occurred. We now turn to that task.

Polarized Politicians

Pennsylvania Extreme 2000

The fundamental transformation of American politics can be summed up by the recent history of a single Senate seat. In 1991, Pennsylvania's three-term senator John Heinz was killed in a plane accident. A Republican, Heinz compiled a moderate record as his party's leading supporter of environmental and labor union causes. In the special election that followed, the Republicans ran another relatively moderate candidate, Richard Thornburgh, a former governor and U.S. attorney general, against Harris Wofford, the interim senator. Wofford, who began his career as the first associate director of the Peace Corps, was significantly more liberal than Heinz. In a campaign orchestrated by James Carville, Wofford ran on a platform of fundamental reform of the health care system in the United States. Thornburgh was beaten easily, and health care became the "hot" issue going into the 1992 presidential elections.

The 1992 election produced another upset in Pennsylvania. Newcomer Rick Santorum defeated eight-term congressman Doug Walgren, a liberal Democrat from the Pittsburgh area. In the House, Santorum compiled one of the most conservative voting records, placing himself well to the right of Heinz and the majority of Pennsylvania House Republicans. In spite of his conservatism, Santorum was able to move up to the Senate by defeating Wofford in 1996. So in a period of five years, this Senate seat was held by one of the most moderate members of the U.S. Senate, then one of the most liberal Democrats, then one of the most conservative Republicans.

The Heinz-Wofford-Santorum transition from moderation to the extremes has been repeated over and over again for the past twenty-five years. It is this process that has increasingly polarized American politics.

To go beyond the anecdotal, in this chapter we provide systematic evidence from the historical record of roll call voting in Congress to demonstrate that the behavior of members of Congress has in fact become highly polarized along a liberal-conservative ideological dimension. This surge reversed a long secular decline in polarization that began at the turn of the twentieth century and lasted until the late 1960s. Many in the Republican Party led by President Eisenhower had accepted much of the New Deal welfare state, and both Democrats and Republicans were solidly behind the foreign policies of anticommunism and containment. John F. Kennedy campaigned to increase defense spending. This consensus led to record levels of bipartisanship and cooperation in Congress. But that consensus was short-lived. By the mid-1970s, the Vietnam War signaled the end of bipartisan foreign policy, while sluggish economic performance led to serious consideration of alternatives to Keynesianism and the welfare state.

Two of us, Poole and Rosenthal (1984), documented the dramatic turnaround of the 1970s in "The Polarization of American Politics." We found that beginning in the mid-1970s, American politics became much more divisive.[1] More Democrats staked out consistently liberal positions, and more Republicans supported wholly conservative ones. The primary evidence in that study, which focused exclusively on the Senate, were the ratings issued by interest groups such as the Americans for Democratic Action and the United States Chamber of Commerce. In *Congress: A Political Economic History of Roll Call Voting*, however, we (Poole and Rosenthal 1997) validated our earlier analysis, using evidence from roll call votes rather than interest group ratings. We further found that the polarization surge had continued unabated through the 100th Congress (1987–88). It has continued through 2004. Our data confirm the more casual observations of polarization in the conflict over aid to the Contras in Nicaragua, the confirmation hearings and votes after the nominations of Robert Bork and Clarence Thomas to the Supreme Court, the rhetoric of the "Contract with America," the budget showdown between Speaker Gingrich and President Clinton in 1995, and the impeachment process in 1998–99.

Measuring Ideology and Polarization: A Quick Primer

How do we know that polarization has occurred? Every aficionado of American politics would label Ted Kennedy (D-MA) and Barbara Boxer (D-CA) liberals, Sam Nunn (D-GA) and Jacob Javits (R-NY) moderates, and Tom DeLay (R-TX) and Jesse Helms (R-NC) conservatives. But how does one demonstrate that Jesse Helms is more conservative than Rick Santorum? And how do we know that Santorum is more conservative than Heinz was, as the two men obviously never served in Congress together? How do we locate Boxer relative to someone even more remote, say William Jennings Bryan, who denounced Republicans for "crucifying mankind on a cross of gold"?

Most political scientists traditionally have measured liberal-conservative positions by using the interest group ratings of the Americans for Democratic Action (ADA), the League of Conservation Voters (LCV), or the U.S. Chamber of Commerce. Groups construct these ratings by choosing the roll call votes that are important to their legislative agendas and determining whether a Yea or Nay vote indicates support for the group's goals. Indices are then constructed from the proportion of votes a member casts in favor of the group. As we have shown, these indices are highly similar across groups (Poole and Rosenthal 1997, ch. 8). The similarity reflects the fact that the interest groups themselves are polarized along the same liberal-conservative lines. Almost any two liberal groups, such as the ADA or LCV, have ratings that are highly correlated, and their ratings are mirror images of any conservative group such as the Chamber of Commerce.

One important limitation in the use of these interest group scores is that they are designed primarily to assess differences among the legislators in a single Congress. Therefore, they do not provide any direct information about the differences between legislators serving at different times, or even the behavior of the same legislator over the course of her career. To illustrate this problem, consider the following example. In 1998, both Helms and Santorum received perfect conservative scores of 0 from the ADA. Paul Wellstone (D-MN) received a perfect liberal score of 100. Kennedy, at 95, did almost as well. In 1980, the ADA had Helms at 11 and Heinz at the moderate score of 50. So to the extent to which the ADA measures really capture member ideology, we might use the "glue" provided by Helms to conclude that Santorum was more conservative than Heinz. This use of overlapping cohorts of legislators is also the basis of the methods developed by Poole (1998; 2005) and Groseclose, Levitt, and Snyder (1999).

But there are additional problems with using interest group ratings. First, all group ratings are based on small, selective samples of roll calls that tend in particular to clump lots of legislators at the extreme scores of 0 or 100. This clumping tends to obscure real differences among legislators as we saw with the zero ADA ratings of Helms and

Santorum in 1998. (In 1997, Helms was again a 0, but Santorum was a 15, more in line with "Inside the Beltway Common Knowledge.") In fact, there is evidence that groups may choose votes strategically in order to divide the legislative world into friends and foes (Fowler 1982; Snyder 1992). This tactic creates an artificially large number of 0s and 100s. Second, because the ratings go from 0 to 100 every year, the range of positions is invariant across time. Not surprisingly, Barry Goldwater (R-AZ) had a 0 rating in 1980. Was he as conservative as Helms and Santorum were in 1998?[2]

Given these problems, we can get much better measures of ideology from scaling methods that use all the roll call votes. These methods all assume that legislators make their choices in accordance with the spatial model of voting. In a spatial model, each legislator is assumed to have a position on the liberal-conservative dimension. This position is termed the ideal point. The ideal point is directly analogous to a rating if the interest group is more liberal or conservative than all of the legislators (Poole and Daniels 1985; Poole and Rosenthal 1997).[3]

Just as the 435 representatives and 100 senators have ideal point locations in the spatial model, we assume that each roll call can be represented by Yea and Nay positions on the liberal-conservative scale. The underlying assumption of the spatial model is that each legislator votes Yea or Nay depending on which outcome location is closer to his ideal point. Of course, the legislator may make "mistakes" and depart from what would usually be expected, as a result of pressures from campaign contributors, constituents, convictions, or just plain randomness. Using our assumptions of spatial voting with error, we can estimate the ideal points of the members of Congress directly from the hundreds or thousands of roll call choices made by each legislator.

To understand better how the spatial positions of legislators can be recovered from roll call votes, consider the following three-senator example. Suppose we observed only the following roll call voting patterns from Senators Kennedy, Specter, and Santorum.

Roll Call	Kennedy	Specter	Santorum
1	YEA	NAY	NAY
2	YEA	YEA	NAY
3	NAY	YEA	YEA
4	NAY	NAY	YEA
5	YEA	YEA	YEA
6	NAY	NAY	NAY

Notice that all of these votes can be explained by a simple model where all senators are assigned an "ideal point" on a left-right scale and every roll call is given a "cutpoint" that divides the senators who vote Yea from those who vote Nay. For example, if we assign ideal points ordered Kennedy < Specter < Santorum, the first vote can be perfectly explained by a cutpoint between Kennedy and Specter, and the second vote can be explained equally well by a cutpoint between Specter and Santorum. In fact, all six votes can be explained in this way. Note that a scale with Santorum < Specter < Kennedy works just as well. But, a single cutpoint cannot explain votes 1 through 4 if the ideal points are ordered Specter < Kennedy < Santorum, Specter < Santorum < Kennedy, Santorum < Kennedy < Specter, or Kennedy < Santorum < Specter. Therefore none of these orderings is consistent with a one-dimensional spatial model.

As two orderings of ideal points work equally well, which one should we choose? Given that Kennedy espouses liberal (left-wing) views and Santorum is known for his conservative (rightist) ones, Kennedy < Specter < Santorum seems like a logical choice.

The real world, however, is rarely so well behaved to generate the nice patterns of the first six votes. What if we observed that Santorum and Kennedy occasionally vote together against Specter, as in votes 7 and 8 below? Such votes cannot be explained by the ordering Kennedy < Specter < Santorum.

Roll Call	Kennedy	Specter	Santorum
7	YEA	NAY	YEA
8	NAY	YEA	NAY

If there are only a few votes like 7 and 8 (relative to votes 1 through 6), it's reasonable to conclude that they may have been generated by more or less random factors outside the model. If there are many more votes like 1 through 6 than there are deviant votes, any of the common scaling procedures will still generate the ordinal ranking Kennedy < Specter < Santorum.[4] In our NOMINATE procedure, the frequency of the deviant votes provides additional information about the nominal values of the ideal points. For example, if there are few votes pitting Santorum and Kennedy against Specter, we place Santorum and Kennedy far apart, to reflect the probability that it was just random events that led them to vote together. Alternatively, if the Santorum-Kennedy coalition were common, we would place them closer together, consistent with the idea that small random events can lead to such a pattern.

It is easy to measure the success of the one-dimensional spatial model. In our example, the "classification success" is simply the proportion of explained votes (that is, types 1 through 6) of the total number of votes. Notice, however, that classification success will be inflated if there are a lot of unanimous votes as in 5 and 6, because any ranking of the senators can explain them. Therefore, it is often useful to assess the spatial model against a null model where all senators are assumed to vote with the majority position. A sensible measure of the improvement of the spatial model over this "majority" model is *Proportional Reduction in Error* (PRE). The PRE is defined as

$$\frac{\text{Majority Errors} - \text{Spatial Errors}}{\text{Majority Errors}}$$

Go back to our three-senator example. We discard the two unanimous votes 5 and 6. There is a single majority error on votes 1 through 4 and 7 through 8 since all six votes have 2-1 majorities. There is one spatial error on votes 7 and 8. The PRE for each of votes 1 through 4 is 1 since there are no spatial errors. The PRE for votes 7 and 8 is zero since there are as many majority errors as spatial errors. The average PRE is 2/3 since overall there are only two spatial errors as against six majority errors $[(6-2)/6 = 2/3]$.

Sometimes there are so many votes like 7 and 8 that it becomes unreasonable to maintain that they are simply random. An alternative is to assume that a Santorum-Kennedy coalition forms because there is some other policy dimension on which they are closer together than they are to Specter. We can accommodate such behavior by estimating ideal points on a second dimension. In this example, a second dimension in which Santorum and Kennedy share a position distinct from Specter's will explain votes 7 and 8. Both dimensions combined will explain all of the votes. Obviously, in a richer example with a hundred senators rather than three, two dimensions will not explain all the votes, but the second dimension will typically add explanatory power.[5] In our discussions below, we will evaluate the importance of higher dimensions by measuring their incremental ability to predict roll call votes correctly.

A cottage industry of specific techniques for recovering ideal points has emerged in recent years. These variations differ not so much in spirit as in their technical assumptions.[6] In fact, the patterns of polarization that we discuss below are robust as to how legislator positions are measured. Nevertheless, we rely on NOMINATE (Poole 2005) because it is the only methodology that allows both for comparison of the dispersion of positions across time and for intertemporal change in the positions of individual legislators. That is, NOMINATE solves the problem of the comparability of Santorum and Goldwater. It also captures some major changes in position, such as the conservative-to-liberal journey of Senator Wayne Morse of Oregon.

To capture these latter effects, the NOMINATE scores we use in this book allow for a linear change in position throughout a legislator's career. One can change from liberal to conservative—but not back again. Although restrictive, this assumption is not particularly important. As a matter of fact, for the period covered by this book, there are only very small changes in legislator positions (Poole and Rosenthal 1997, pp. 73–74). Large changes occur only for those legislators who switch parties (McCarty, Poole, and Rosenthal 2001). To account for these jumps, we estimate two separate ideological paths for these "party-switchers."

To match the common-language designation of liberals with the left and conservatives with the right, we adjust the NOMINATE scores so that each member's *average* score lies between −1 and +1, with −1 being the most liberal position and +1 the most conservative. For the example that introduced this chapter, Heinz ended his career at 0.017, Wofford ended at a liberal −0.40, and his replacement, Santorum, is currently located at a conservative +0.44.

As the comparison of Wofford and Santorum shows, party, at least as much as constituency, has a strong influence on ideal points (McCarty, Poole, and Rosenthal 2001). The biggest changes are indeed associated with legislators who change party during their careers. Morse, for example, moved from −0.24 to −0.83. Each legislator adjusts his position, to some degree, as a function of party affiliation. Heinz may well have had a more liberal voting record had he been a Democrat. On the other hand, party is a much coarser measure than a NOMINATE score. There is always substantial diversity of NOMINATE positions within each party and, at times, ideological overlap between the parties.

Although we computed the NOMINATE scores using all the roll calls in the history of the United States Congress, in this chapter

1878

we start all time series with the 46th Congress, which was elected in
1878. This was the first Congress elected after the presidential election of 1876, which ended Reconstruction and marked the restoration
of a competitive, national two-party system. A second reason for
beginning our time series analysis here is that the election of 1876 initiated the most bi-polar period after the Civil War in American political history. As documented by C. Vann Woodward in *Reunion and
Reaction* (1951), Samuel Tilden undoubtedly won the 1876 presidential
election, but a coalition of Republicans and southern Democrats in
Congress threw the election to Rutherford B. Hayes by awarding
Hayes *all* of the contested electoral votes. The southerners were
rewarded with the withdrawal of federal troops from the secessionist
states. This event essentially ended the reign of the pro–Civil Rights
forces in the Republican Party. The post-Reconstruction Democrat-Republican party system emerged. The ensuing congresses near the end
of the 19th century were the most polarized since the end of the Civil
War. They provide us with a benchmark to assess polarization in our
own times.

During most of the period treated in this book, a single liberal-
conservative dimension does an excellent job of accounting for how
members vote, be it on minimum wages, gun control, or the shop-
ping list of issues represented by the Contract with America or a
presidential State of the Union address. One way of directly measuring
the predictive power of the liberal-conservative dimension is to compute the percentage of votes on which a legislator actually votes for
the roll call alternative that is closest to her on the dimension. This
"classification" success exceeds 84 percent across all congresses since
1789.

One issue area, however, clearly did not fit the standard liberal-
conservative pattern—civil rights for African Americans. For much of
the post–WWII era, the voting coalitions on racial issues were distinct
from those on other issues. This issue is represented in our spatial
model by a second dimension, with Southern Democrats at one end
and eastern liberal Republicans, such as Jacob Javits of New York,
at the other. We find that it is important to allow for these two political dimensions in the middle of the twentieth century. Consequently,
we present results for the two-dimensional NOMINATE estimations.
Just as one-dimensional scores run from -1 to $+1$, in two dimensions
a legislator's career average scores must lie in a circle with a radius of
one.

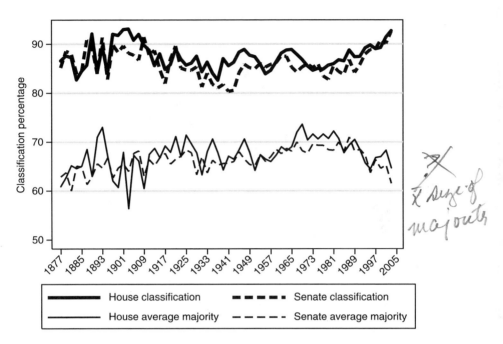

Figure 2.1
Classification of Roll Call Votes, 1877–2004
Source: Computed from Two-Dimensional NOMINATE Model. Only roll calls with at least 2.5% in the minority are included.

The Decline and Surge of Polarization

From our estimates of legislator preferences and the corresponding measurement of polarization, we can identify five distinct, yet complementary, trends that add up to a fundamental transformation of recent American politics.

1. Almost all political conflict in Congress is expressed in the liberal-conservative terms of the first dimension. Consequently, most roll call votes can be interpreted as splits on the basic liberal-conservative dimension. Other dimensions, such as a civil rights dimension, have largely vanished, as the coalitions on those issues have increasingly begun to match those of the liberal-conservative dimension.

2. The dispersion of positions of members on the liberal-conservative dimension has increased. Compared to the 1960s, extreme conservative as well as extreme liberal positions are more likely to be represented in Congress.

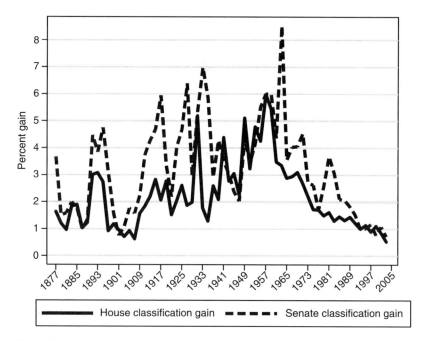

Figure 2.2
Classification Gain of Second Dimension
Source: Computed from Two-Dimensional NOMINATE Model.

3. The ideological composition of the two political parties has become more homogeneous. Intra-party regional differences, such as those between northern and southern Democrats, have abated.

4. The positions of the average Democrat and average Republican member of Congress have become more widely separated. That is, the difference in the party means has increased over time.

5. There is less overlap in the positions of the parties. There are no longer any liberal Republicans or conservative Democrats in Congress. The moderates are vanishing.

As we have indicated, the surge in polarization began in the 1970s. The decline in polarization that took place between the turn of the century and the 1960s just reverses the pattern for the surge: a decline in classification, less dispersion, more intra-party heterogeneity, decrease in difference in party means, more overlap of positions. We now turn to documenting these points.

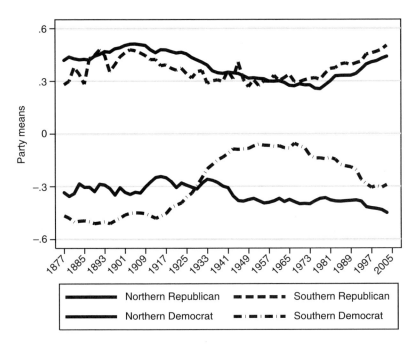

Figure 2.3
Party Means in the U.S. House by Region
Source: Computed from NOMINATE scores at PooleandRosenthal.com
Note: The range of NOMINATE scores is approximately −1.0 to +1.0. The South is
defined as the eleven states of the Confederacy plus Kentucky and Oklahoma.

*Roll call votes can be interpreted as splits on a basic liberal-conservative
dimension. Other dimensions have vanished.*

Figure 2.1 shows that in both chambers, the two-dimensional spatial
model accounts for most individual voting decisions throughout this
period. Classifications were highest at the turn of the twentieth century, exceeding 90 percent in the House and reaching nearly 90 percent
in the Senate. In both chambers, classifications once again exceed 90
percent. In the last three congresses, classification is higher than at any
time since the end of World War I.

The very high rates of classification success we observe do not happen simply because most votes in Congress are lopsided votes where
members say "Hurrah." On the contrary, as the figure indicates, Congress has had mostly divisive votes, with average winning majorities
between 60 and 70 percent.

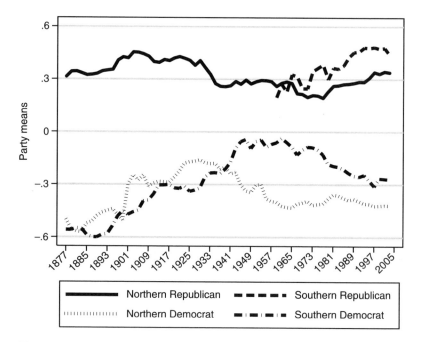

Figure 2.4
Party Means in the U.S. Senate by Region
Source: Computed from NOMINATE scores at PooleandRosenthal.com
Note: The range of NOMINATE scores is approximately −1.0 to +1.0. The South is defined as the eleven states of the Confederacy plus Kentucky and Oklahoma. Because of small numbers, the Southern Republican mean is computed only after 1956.

The high rate of classification success also does not result from an important second dimension. An important second dimension was present in both chambers at midcentury, as shown in figure 2.2. From the late 1960s onward, however, the second dimension has abruptly declined in importance. In the Bill Clinton and George W. Bush eras, it improves classification only by about one percent.[7] Clearly, most roll call votes can now be viewed as splits on a single dimension. This dimension corresponds to the popular conception of liberals versus conservatives.

The positions of the average Democrat and average Republican member of Congress have become more widely separated.

Figures 2.3 and 2.4 show the means of the political parties on the first dimension for the post-Reconstruction period for the House and Senate, respectively.

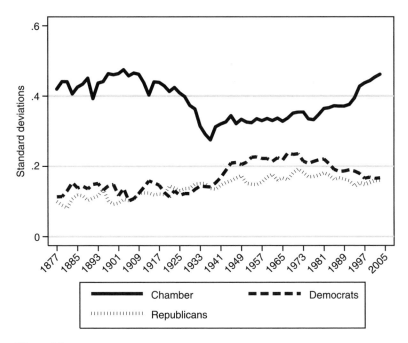

Figure 2.5
Standard Deviations of House NOMINATE Positions
Source: Computed from NOMINATE scores at PooleandRosenthal.com
Note: The range of NOMINATE scores is approximately −1.0 to +1.0.

In both chambers, the Republicans became more moderate until the 1960s.[8] The Republican mean bottomed out in the 1960s and then moved in a sharply conservative direction in the 1970s. The pattern for the Democrats is almost exactly the opposite. Consequently, the two party means moved closer together during the twentieth century until the 1970s and then moved apart.

On the second dimension, this pattern reverses. As figure 2.2 shows, the second dimension's importance to classification peaks during the period when the civil rights issue was active, from the 1930s through the 1960s. In contrast to the story for the first dimension, the party separated on the second dimension during this period because southern Democrats had a conservative position on race. But the lack of polarization on the first dimension in the civil rights period is not simply the consequence of the relevance of a second dimension. First-dimension polarization started its decline well before the civil rights issue arose. Moreover, as we explain later in the chapter, the decline

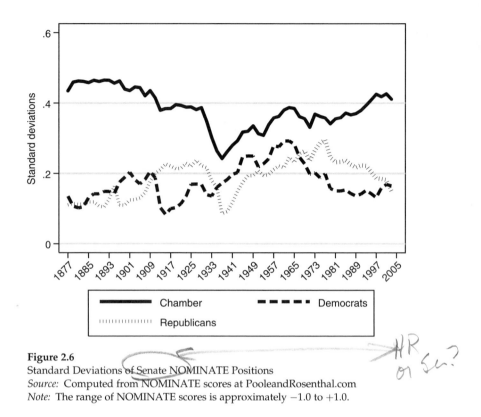

Figure 2.6
Standard Deviations of Senate NOMINATE Positions
Source: Computed from NOMINATE scores at PooleandRosenthal.com
Note: The range of NOMINATE scores is approximately −1.0 to +1.0.

and surge of polarization is found in the North even when we completely ignore the votes of southerners.

*The dispersion of positions of members on the first dimension has increased;
the parties have become more homogeneous.*

Since the mid-1970s, the dispersion of members of Congress has systematically increased in both chambers. The pattern is disclosed by figures 2.5 and 2.6. Dispersion is shown by the standard deviation for all
members on the first dimension. The increasing standard deviation
shows that members are tending to appear more at either the conservative end or the liberal end of the dimension. Moderates are vanishing.
Polarization along the dimension has reached the levels present during
the intense conflicts over regulatory policy and monetary policy at the
end of the nineteenth century.

The figures also show that, at the same time, the parties are becoming more homogeneous. The standard deviations for both parties

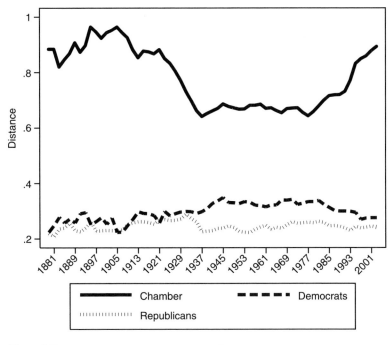

Figure 2.7
Average Two-Dimensional Distances in the House

have fallen in the past thirty years in the Senate. The parties now represent polarized blocs; voting coalitions that cut across the blocs are infrequent.

The results we have presented for standard deviations on the first dimension are validated by an approach that considers both dimensions simultaneously. For each pair of members of a chamber, one can compute the two-dimensional distance between the pair. For each party, we average these distances for all pairs in the party to get within-party distances. We also average the distances for all pairs of one Republican and one Democrat to get between-party distances. Like the overall standard deviation, between-party distances have increased since the 1970s (see figures 2.7 and 2.8). The within-party distances fell, although not as precipitously as the standard deviations. These results demonstrate that the surge and decline of polarization persists, even when the civil rights dimension is explicitly taken into account.

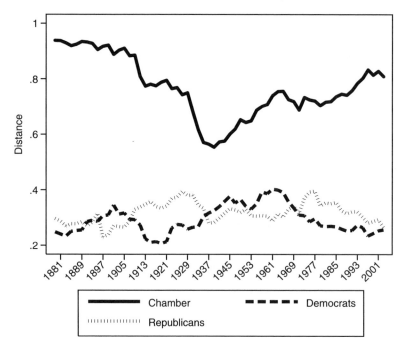

Figure 2.8
Average Two-Dimensional Distances in the Senate

The moderates are vanishing from Congress.

In fact, this loss is synonymous with polarization. One way to see the disappearance of moderates is to calculate the percentage of the total membership that have ideal points closer to the mean of the other party than to the mean of their own party. Figure 2.9 discloses a clean pattern for the House: almost no overlap until the late 1950s, a sharp increase in the 1960s, and a drop back to no overlap by the end of the 1990s. The story for the Senate is the same, with an important exception. Overlap there also increased in the 1920s and 1930s. Progressive Republican senators from farm belt states frequently voted with the Democrats. There is a much smaller uptick in the House because the farm belt states have relatively few members of the House. The farm belt story also relates to House-Senate differences in earlier figures in this chapter.

Another way of looking at vanishing moderates is to note how many Democrats have ideal points to the right of the leftmost Republican.

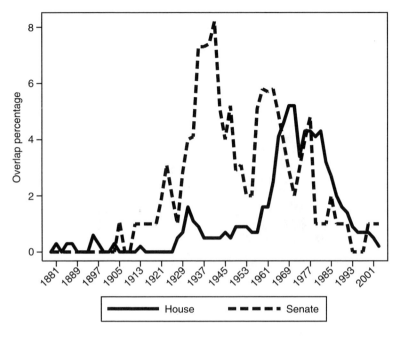

Figure 2.9
Party Overlap in Congress

Over the past ten years, only one senator, Zell Miller of Georgia, fit into this category. As the histogram in figure 2.10 shows, the two parties in the 108th House (2003–04) are completely separated.

We have documented the surge and decline in polarization. What brought it about? In the remainder of this chapter, we examine a number of distinct hypotheses about the causes of the polarization surge. In the next section, we explore the extent to which the link between constituency interests and congressional voting has changed during the surge. It is important, given our arguments, that the congruence between constituency income and congressional voting has increased substantially. But the increased link to constituency interest is only part of the story. The surge in polarization cannot be explained solely by constituency characteristics. We find that for a given constituency, the difference between Democratic and Republican representatives has grown. We then consider many other hypotheses that others have proffered to explain polarization, including those related to the southern realignment, enhanced capacities for party leadership, congressional apportionment, and primary elections. These alternative

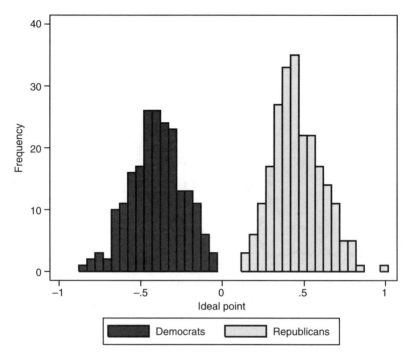

Figure 2.10
Distribution of Ideal Points in 108th House (2003–04)

explanations are never lead dancers and rarely get picked for the chorus line.

Polarization and Representation

Political scientists and economists have often tackled the question of representation and accountability by examining how well characteristics of a given electoral constituency explain the behavior of their representatives. Essentially adopting the "delegate" position in Burke's famous dichotomy, these scholars have defined good representation as what occurs when a representative's behavior is strongly associated with measures of her constituency's preferences and interests.[9]

Studies of roll call voting in the House have shown that the behavior of representatives deviates in large and systematic ways from the preferences of the average or median constituent. This finding persists even when the mismeasurement of constituency interests is not at issue.

For example, senators from the same state do not vote identically.
Most obviously, senators from the same state but different parties pursue very different policy goals. The difference is picked up in their
polarized NOMINATE scores. If the two senators are from the same
party, they are, of course, more similar. Even here, however, there are
differences. These differences occur even when the senators have similar NOMINATE scores, like John Heinz and Arlen Specter, and not
just when they differ sharply, like Rick Santorum and Arlen Specter.
The ideological model in fact outperforms a model that scores a prediction failure only when two senators are from the same state and party
but vote differently (Poole and Rosenthal 1997). In addition, Poole and
Rosenthal developed a version of NOMINATE where they could study
those aspects of roll call voting that were not "explained" by ideological position. How the two senators from the same state deviated from
ideology was correlated, but the correlations were not particularly
strong, even if the two senators were from the same party.

Congressional districts, being single-member, do not allow the same
natural experiment that is possible for the Senate. It is possible, however, to compare the voting behavior of a member to that of her succes-
sor. Poole and Romer (1993) found that same-party replacements of
House members had NOMINATE scores that could be very different
from those of their predecessors. True, a relatively liberal Democrat
was likely to be replaced by another liberal Democrat. Nonetheless,
the within-district variation of same-party replacements was about
half the total variation of positions in the party. A representative has a
great deal of latitude in either building a coalition of supporters or in
expressing his or her personal ideology.

Given that constituency interest fails to explain all, or even very
much, of the variation in roll call voting behavior, scholars have focused on the importance of party and ideology. These factors play little
role in a world of Burkean delegates or Downsian competition, but empirical studies have routinely verified their importance as determinants
of legislative behavior. While scholars generally agree that no one factor can explain legislative behavior, there is an ongoing debate about
the relative importance of ideology, constituency, and party as consid-
erations in casting roll call votes.

Our analysis reveals several important clues about polarization. The
first and most important is that the contributions of party, constituency, and ideology in explaining roll call behavior have changed
dramatically over the past thirty years. Not surprisingly, given our

results about polarization, political party is a much more consequential factor in explaining NOMINATE scores of representatives in 2004 than it was in the 1970s. As we will see, this is not because constituency factors are less important. In fact, if we measure constituency representation as the multiple correlation between constituency interests and a representative's behavior, representation has improved substantially. In other words, a set of simple constituency demographics better explains NOMINATE scores now than it did thirty years ago.

At first blush, the simultaneous increase in the importance of party and constituency seems counterintuitive. But it is entirely consistent with polarization. Because most voters in congressional elections are ill-informed about the specifics of the respective member's voting record, they often vote on the basis of partisan cues and reputations. As the parties polarized, these cues became much more informative, leading to the election of members with records more reflective of their districts.

The personal ideologies of members of congress is not waning as a component of roll call voting. It is often hard to measure the ideological component directly or to distinguish it from mismeasured constituency characteristics.[10] Therefore, we use the racial, ethnic, and gender identity of the representative as a proxy. We find that, even controlling for party and the ethnic and racial composition of the district, these factors are significant predictors of roll call voting behavior. This finding suggests that accounts of polarization that focus primarily on increased partisan homogeneity (Bishop 2004) are incomplete. If the voters in a congressional district were completely homogeneous in their preferences, switching the representative from male to female or from black to white shouldn't make a difference. It does.

Constituency, Party, and Ideology

To provide evidence for our claims, we estimate econometric models of the following form:

$$\text{NOMINATE}_i = \alpha + \beta R_i + \gamma \mathbf{C}_i + \delta \mathbf{P}_i + \varepsilon_i$$

where

$R_i = 1$ if the representative of district i is a Republican and 0 otherwise

$\mathbf{C}_i$ is a vector of constituency characteristics of district i

$\mathbf{P}_i$ is a vector of personal characteristics of the representative from district i

ε_i is the error term

α, β, γ, and δ are the corresponding coefficients.

Before we turn to the results, it is useful to discuss the interpretation of the basic model and several restricted versions. First, note that if we estimated the restricted model $\gamma=0$, $\delta=0$, then our estimate of β would reflect polarization as measured by the difference in party means. In the restricted model with just $\delta=0$, however, β can be interpreted as the polarization of the parties within a given district.[11] Thus, focusing on β in the restricted model helps to distinguish between two distinct hypotheses about polarization.

The first hypothesis is that polarization has arisen because of better matching between representatives and districts. In other words, conservative districts are more likely to elect Republicans and liberal districts are more likely to elect Democrats. In such a situation, we could observe an increase in polarization even if there were not more divergence in the candidates running in each individual district. Under this hypothesis, $\beta_{\delta=0}$ would not increase over time. The second hypothesis is that polarization has arisen because of greater divergence between the parties on the district level. Thus, for a given type of district, the Republican representatives are more conservative and the Democratic representatives are more liberal. This hypothesis predicts that $\beta_{\delta=0}$ should increase over time.

Now consider the effect of constituency characteristics $\mathbf{C}$. It is useful to distinguish between direct and indirect constituency effects. The direct effects represent the impact of those characteristics when the party of the member and the member's personal or ideological characteristics are controlled for. They are estimated as the vector γ in the unrestricted model. But $\mathbf{C}$ has an indirect effect on the legislator's ideal point through its effects on the party and other characteristics of the representative. These indirect effects can be captured by comparing the direct effects and the estimates of $\gamma_{\delta=0,\beta=0}$ that capture the total effects.

The distinction between total, direct, and indirect effects is also crucial in distinguishing among several arguments about the representational consequences of polarization. If polarization is simply the result of parties fleeing the voters, we would expect to see a decline in the total effect of constituency variables. Alternatively, if politicians are responding to more extreme voter preferences, the direct effect of constituency would go up. An additional possibility is a mixture of these two extremes. Polarization may provide voters with clear choices, enhancing the correlation between the representative's party and the set of constituency variables, **C**. In such a scenario, polarization increases the indirect effect but not necessarily the direct effect.

The Data

Below we present the results of the model for four different terms of the U.S. House of Representatives: the 93rd (1973–74), the 98th (1983–84), the 103rd (1993–94), and the 108th (2003–04). These were chosen to represent roughly each of the past four decades.[12]

The dependent variable for this analysis is each House member's first-dimension NOMINATE score. We include the scores for all members who vote a sufficient number of times to obtain a score. Thus, some districts will appear in the data set multiple times because of deaths and resignations.[13] Because the Democratic Speakers of the House rarely cast roll call votes, only 434 districts are represented in the samples for the 93rd and 98th Houses. In our four samples, the only independent member in the House was Vermont's Bernard Sanders. He caucuses with Democrats, so we treat him as one.

We deploy a number of congressional district characteristics that are complied by the decennial census. The measures were chosen on the basis of previous studies and consistency of measurement over time. The first characteristic, median family income, plays an important role in many of our arguments. For comparability purposes, we measure it in thousands of dollars and adjust it to the price level of 2000 using the Labor Department's CPI-U series. We also measure the education level of the district. To do so, we compute the percentage of the district residents twenty-five years or older who have college degrees and the percentage who graduated from high school and attended some college. We also capture the ethnic and racial composition of the district by measuring the percentage of constituents who identify as African-American and the percentage who identify as Hispanic.[14] We control for America's historical regional cleavage with a indicator variable for districts in the South.[15] To capture ideological effects, we indicate a representative's membership in racial, ethnic, and gender groups.

Results: Income's Increasing Importance

In tables 2.1–2.4, we present the results of the full specification of the model along with two restricted versions that allow us to assess various hypotheses. In each table, model A contains only constituency

Table 2.1
Determinants of NOMINATE Scores, 108th House (2003–04)
(standard errors in parentheses)

	Model A	Model B	Model C
Republican		0.799	0.797
		(0.017)	(0.016)
Family income in thousands of $	0.009	0.002	0.002
	(0.003)	(0.001)	(0.001)
% black constituents	−1.209	−0.261	−0.117
	(0.130)	(0.055)	(0.086)
% Hispanic constituents	−0.574	−0.085	0.007
	(0.115)	(0.047)	(0.065)
% with some college	2.077	0.545	0.526
	(0.414)	(0.167)	(0.170)
% college degrees	−1.382	−0.473	−0.441
	(0.366)	(0.146)	(0.147)
Southern	0.355	0.144	0.133
	(0.041)	(0.017)	(0.017)
African-American member			−0.095
			(0.043)
Hispanic member			−0.071
			(0.049)
Female member			−0.045
			(0.021)
N	440	440	440
R^2	0.357	0.899	0.902

characteristics. The coefficients from model A reflect the total effects of these factors. In model B, we add the indicator variable for the member's party. As we discussed above, we can interpret the coefficient on party as the average within-district polarization. Model C includes the full specification. Here we interpret the coefficients on personal characteristics as ideological effects and the coefficients on constituency characteristics as direct constituency effects.

We begin with the most recent Congress, the 108th House, in table 2.1. All of the constituency variables in model A are statistically significant. Family income, a southern location, and college *attendance* are correlated with more conservative scores, whereas African-American and Hispanic constituents and college *degrees* lead to more liberal scores.[16] Even though model A is relatively sparse, it captures more than 35 percent of the variation in NOMINATE scores. This is relatively strong explanatory power given that Poole and Romer's results

Table 2.2
Determinants of NOMINATE Scores, 103rd House (1993–94)
(standard errors in parentheses)

	Model A	Model B	Model C
Republican		0.680	0.678
		(0.015)	(0.015)
Family income in thousands of $	0.008	0.000	0.000
	(0.003)	(0.001)	(0.001)
% black constituents	−0.981	−0.451	−0.121
	(0.114)	(0.049)	(0.078)
% Hispanic constituents	−0.415	−0.218	−0.109
	(0.116)	(0.049)	(0.070)
% with some college	1.135	0.539	0.516
	(0.359)	(0.151)	(0.151)
% college degrees	−0.956	−0.508	−0.444
	(0.374)	(0.157)	(0.153)
Southern	0.230	0.140	0.120
	(0.039)	(0.016)	(0.016)
African-American member			−0.224
			(0.041)
Hispanic member			−0.090
			(0.053)
Female member			−0.044
			(0.022)
N	437	437	437
R²	0.258	0.869	0.880

about replacement suggest a low upper bound to the explanatory power of constituency.[17]

Moving to model B, we get an estimate of within-district polarization of .799. The total difference in party means is .864. Consequently, we find that differences in constituencies account for less than 10 percent of the total party polarization.

In model C, we examine the role of personal characteristics. The results show that African-American and female members have significantly more liberal voting records, with the liberal effect for Hispanic members just shy of statistical significance. These results are surprising perhaps only to hardcore Downsians, but more interesting is the large mitigation in the constituency effects when the individual characteristics and party are included. For example, the coefficient on the percentage of African Americans in the district drops by about 90 percent in absolute magnitude when party and individual characteristics are

Table 2.3
Determinants of NOMINATE Scores, 98th House (1983–84)
(standard errors in parentheses)

	Model A	Model B	Model C
Republican		0.611	0.612
		(0.017)	(0.017)
Family income in thousands of $	−0.002	0.001	0.000
	(0.003)	(0.001)	(0.001)
% black constituents	−0.898	−0.428	−0.238
	(0.115)	(0.059)	(0.081)
% Hispanic constituents	−0.877	−0.347	−0.287
	(0.151)	(0.077)	(0.099)
% with some college	1.618	0.856	0.896
	(0.427)	(0.215)	(0.216)
% college degrees	−0.652	−0.981	−1.005
	(0.479)	(0.240)	(0.238)
Southern	0.204	0.222	0.194
	(0.037)	(0.019)	(0.020)
African-American member			−0.182
			(0.054)
Hispanic member			−0.036
			(0.072)
Female member			−0.028
			(0.035)
N	437	437	437
R^2	0.233	0.808	0.814

included. In fact, in the full model, the effect of African-American constituents is statistically zero.[18] This result suggests that the representation of African Americans comes almost entirely indirectly through the choice of party and through the ability to elect African-American members of Congress. A similar story holds for Hispanic representatives. The effects of income, education, and region are also primarily indirect.

Given the baseline of the most recent Congress, we can conduct similar analyses of earlier terms to gather clues about polarization and the changing nature of congressional representation. We first note the increasing explanatory power of party, constituency, and individual characteristics. Figure 2.11 plots the R^2 for each of the models for each congressional term.

In the constituency-only model (A), the explanatory power rises from 19 to 36 percent. Polarization does not seem to have made members' voting records less representative of their districts. It is important

Table 2.4
Determinants of NOMINATE Scores, 93rd House (1973–74)
(standard errors in parentheses)

	Model A	Model B	Model C
Republican		0.588	0.590
		(0.018)	(0.018)
Family income in thousands of $	−0.002	−0.002	−0.003
	(0.003)	(0.002)	(0.002)
% black constituents	−0.782	−0.322	−0.046
	(0.122)	(0.067)	(0.093)
% Hispanic constituents	−0.933	−0.332	−0.212
	(0.178)	(0.098)	(0.125)
% with some college	1.943	0.902	0.930
	(0.697)	(0.377)	(0.384)
% college degrees	0.099	−0.532	−0.390
	(0.611)	(0.330)	(0.329)
Southern	0.187	0.214	0.169
	(0.043)	(0.023)	(0.025)
African-American member			−0.275
			(0.066)
Hispanic member			−0.119
			(0.101)
Female member			−0.017
			(0.045)
N	441	441	441
R^2	0.188	0.764	0.774

to note that this increase in explanatory power is not simply a product of the southern realignment. When we run the model on northern and southern districts separately, we obtain similar increases in R^2 from 1973 to 2003 for both regions. In the North, the R^2 increased from .184 to .310 while the South witnessed an increase from .213 to .411. The models including party and member characteristics also show substantial gains in explanatory power.

Our estimates of the relationship of district income to congressional voting confirm our arguments about the increasing political salience of income. Figure 2.12 plots the estimated difference in NOMINATE score of the member representing the highest-income district and one representing the lowest-income district (holding all other district characteristics constant).

Consider first the results from the constituency-only model (the first bar of each pair). Clearly, the effect of family income has risen substan-

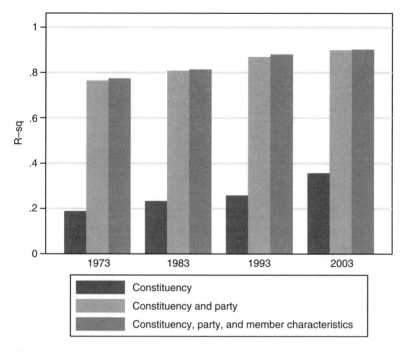

Figure 2.11
Explanatory Power of the Models

tially. In the 1973–74 and the 1983–84 Houses, the effect of income was negative and not statistically significant. But in 1993, the income effect is positive and significant, and it grew larger in the most recent congress. The income effect in 2003–04 is substantively large. An increase in family income of two standard deviations is associated with a .225 shift to the right, larger than the shift associated with reducing the percentage of African Americans by the same two standard deviations. The second and third bars in figure 2.12 represent the estimated income effects from models B and C, which control for party and member characteristics. The estimated effects are much smaller when we control for party, suggesting that most of the increased relationship between district income and congressional voting originates in the increased propensity of Republicans to win election in high-income districts. Nevertheless, the results from the 2003–04 House suggest that there is now a significant effect of income independent of its effect on the selection of representatives.

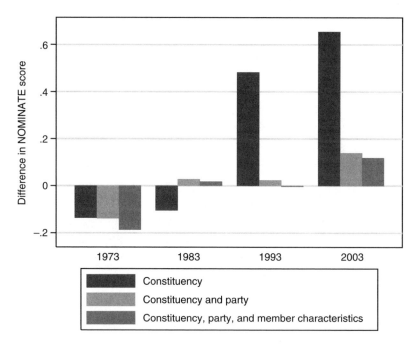

Figure 2.12
Effect of District Income on Left-Right Position
Note: Estimated difference between richest and poorest district for each model.

The increased magnitude of the income effects represented by figure 2.12 is attributed to two distinct factors. The first is the increased size of the coefficient on income. The second is that increasing income inequality has increased the gap between the richest and poorest districts. This income gap grew (in year 2000 dollars) from $56,000 in 1973 to $70,000 in 2003. Almost all of this increase is attributable to increasing incomes in the highest-income districts. This increase in inter-district inequality accounts for about 20 percent of the current difference in NOMINATE scores between high-income and low-income districts.

The results from model B, however, suggest that polarization is not simply the better sorting of representatives to districts. Figure 2.13 illustrates the growth in the estimates of the effects of member partisanship, once we control for constituency characteristics.

Our estimate of within-district polarization from model B has risen from 0.588 in 1973 and 1974 to 0.799 in 2003 and 2004. Over the same period constituency sorting has also increased. In the 1973–74 House, the unconditional difference in party means was essentially the

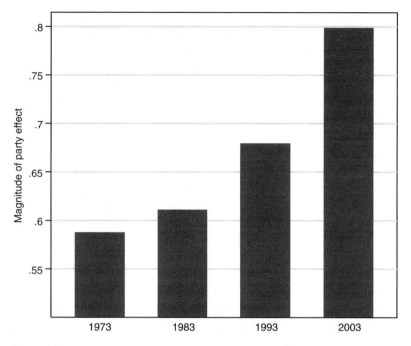

Figure 2.13
Partisan Difference on Left-Right Scale
Note: Estimates of party coefficient in Model B.

same as our estimate of within-district polarization. This result holds because the constituency characteristics were much more weakly related to the party of their representative in the 1970s than they are today.[19] Partisan sorting has increased and is partly responsible for the increase in the total effects of the constituency variables. But, the increased sorting is dwarfed by the increase in within-district polarization.

When viewed over time, the results on member characteristics tell a mixed story. Clearly, Hispanic and female members generated more distinctive voting records. Neither the Hispanic nor the female coefficients are significant in the 1970s and 1980s, but both have become so more recently.[20] Surprisingly, however, African-American representatives have become less distinctive, if we control for party and constituency.[21] As we do not find a similar change for females and Hispanics, it would be hard to argue that this finding is due to greater Democratic Party pressure for African-American representatives to conform. Much of the effect is the consequence of the departure of white southern Democrats, which means that the entire Democratic Caucus votes more like the Congressional Black Caucus. It is also a reflection both of the recent success of some African-American candidates such as Sanford Bishop and Julia Carson in nonmajority minority districts and of the entrance of the post–Civil Rights generation of black leaders typified by Harold Ford Jr.[22]

Summary

Although we argue in parts of this book that polarization has been elite-driven, our results here suggest that it does have some basis in the preferences of voters. Polarization has been associated not with a decline, but rather a strengthening, of the association between the demographic characteristics of House districts and the voting behavior of their members. This finding is the "choice, not an echo" benefit of polarization.

Also crucial to our principal arguments is our finding that polarization has been associated with a strengthening of the relationship between the economic well-being of a district and the representative's ideal point. A nonfactor in 1973, district income has both a direct and an indirect effect on the conservatism of the district's House member now. In chapter 3, we find out the reason. Voters are increasingly voting their pocketbooks.

Alternative Explanations

Although this book is primarily focused on the links between political polarization and the unequal economic performance of the past thirty years, a number of other plausible arguments have been put forward to explain congressional polarization.

The Southern Realignment

When V. O. Key (1949) penned his classic *Southern Politics in State and Nation*, the Democratic Party was monolithic in its control of southern local politics and was the only relevant intermediary between southerners and national politics. The southern Republican Party was, ironically, a more liberal alternative, but one available only to voters in the mountainous, impoverished regions of Virginia, Kentucky, and Tennessee. The Democratic dominance of the South combined with the congressional seniority system and the party presidential nomination

Figure 2.14
Difference in Republican Two-Party Vote between South and North, 1948–2004
Note: The South is defined as the eleven states of the Confederacy plus Kentucky and Oklahoma.

rule requiring a two-thirds majority (until 1936) guaranteed that the Democratic Party would do the South's bidding in national politics.

With the possible except of partisan polarization, no other change to the American polity is as important as the transformation of the southern United States from the core of the Democratic Party to the reddest of Republican strongholds. The trajectory of these changes is revealed in figures 2.14–2.17.

The transition began with a shift in presidential voting, starting with the Goldwater candidacy in 1964. By 1972, the South was solidly Republican. The only time after 1964 that a Democratic presidential candidate performed better in the South than in the North was 1976, when Jimmy Carter, a governor from the Deep South, defeated Gerald Ford. Bill Clinton, another southern governor, did relatively well in the South, but he won his two elections on the basis of northern votes. By 2000, another southern Democratic presidential nominee even lost his home state.

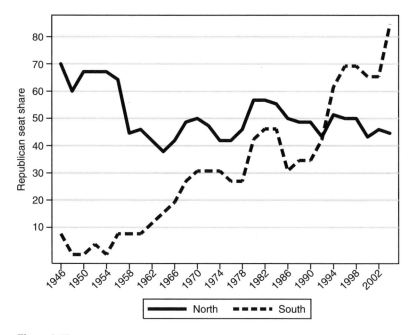

Figure 2.15
Republican Percentage of Seats in U.S. Senate
Note: The South is defined as the eleven states of the Confederacy plus Kentucky and
Oklahoma.

The realignment moved slowly down the ballot. Southern Republicans gradually increased their numbers in Congress, but they did not obtain a majority of southern seats in the House and Senate until the 1994 elections. State and local politics long seemed immune to the Republican advance. Nevertheless, the once-formidable Democratic advantage in the southern state legislatures has been reduced to ten Senate seats and a single House seat.

The conventional view is that the southern Republican Party was built on a foundation of racial conservatism following the Democratic Party's success in passing the 1964 Civil Rights Act and the 1965 Voting Rights Act. Without denying the importance of race in the realignment, we present evidence in the next chapter suggesting that the standard view may need to be altered in important ways. As we show, the changes in the South do not contradict, but rather complement, our basic story.

It is important to keep in mind that many of the nation's economic and demographic changes were magnified in the South. Economic

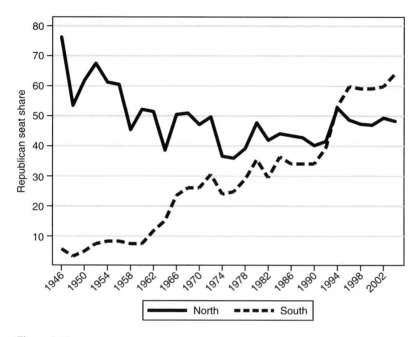

Figure 2.16
Republican Percentage of Seats in U.S. House
Note: The South is defined as the eleven states of the Confederacy plus Kentucky and Oklahoma.

growth in that region has been torrid for the past thirty years. Real per capita income grew 130 percent in the South between 1959 and 1989 compared to 95 percent in the rest of the nation. The eight fastest-growing states in the nation were all former members of the Confederacy. The gains were as unequally distributed as elsewhere.

A cause and consequence of this growth was the large migration to the South of middle- and upper-class whites who lacked the old southern enmity toward the GOP. The migrants included both George H. W. Bush and Newt Gingrich. And, with the exception of Texas and Florida, the South is only now beginning to feel the effects of the new waves of immigration. Even without the additional factor of race, the conditions were ripe for southern politics to reflect the same types of political alignment found in the rest of the country.

In table 2.5, we present evidence to suggest that the southern realignment was related to economics. By the early 1970s, the southern districts represented by Republicans were considerably more well-heeled

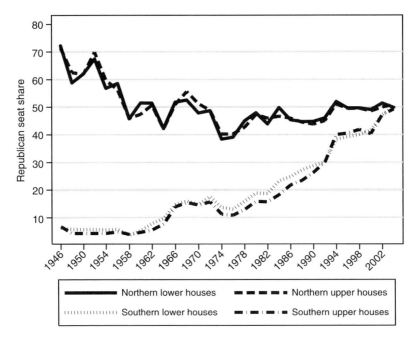

Figure 2.17
Republican Percentage of Seats in State Legislatures
Note: The South is defined as the eleven states of the Confederacy plus Kentucky and
Oklahoma.

Table 2.5
Income and Party in Southern House Seats

Southern House seats	Median family income in 2000$
Republican seats, 93rd House	$38,629 ($n = 37$)
Democratic seats, 93rd House	$34,104 ($n = 83$)
Difference	$4,525 $t = 3.19$
Republican seats, 108th House	$49,355 ($n = 84$)
Democratic seats, 108th House	$41,066 ($n = 57$)
Difference	$8,288 $t = 4.66$

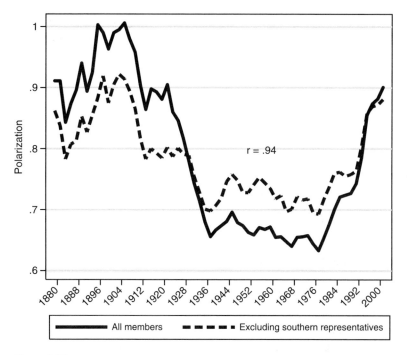

Figure 2.18
Southern Effect on Polarization in U.S. House, 1879–2001
Note: Measures of distance between two parties with and without southern members.

than those represented by Democrats. The median family income was about $4,500 greater in real terms in Republican districts than in Democratic ones. By 2004, the real income gap had grown to $8,300. Republican gains appear to be primarily the consolidation of control of high-income districts rather than the capture of middle- and lower-income districts.[23]

Whatever the cause of the southern realignment, a major consequence of the shift in allegiances was that many of the moderate and conservative southern Democrats in Congress were replaced by conservative Republicans. Clearly, this shift contributed to the establishment of the Republicans as the conservative party. But the realignment-induced replacement effect cannot be the whole story. In figure 2.18, we show the polarization measure for the entire House from the NOMINATE scaling used throughout this book. We also show the result from a separate scaling for the House minus its southern members. The two series are very highly correlated and follow the same U-shaped trajectory. The figure suggests that polarization among nonsouthern legislators is the driving force. The South significantly dampened polarization through the 1970s and 1980s; total House polarization exceeds nonsouthern polarization only in the mid-1990s.

A "southern" theory of polarization (at least the simple version) flounders on its inability to explain an equally prominent feature of the past thirty years: the disappearance of liberal Republicans outside the South. In 1973, the Senate had three Republicans positioned near the median Democrat: Clifford Case (NJ), Ed Brooke (MA), and Jacob Javits (NY). Their seats are currently held by Frank Lautenberg, John Kerry, and Charles Schumer, all from the liberal wing of the Democratic Party. Other liberal Republican seats from 1973 have been transmuted to the Republican right. Hugh Scott's (PA) seat is now held by Rick Santorum, and Pat Roberts (KS) is Jim Pearson's current replacement.

A second hypothesis about the link between realignment and polarization centers on how the southern stampede to the Republican Party altered the basic dimensions of political conflict. During the post-Reconstruction period, two spatial dimensions account for between 85 and 90 percent of roll call voting decisions. The primary dimension divides the two major parties, and the second dimension picks up regional divisions within the two major parties. As we have discussed, the first dimension is picking up, roughly speaking, the conflict between rich and poor. In contrast, during the civil rights conflicts of the mid–twentieth century, the second dimension was based on race— North versus South. Since the early 1970s, however, the importance of the second dimension has steadily declined, and congressional voting has become increasingly unidimensional. Racial issues formerly divided both parties internally but have now ceased to do so. To demonstrate this point, we have compared the fit of the one-dimensional NOMINATE model to the two-dimensional fit for votes on legislation related to civil rights. Figure 2.19a shows the aggregate proportional reduction in error (APRE)[24] for the one-dimensional model and the incremental improvement of the two-dimensional model for votes on race and civil rights.

During the post-Reconstruction period, voting on civil rights for African Americans was effectively kept off the congressional agenda except for a scattering of votes on lynching. The elections of 1936 pro-

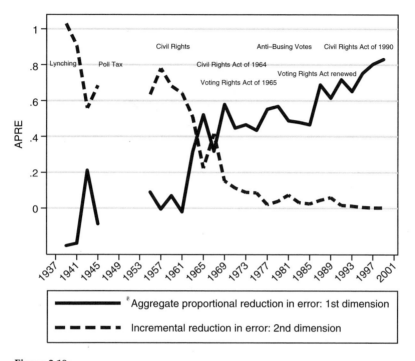

Figure 2.19a
Civil Rights, 1937–2000
Note: Congresses with fewer than two votes not included.

duced a majority of northern Democrats in both houses of Congress. Consequently, votes on civil rights for African Americans became more numerous—anti-lynching, voting rights in the armed forces during World War II, and then basic civil rights laws.

Figure 2.19a shows that when race on reappeared on the agenda of Congress in the late 1930s, the votes are largely explained by a second dimension separating northern and southern Representatives, regardless of party. Beginning in the late 1950s, the second dimension began to disappear. The movement of this issue to the first dimension sped up dramatically after the passage of the landmark 1964 Civil Rights Act and the election of a northern Democratic majority in the 1964 elections.

The timing of this transition roughly corresponds to that documented by Carmines and Stimson (1989), who stress the effects of the 1958 congressional elections and 1960s civil rights legislation on the polarization of American politics due to the issue of race. Although we

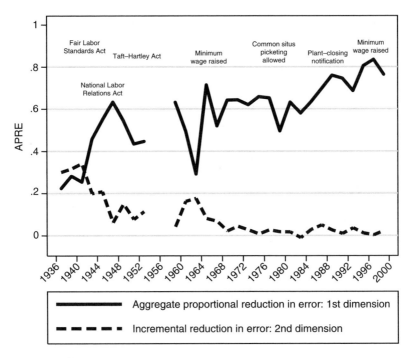

Figure 2.19b
Labor and Minimum Wage Votes, 1937–2000
Note: Congresses with fewer than two votes not included.

concur on the timing, we disagree about the nature of the transformation. For Carmines and Stimson, American politics has become the
politics of race. We are suggesting that racial politics has become more
like the rest of American politics.

To demonstrate this point, figures 2.19b and c plot the fit of the first
dimension and the incremental fit of the second dimension for two canonical sets of economic left-right issues. The first consists of votes on
labor regulation and the minimum wage. Except for a brief period in
the late 1930s, voting on these issues has largely been explained by the
first ideological dimension. Figure 2.19c extends the analysis to a broad
category of "government management" votes from the classification
scheme developed by Clausen (1973). Clearly, these issues have an-
chored the first dimension for the past seventy years and the power of
the first dimension to explain these votes rose during the period of polarization. Therefore, it seems far more likely that the voting cleavages
over race are converging to the preexisting economic cleavages, rather
than the other way around.

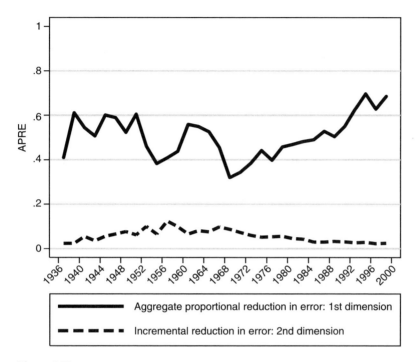

Figure 2.19c
Government Management Votes, 1937–2000

The trend toward increasing unidimensionality that began in the early 1970s in both the House and Senate cannot be adequately explained in terms of partisan control of Congress, changes in congressional rules, or agenda selection effects. Rather, it is clear that it must reflect a long-term change in the substance of party conflict. These trends closely track the exodus of the South from the national Democratic Party coalition. Southern realignment clearly changed the dimensionality of political conflict, but it is not at all clear how the change in dimensionality generated greater polarization.

Even though the replacement and dimensionality stories are incomplete, the South is certainly an important part of the story. First, Perlstein (2001) identifies the South as an important organizational nucleus for the conservative movement that has come to dominate Republican Party politics in the years since Goldwater's defeat in 1964. In the 1960s southern Republican congressmen were centrists typified by George H. W. Bush (TX) and Howard Baker (TN). But many, if not all, of the southern Republican legislators elected to Congress in the 1970s and 1980s were conservatives who got their start in politics during Goldwater's campaign. The South provided fertile soil for a movement that eventually spread to the rest of the country.

Second, had the Democratic Party maintained the allegiance of southern voters, the Republicans would have been denied an electoral majority for their low-tax and anti-regulation platform. The electoral cushion provided by southern votes allowed the Republicans to pursue noncentrist policies and win elections. As we document in the next chapter, southerners are not uniformly voting against their economic interests. On the contrary, like other Americans, southerners split along income lines. The richer the southerner, the more likely he is to vote Republican.

Partisan Reforms in Congress

Another proposed explanation for polarization lies in the series of reforms undertaken in the House since the 1970s (see Rohde 1991). According to such accounts, power in Congress was decentralized among its committees until a series of post-Watergate reforms strengthened the majority party caucus at the expense of committees.[25] Party power was further centralized in 1995 when Newt Gingrich and the Republican Conference exercised enormous discretion in the selection of committee chairs and imposed term limits on them.

The centralization of party power may effect polarization measured by NOMINATE scores in two ways. First, it may generate "artificial extremism" (Snyder 1992) if party leaders use their agenda control to select issues on which to divide their partisans from the other side. In the extreme, if every vote is on an issue that divides Democrats and Republicans, the voting patterns may look extremely polarized even if the parties are not very far apart. Polarization would be a statistical artifact. Second, increased party leadership might also exacerbate polarization if leaders were better able to force their moderate wings to vote with the party majority.

The completeness of either of these claims is doubtful as a simple matter of face validity. First, the explanations are very House-centered, so that explaining the polarization of the Senate and various state legislatures becomes a tortuous exercise. It is probably true that partisan leadership has become more prominent in the Senate but reform there has been less ambitious than in the House. The Senate's supermajority requirement embedded in its cloture rule also makes it extraordinarily difficult to pursue the partisan strategies that would create artificial extremism. Second, these stories are hard to reconcile with the increase in constituency representation that we documented earlier. Nevertheless, it is worthwhile to examine these hypotheses in some detail.

Because no one wants to read a book, much less write one, based on a statistical artifact, we begin with the "artificial extremism" hypothesis. The idea of artificial extremism was first applied to the use of interest group ratings. Snyder (1992) shows that if the votes chosen by a group produce a distribution of cutting lines with a variance less than the distribution of legislator ideal points, the distribution of ratings will be artificially bimodal. Fortunately, there are many reasons to be confident that this is not a large problem for scaling techniques such as NOMINATE. First, unlike interest group ratings, NOMINATE uses almost all the votes in a given term to estimate each ideal point. Interest groups can select only those votes that divide friend from foe, but no such selection bias exists when all votes are used. Thus, despite any increase in partisan control over the agenda, there are a wide variety of roll call cutpoints each term. The second reason that artificial extremism is unlikely to be an issue lies in a critical difference between interest group ratings and NOMINATE scalings. In an interest group rating, the distance between two legislators is directly proportional to the number of roll call cutpoints that separate them. Because NOMINATE uses the technique of maximum likelihood estimation, this is generally not the case. So as long as the distribution of cutpoints is sufficiently wide, an increase in the density of cutting lines between the two parties will not necessarily lead to an increase in polarization.

To assuage any remaining concerns, we conducted an experiment. We reran NOMINATE for the 1st through the 105th Congresses *constraining each House to have the same distribution of roll call margins.*[26] The average distribution of margins for all 105 Houses was used as the common margin and the number of roll calls for each House was set at 400. The distribution is shown in table 2.6.

To construct the artificial data for each House, we sampled each margin category *with replacement* to get the required number. For example, if for some Houses there were 75 roll calls with margins in the range 66-70, then 44 roll calls from those 75 were drawn with replacement. If there were no roll calls in the range, no roll calls could be included. But this caveat cannot affect our basic results about contemporary polarization, as no House since the 78th (1943–44) had a missing margin.

Table 2.6
Roll Call Weights

Majority size	Frequency	Relative frequency
50–55	92	0.23
56–60	80	0.20
61–65	60	0.15
66–70	44	0.11
71–75	32	0.08
76–80	24	0.06
81–85	20	0.05
86–90	16	0.04
91–95	20	0.05
96–97.5	12	0.13

Table 2.7
Comparison of Actual and Simulated Polarization Measures

Data series	Pearson correlation (r)
1st-dimension means	
Chamber	0.973
Republicans	0.967
Northern Democrats	0.950
Southern Democrats	0.996
Within- and between-party distances	
Between	0.992
Republicans	0.854
Democrats	0.984

Table 2.7 reports Pearson correlations between several of the polarization measures used in the chapter and the same measures computed from the artificial data. The correlations are over the sixty Houses studied in this book. It can be seen that the results are, from the standpoint of substantive interpretation, essentially identical. The lowest correlation is for the within-party distances for the Republicans (0.854).

We thus find that the pattern of polarization would be essentially the same even if the agenda were held constant. Of course, this experiment does not prove that the *level* of polarization is not inflated by artificial extremism, but it casts grave doubts on the role of artificial extremism in the *increase* in polarization.

We now ask the question of whether increased polarization is a reflection of the enhanced ability of party leaders to impose discipline on party members. This question has bedeviled the recent literature on legislative behavior because increased party pressure is, in general, observationally equivalent to better matching of legislator preferences and party. In the previous section, we provided evidence that polarization was a combination of increased sorting and increased party effects. But the analysis cannot distinguish between pressures internal to the legislature, such as those from leaders and caucus majorities, and those that are external, emanating from primary electorates, partisan constituents, and contributors.

One approach to distinguishing between internal and external pressure is to look for "selective" party pressures on close or important votes. Essentially, this approach seeks to determine the extent to which certain roll calls are more partisan than others and postulates that the variation is due to the activity of party leaders and whips. A version of the approach was first developed by Snyder and Groseclose (2000). Because, as they argue, rational leaders would expend little effort whipping on lopsided votes, those votes can be used to estimate measures of preferences uncontaminated by party effects. Therefore, after estimating legislator preferences using 65–35 divisions or greater, they regress each vote on the measure of preferences and a party dummy variable. They find that the party variable is statistically significant on a large percentage of the close roll calls but, as expected, on few lopsided ones.

In our paper "The Hunt for Party Discipline in Congress" (McCarty, Poole, and Rosenthal 2001), we criticize the Snyder-Groseclose approach on several methodological grounds and propose a different technique for uncovering selective party pressure. We assume that on each roll call there is a separate cutting line for each party. If there is no party effect, the two cutting lines will be identical, just as in the standard spatial model. If party discipline is applied, however, some Republicans to the left of the common cutpoint will vote with their party and some Democrats to the right will vote with theirs. The result is a separate cutpoint for each party. Because party discipline generally involves getting moderates to vote with extremists, the cutpoint for the Democrats should be to the right of the cutpoint for Republicans.

For a more concrete example, consider the one-dimensional spatial configuration illustrated in figure 2.20. If the cutpoint is constrained to be the same for both parties, this produces the standard spatial model.

Legislator	1	2	3	4	5	6	7	8	9	10	11	12	13	14	15	16	17
Party	D	D	D	D	R	D	R	D	R	R	D	D	R	R	R	R	R
Vote	Y	Y	N	Y	Y	Y	Y	Y	N	N	Y	N	N	N	Y	N	N

Common cutpoint — *Predicted Yea | Predicted Nay*

Rep. cutpoint — *Predicted Yea | Predicted Nay*

Dem. cutpoint — *Predicted Yea | Predicted Nay*

Figure 2.20
Cutpoint Models

For example, in figure 2.20, with a common cutpoint, there are three classification errors, legislators 3, 11, and 15. When each party can have its own cutpoint, this produces a model that allows for party discipline. Moderate Democrats to the right of some Republicans can vote with the majority of their party. Moderate Republicans to the left of some Democrats can vote with the majority of their party. The best cutpoint for the Republicans in figure 2.20 remains the common cutpoint. Legislator 15 is the only R classification error. But the best cutpoint for the Democrats is to the right of the common cutpoint. The D cutpoint leaves only legislator 3 as a classification error for this party. Rather than estimate either the one-cutpoint model or the two-cutpoint model via a metric technique, such as NOMINATE, one can simply find the joint rank order of legislators and cutpoints that minimizes classification error. Poole (2000) presents an efficient algorithm that closely approximates the global maximum in correct classification.[27]

To assess the importance of selective party pressure, we simply compare the predictive success of the two-cutpoint model to that of a one-cutpoint model. When party pressure is important, the two-cutpoint model should perform much better. The upshot of our results, reproduced in figure 2.21, is that the correct classification gains of the two-cutpoint model are modest and that there is no evidence that selective party pressures have increased.[28]

Of course, it's entirely possible that even if the ability to apply selective pressures has not increased, general party pressure (which would be reflected in each member's ideal point) has increased. But, as we have already noted, it is impossible at this point to distinguish between general party effects that are internal to the legislature and those that

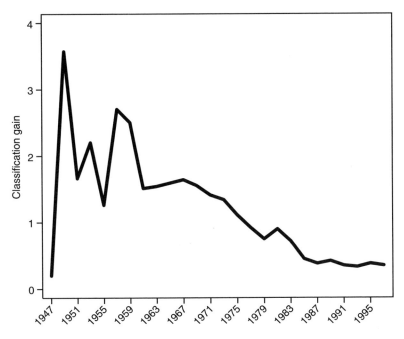

Figure 2.21
Classification Gain, One Cutpoint versus Two Cutpoints
Note: The classification gains are for a one-dimensional voting model. All representatives
were scaled together, and a separate cutpoint was then estimated for each party. The
classification gains are similar to those scalings in which each party has an independent
rank order of ideal points as well as a separate cutpoint.

are external. We can only hope to convince the reader that the prepon-
derance of the evidence presented throughout the book speaks in favor
of our externalist account.

Apportionment and Redistricting

Following the 2000 census reapportionment, congressional incumbents
were all but invincible in the 2002 elections. Indeed, two years later, almost all the incumbents who lost were beaten by other incumbents
in contests engineered by the controversial Tom DeLay–inspired mid-
decade redistricting in Texas. These events have brought the politics of
congressional districting under the punditry microscope.

As important as these controversies surrounding apportionment and
redistricting are, it is not obvious that they are much more than a
symptom of our political maladies rather than their cause. As polarization and partisanship have increased in the electorate, it would be

surprising if congressional incumbents were not more secure, independent of how their districts are drawn. And clearly, norms against redrawing the boundaries at mid-decade are hard to sustain when partisan balance is so even and the ideological stakes are so high. The strongest argument against overemphasizing the politics of apportionment is the fact that the United States Senate (which of course is never redistricted) has endured an almost identical history of polarization. It would be premature, however, to dismiss a link between districting and polarization out of hand, as the last three post-apportionment elections (1982, 1992, and 2002) have led to above-average increases in the polarization in the House. It behooves us to take a closer look.[29]

Arguments about the role of congressional apportionment in enhancing legislative polarization tend to stress two factors. The first is the creation of majority-minority districts designed to promote the election of racial and ethnic minorities to Congress. Creation of such districts often requires the concentration of black or Hispanic voters into districts where they constitute a large majority. A by-product of such concentration is the "bleaching" of majority white districts by removing minority voters. The result is an increase of African-American and Hispanic representatives who anchor the left end of the scale and conservative Republicans who represent almost entirely white districts. Although majority-minority districting undoubtedly has such effects, it is easy to overstate its significance in the big picture. First of all, very few states have majority-minority districts. More than two-thirds of the majority-minority districts are located in just five states: California, Florida, Illinois, New York, and Texas. In many of these cases, minority voters are sufficiently concentrated so that majority-minority districts can be formed easily with minimal effects on the boundaries of other districts. Eliminating these states from the calculations does not qualitatively alter the time series on polarization in the U.S. House.[30] There is a second reason to believe that racial gerrymandering has not had much impact. Earlier in this chapter, we showed that whereas African-American legislators have much more liberal voting records than white legislators, if we control for party, white representatives are not particularly sensitive to the size of the black population of their districts. Even if the "bleaching" effect alters the partisan balance, it does not increase partisan polarization among white representatives.[31]

A second common argument about apportionment is that the opportunity and technical ability to engage in partisan gerrymandering have gone up over time. Such gerrymandering is assumed to create much more homogeneous congressional districts, which accommodate more extreme legislators. Advocates of this hypothesis stress the near-absence of incumbent losses in the previous two electoral cycles. In a less anecdotal vein, Cox and Katz (2002) analyze congressional elections in light of the landmark "one person, one vote" Supreme Court decision in *Baker v. Carr*. This decision forced every state with more than one representative to redistrict after every decennial census. Cox and Katz show that the decision had a substantial impact on the rise of the incumbency advantage. There are reasons to be skeptical of a large connection between partisan districting and polarization. The first reason is theoretical. A seat-maximizing partisan gerrymander involves creating small majorities for the dominant party in a large number of districts and creating large majorities of the opposition party in a small number of districts. Purely partisan gerrymanders would not necessarily reduce the number of competitive districts.

Consequently, Cox and Katz argue that the incumbency effect arose precisely where pure partisan gerrymanders were politically infeasible. When the dominant party cannot impose its districting preferences, the result is a cross-partisan compromise, incumbency protection. Because such plans often involve enhancing the partisan homogeneity of districts, they have the potential to exacerbate polarization. But the effect is not obvious. Our recent polarization is primarily manifested in new cohorts of legislators that are more extreme than the departing cohorts. The average ideological movement of incumbent politicians has been much smaller.[32] By prolonging the careers of incumbents, incumbent-protecting gerrymanders may have impeded even greater polarization.

The final way in which apportionment may have contributed to polarization has not received nearly so much attention, but it may be the most significant. As a result of the shifts of population from the Northeast and the Middle Atlantic to the South and West, the last three decennial apportionments have resulted in a large net shift of seats to the Sunbelt. Following the 2000 census, the South gained five congressional seats and the Mountain West gained four. These gains came almost entirely at the expense of the Middle Atlantic and the industrial Midwest. Because the parties in the Sunbelt (especially in the once-solid South) are more polarized than in the Rust Belt, the result has been an increase in polarization due to the regional reallocation of seats.

Tables 2.8a-d provide the mean NOMINATE position of the Democratic and Republican members broken down by whether their state

Table 2.8
Mean NOMINATE Positions Following Reapportionment

Table 2.8a
2000 Reapportionment

Apportionment outcome	Democrats	Republicans	Difference
Loser	−.414	.421	.835
Unchanged	−.394	.438	.832
Winner	−.407	.544	.951

Table 2.8b
1990 Reapportionment

Apportionment outcome	Mean Democrat	Mean Republican	Difference
Loser	−.374	.311	.685
Unchanged	−.263	.360	.623
Winner	−.324	.456	.780

Table 2.8c
1980 Reapportionment

Apportionment outcome	Mean Democrat	Mean Republican	Difference
Loser	−.380	.250	.630
Unchanged	−.195	.315	.510
Winner	−.280	.424	.704

Table 2.8d
1970 Reapportionment

Apportionment outcome	Mean Democrat	Mean Republican	Difference
Loser	−.371	.259	.630
Unchanged	−.225	.252	.477
Winner	−.266	.338	.604

was a winner, a loser, or unaffected by reapportionment. In each of the last three apportionments, the mean difference between the parties in the "winning" states is substantially larger than the partisan differences in "losing" and unaffected states. The last apportionment for which this was not true was in 1970, just before the current wave of polarization began. The principal way in which reapportionment appears to influence polarization is not through partisan gerrymandering within states. It is the reallocation of seats across states forced by the decennial census.[33]

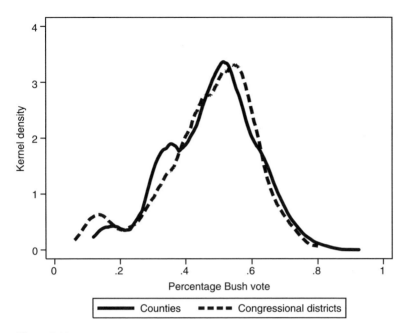

Figure 2.22a
Distribution of the 2000 Bush Two-Party Vote by Counties and Districts
Note: Counties are weighted by population. Both densities estimated using bandwidth =.025.

An important implication of all of the reapportionment-based arguments is that the distribution of voter preferences across districts is more polarized than the underlying distribution of preferences. But we see little evidence that the difference in those distributions is large. To illustrate this point, consider the distribution of presidential vote, a common measure of district partisanship and ideology. If the districting process is contributing to polarization, we would expect that the distribution of the presidential vote across districts to have "fatter" tails that the distribution of the vote across geographic units that are not subject to political manipulation. Figures 2.22a-d show estimates of the distribution of the Republican presidential vote across districts and across counties for the last four apportionments.[34] Contrary to the districting hypotheses, these distributions are very similar. The densities in the tails of each distribution are almost identical. Following the 2000 election, there are slightly fewer counties voting around 30 percent for Bush relative to districts and a few more very anti-Bush districts. This is presumably the effect of majority-minority districting.

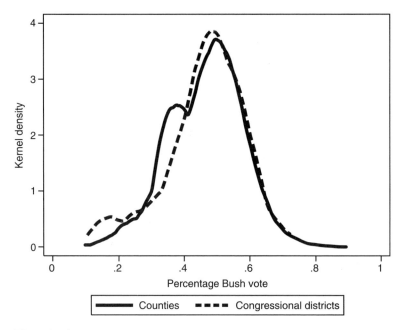

Figure 2.22b
Distribution of the 1992 Bush Two-Party Vote by Counties and Districts
Note: Counties are weighted by population. Both densities estimated using bandwidth
=.025.

A similar effect is apparent following the 1990s apportionment. The
1970s and 1980s apportionment did not produce "fat tails" either, but
rather a pro-Republican bias where the distribution of presidential vote
across districts lies distinctly to the right of the county distribution.
That is, although there was a pro-Republican bias in districting, there
was no bimodal distribution of districts that would protect incumbents. In all four years captured in figures 2.22a-d—most emphatically
in 1992 and 2000—there were many congressional districts where the
Republican presidential vote percentage was close to 50. Incumbents
win such districts not because they benefit from gerrymandering but
because they enjoy an incumbency advantage. Districting does seem
to distort the underlying distribution of preferences, but it would be
very hard to argue that there is a significant tendency toward more
polarized distributions.

Given the lack of strong evidence of a link to districting in the
House, we return to perhaps the biggest objection against such a link:

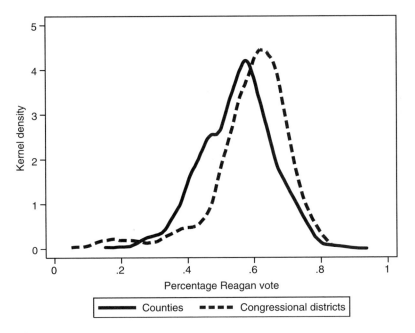

Figure 2.22c
Distribution of the 1980 Reagan Two-Party Vote by Counties and Districts
Note: Counties are weighted by population. Both densities estimated using bandwidth
=.025.

the polarization of the Senate. The Senate is never reapportioned or redistricted, so an apportionment story requires that polarization in the House cause polarization in the Senate. It is not clear what sort of mechanism might underlie such an effect. It is possible that changes in House apportionment alter the pool of competitive Senate candidates, or that the effects of apportionment strengthened the hand of each party's extreme factions. But any such mechanism would seem to require that changes in House polarization occur before changes in the Senate. In the spirit of a Granger causality test, we regressed biennial changes in Senate polarization on the contemporary change in House polarization and the lagged changes in House polarization for the . post–World War II period.[35] The results are shown in table 2.9.

Only the contemporary change in House polarization, not its lagged values, is correlated with changes in the Senate series. Thus, we find no evidence of Granger causation. Similarly, we find little support of an effect of Senate polarization on House polarization.

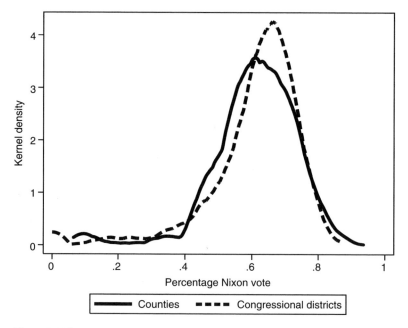

Figure 2.22d
Distribution of the 1972 Nixon Two-Party Vote by Counties and Districts
Note: Counties are weighted by population. Both densities estimated using bandwidth
=.025.

Table 2.9
Change in Senate Polarization
(standard errors in parentheses)

	Coefficient
Change in House polarization at t	0.748
	(0.255)
Change in House polarization at $t-1$	0.020
	(0.244)
Change in House polarization at $t-2$	−0.008
	(0.214)
Constant	0.001
	(0.006)
N	27
R^2	.289

Although congressional apportionment is obviously an important determinant in the determining the quality of representative government, it plays but a bit part in our choreography.

Party Primaries and Polarization

Another of the common folk explanations of political polarization lies in the role of primary elections in nominating congressional candidates. It is widely assumed that moderates have an increasingly difficult time winning their party's contests. Such a dynamic would then present increasingly stark choices to the general electorate.

This account has important limitations, however. The first is that the widespread adoption of the primary as a nomination device for Congress took place at the end of the nineteenth century and the first half of the twentieth. As we have seen, this corresponds to an era of declining polarization. By the time polarization began escalating, primaries were nearly universal. So any general claim that primary elections are the principal cause of polarization seems weak. Nevertheless, it is still worth entertaining the idea that institutional differences in the selection of legislative candidates do contribute to polarization.

Gerber and Morton (1998) provide evidence for the claim that laws dictating the ease with which independent voters can participate in partisan primaries has an important effect on the divergence of the general election candidates in congressional districts. They argue that states with "closed" primaries, which allow only registered partisans to vote in their party's primary, produce much more polarized general elections than states that allow independents to vote in primaries and partisans to vote in any primary. They cannot observe the positions of both candidates, but they claim support for their hypothesis by finding that winning candidates are more extreme relative to the district median in closed primary states.

Without calling into question their presentation of the evidence for this claim, we can say that it is not clear that such differences in primary laws have contributed much to polarization. First, it is important to remember that factors that lead to greater within-district candidate divergence may or may not lead to greater system-wide party polarization. Such an effect requires that the more extreme Democratic nominees continue to win in liberal districts and the more extreme Republican nominees continue to win in conservative districts. Therefore, to test to see whether closed primaries increase polarization, we conduct a simple difference in means tests on the NOMINATE scores

Table 2.10
Effect of Primary System on House Polarization: Mean NOMINATE Position by Party and Primary Type

System/Party	Democrats	Republicans
Closed	−.376	.387
	($n = 86$)	($n = 68$)
Open/Mixed	−.302	.359
	($n = 183$)	($n = 99$)
t-statistic	−3.011	1.091

Table 2.11
Effect of Primary System on Senate Polarization: Mean NOMINATE Position by Party and Primary Type

System/Party	Democrats	Republicans
Closed	−.315	.382
	($n = 18$)	($n = 14$)
Open/Mixed	−.361	.288
	($n = 40$)	($n = 30$)
t-statistic	1.079	1.248

from legislators nominated in closed primaries versus those in more open procedures. As Gerber and Morton do, we use Bott's (1990) classification of closed primary systems as of 1990 and conduct the test on the House and Senate elected that year. Table 2.10 presents the results for the House by party.

It appears that the closed system does indeed produce significantly more liberal House Democrats but has little effect on the distribution of Republican members. Although polarization is therefore greater in states with closed primaries, the aggregate effect is small. Only 35 percent of the House is elected under that system, so its aggregate contribution to polarization is on the order of 0.03, a tiny fraction of the NOMINATE scores—which, recall, run from −1 to +1.

Turning to table 2.11, which conducts the same analysis for the Senate, we find little evidence for any effect. In fact, closed states produce more conservative Democrats, though the difference is not significant. The conservative effect on Republicans is substantively large but is not statistically significant because of the small sample size.

Finally, even if one could establish a cross-sectional relationship between primary systems and polarization, the fact that closed primary systems have not become more common suggests that it cannot ex-

Table 2.12
Change in Polarization Since 1972 by Election Type

Election type	Average change in polarization	Standard error
Presidential	.021	.007
Midterm	.023	.010
t-value	−0.252	

plain the long-term trends. Closed primaries should have been producing as much polarization in 1960 as they did in 1990.

Perhaps the source of the effect of primaries on polarization is not
institutional but rooted in changes in participation and behavior of the
electorate. David King (2003) argues that the decline in participation in
legislative primaries is the major culprit. He speculates that declining
participation has made each party's primary electorate more homogeneous ideologically, resulting in more extreme candidates. There are a
number of reasons to be skeptical of such explanations. The first is that
the claim that primary electorates have become more partisan over
time is hard to verify directly. The National Election Study and other
sources of survey data have not consistently queried voters specifically
about their participation in primaries. King's deduction is based on a
series of indirect claims:

1. Participation in congressional primaries has fallen.

2. Partisans are more likely to participate in general elections.

3. Therefore, they are most likely to continue participating in congressional primaries.

4. Partisan identifiers are more ideological.

5. Therefore, the primary electorate has become more ideological.

Not an unreasonable chain of logic, but not a substitute for direct
proof. The second cause for concern is that the mechanism creating
polarization is almost identical to the mechanism by which closed
primaries are claimed to create it. As closed primary electorates are
the most partisan, tables 2.9 and 2.10 would seem to cast doubt on
King's hypothesis as well.

In the absence of direct confirmation or refutation of the hypothesis, we propose to use the natural variation in the size of the primary electorate induced by the presidential election cycle to test it. If

smaller primary electorates contribute to polarization, we would expect to see the polarization indices increase following midterm elections. Table 2.12 reports the result of a t-test matching the change in
polarization (as measured by the difference in party means) following
a presidential election with the change from the preceding midterm
election for each election since 1972.

This result provides no support for the primary participation hypothesis. The increases in polarization associated with midterm elections
are not significantly greater than those associated with presidential
elections. Apart from the large increase associated with the 1994 midterm Republican takeover, the average increase is greater following
presidential elections.

In summary, the evidence for the culpability of primaries is very
thin.

Seeking the Sources of Congressional Polarization

In this chapter, we have documented the rise of polarization in the two
houses of Congress. We have ruled out a broad spectrum of alternative
explanations for our finding. These range from method artifact to the
political realignment of the American South to institutional changes
within Congress and the structure of congressional elections and primaries. None of the alternatives provides a convincing theoretical explanation. Nor does any correlate empirically with the time-series of
polarization. Certainly none of these alternatives is as cheek to cheek
with polarization as were the time series of inequality and immigration
that we showed in chapter 1.

We did find, however, that constituency characteristics had become
more linked to congressional ideology in recent decades and, in particular, that median income had become more linked to conservatism. We
therefore turn to economic and demographic factors in the next three
chapters.

3 Income Polarization and the Electorate

What has happened to voters as politicians have polarized? A hint at the answer is contained in our finding that the liberal-conservative ideologies of members of the House of Representatives are increasingly tied to the median incomes of their constituents. In this chapter, we explore how the political preferences of individual voters have become increasingly related to their incomes. High-income voters increasingly identify with the Republican Party and vote for Republican presidential candidates. Low-income voters are increasingly in the Democratic camp. This finding controverts recent punditry.

The 2004 election, in particular, was not just a contest featuring Bush, Kerry, and their parties. It was also a battle of pundits over the extent and nature of America's electoral divide. Some saw the country as red and blue, the colors used in the famous electoral maps showing the Democrats winning the coasts, major urban areas, and college towns, with the Republicans getting the rest. Red and blue analysis became fashionable despite some claims that the country is purple, with most areas splitting their votes between the parties at fairly equal rates. A conventional wisdom about the electoral divide quickly emerged. When 22 percent of voters told election pollsters that moral values were their top issue and thirteen states voted to ban same-sex marriage, "guns, God, and gays" became the mantric explanation for Bush's victory.[1]

Academics have been somewhat more circumspect in their analysis of electoral polarization. Dimaggio et al. (1996), Evans (2003), and Fiorina (2004) find no evidence that the overall electorate is more polarized on most social and economic issues. Indeed, on many issues the electorate is moving toward consensus. The one not-so-minor exception in these studies, however, is that those voters who identify strongly with the major parties are increasingly divided, with Democratic identifiers

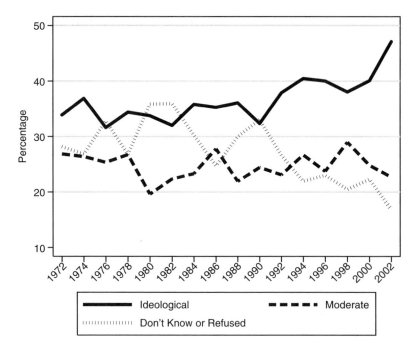

Figure 3.1
Ideological Self-Placement
Note: Respondents to National Election Study. Respondents identifying as liberal or conservative (including "strongly" and "slightly") are grouped into the ideological category.

consistently taking more liberal positions and Republicans taking more conservative ones.[2] Similarly, there is evidence that partisan affiliation in the mass public is increasingly polarized by liberal and conservative views. Green, Palmquist, and Schickler (2002) report that the difference between the "percentage of Republicans who call themselves conservatives" and the "percentage of Democrats who call themselves conservatives" has doubled between 1972 and 1996, moving from 25 to 50 percent.[3] Figure 3.1 also shows that the overall percentage of voters calling themselves liberal and conservative has grown steadily since 1990, while the number refusing to take an ideological label has declined.

One thing that public and academic discourses have in common is that neither has paid much attention to how changes in the American economy have contributed to electoral polarization. Thomas Frank, a journalistic proponent of "values" theory, sums up the conventional wisdom: "One thing is certain in the search to unravel the mystery of the 'great divide': we know for sure the answer isn't class. We can rule that uncomfortable subject out from the start"[4] (2004b).

For the most part, political scientists have been no more eager to broach the "uncomfortable subject." Although much recent work in comparative political economy has sought to link inequality to political conflict and back to economic policy, few of these insights have been applied to American politics.[5] Only very recently has interest in the links between inequality and American politics increased. Bartels (2002), Gilens (2005), and Jacobs and Page (2005) find strong evidence that congressional voting and public policy are much more responsive to the opinions of high-income citizens than poorer ones. Bartels (2004) also finds a significant effect of partisan control of the presidency on the growth of inequality. Despite this progress, however, a recent report of the American Political Science Association declares that "inequality in American government is understudied [sic]."[6]

Perhaps one reason for the dearth of interest is that income or wealth has not been seen as a reliable predictor of political beliefs and partisanship in the mass public, especially in comparison to other cleavages, such as race and region, or in comparison to other democracies. For example, a major recent work on partisan identification by Green, Palmquist, and Schickler (2002) makes little or no use of income as predictor of partisan attachments.[7] Studies of "class voting," conducted primarily by sociologists, have found that the American electorate has become less divided on occupational and subjective class identities since the New Deal.[8] If political conflict does not have an income basis, it makes little sense that changes in economic inequality would disturb existing patterns of political conflict.

That American politics has not always been organized as a contest of the haves and the have-nots does not mean that it will always be that way. If income and wealth are distributed in a fairly equitable way, politicians gain little by organizing politics around nonexistent conflicts. In this context, it is interesting that much of our empirical knowledge about the nature of American political attitudes and partisanship is drawn from surveys conducted during an era of relatively equal economic outcomes.

Partisanship was, in fact, only weakly related to income in the period following World War II. In the presidential election years of 1956 and 1960, National Election Study respondents from the highest income quintile were hardly more likely to identify as a Republican than were respondents from the lowest quintile. In contrast, in the

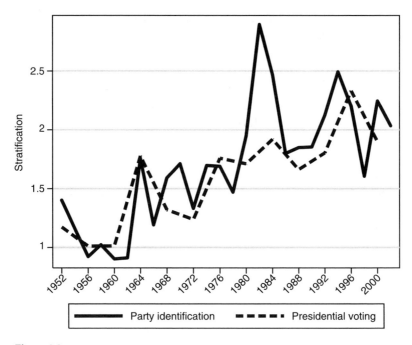

Figure 3.2
Party Stratification by Income
Source: The American National Election Study
Note: Stratification is the Republican proportion of the top income quintile divided by
the Republican proportion of the bottom quintile.

presidential election years of 1992, 1996, and 2000, respondents in the
highest quintile were more than twice as likely to identify as Republican as were those in the lowest.

We can measure the income basis of partisanship through an index
of party-income stratification. Our index is simply the proportion of
Republican identifiers in the top income quintile divided by the proportion of Republican identifiers in the bottom quintile.[9] As seen in figure 3.2, the stratification of partisanship by income has grown steadily
over the past forty years, leading to an increasing rich-poor cleavage
between the parties.

In figure 3.2, we also plot stratification for the presidential vote. Here
we compute the ratio of the fraction of Republican voters among voters
for the two major parties in the top quintile to the same fraction in the
bottom quintile. The upward trend in stratification is also evident for
the presidential vote.

Of course, the simple bivariate relationship between stratification and income does not show that the party system is increasingly organized along income lines. These results could be due to changing income characteristics of party constituencies based on other cleavages. We do not deny this claim (in fact, we present some evidence for it below), but we insist that regardless of the mechanism that created the stratification of partisanship by income, the mere existence of substantial income differences across the constituencies of the two parties has important implications for political conflict. As parties are generally presumed to represent the interests of their base constituencies, the income stratification should contribute to the parties pursuing very different economic policies. Moreover, public policy may be shifting away from policies that are based on self-identified racial, ethnic, or gender characteristics. The shift could be to policies, such as preferred access to higher education for children from poor homes or earned income tax credits for working families, that are income- or wealth-based. Such a shift would reinforce interest in studying the income stratification of partisan identification.

To explore the relationship between the economic and political transformations we have discussed, the rest of this chapter attempts to provide some explanations for the increased party-income stratification. The main source of data is the National Election Study (NES) conducted by the Survey Research Center of the University of Michigan. The NES has sampled the American electorate every two years starting in 1952 (1954 excepted) and is the only longitudinal data source that has been on the dance floor for all of the past fifty-plus years. In order to address directly the alternative viewpoints raised by the proponents of "moral values" explanations, we also use the much larger recent samples provided by the Pew Research Center for the People and the Press.

In our analysis of the NES data, we focus on partisan identification because it is the one item present in every study from 1952 to 2002. Moreover, unlike presidential vote intention or choice, it is less influenced by election-specific factors. We are able, however, to show that our results for partisanship largely replicate for presidential vote choice, although, as is to be expected, the results are somewhat noisier.

Logically, there are four non–mutually exclusive reasons why income stratification might have increased. First, there could be a _response_ effect. That is, there can be a temporal increase in the coefficient for income in our model of partisanship. Below we argue that this increase is consistent not only with party polarization on economic policy issues, but also with increased salience of economic issues. Second, there may be an *inequality* effect. Increased inequality might have made low-income groups relatively poorer and high-income groups richer, so that with even a constant *response* effect, stratification would grow. Third, increased stratification might be a result of a change in the joint distribution of other demographic characteristics and income. Pro-Democratic groups may have gotten poorer while pro-Republican groups got richer. For example, African-American partisanship may have remained unchanged, but the relative poverty of African Americans may have increased. Fourth, groups with high incomes may have moved toward the Republicans while poorer groups moved toward the Democrats. For example, the relative poverty of African Americans may have remained unchanged but their propensity for Democratic identification increased.

To quantify each of these effects, we estimate a model of party identification and its relationship to income and other characteristics. We then use the estimates of this model as well as data about the changing distribution of income to calculate the level of party-income stratification under many different counterfactual scenarios. The results show that almost all of the increase can be attributed to an increased effect of income on partisanship and changes in party allegiances of certain groups. A significant portion of the stronger income effect reflects a greatly increased income effect in the South. Changes in the incomes of various groups and the widening income distribution do not play as large a role.

A Simple Model of the Relationship between Income and Partisanship

To provide structure for our empirical analysis, we begin with the canonical prediction of political-economic models of voter preferences over tax rates and the size of government. These models predict that a voter's preferred tax rate is a function of both her own income and the aggregate income of society.[10] If we assume that tax schedules are either proportional or progressive, people with higher incomes prefer lower tax rates because they pay a larger share of taxes but receive only an equal share of public expenditure. Alternatively, when aggregate income is larger, higher tax rates produce more money for redistribution and public goods. Thus, *ceteris paribus*, citizens prefer higher tax rates as aggregate income increases.

How much higher? In a seminal paper, Duncan Foley (1967) assumed that people paid a proportion of their income as taxes but received, as redistribution, an equal share of the tax revenues. People with incomes below the mean would benefit as their equal share would be greater than their taxes. Those above the mean would lose. Foley's model implies sharply polarized preferences. All below the mean income would favor a tax rate of 100 percent; all above it would favor 0 percent. In turn, in simple models of politics, the median voter is thought to be decisive. Because income distributions are skewed with median income considerably less than mean income, Foley's model suggests that a democracy should have a high degree of redistribution.

Redistribution, however, cannot be carried out without some cost to aggregate income. Specifically, high taxation should reduce labor supply.[11] Alternatively, there could be a deadweight loss that occurs in the collection and redistribution of tax revenues. When taxation is costly, preferences on taxation become a continuous function of income. There is no longer Foley's discontinuity at the mean.

A straightforward, tractable model of the cost of taxation was developed by Bolton and Roland (1997). They assumed that redistribution generates a deadweight loss that is quadratic in the tax rate. Specifically, the deadweight loss from a dollar of taxation is αt^2, where α is a parameter and t is the proportional tax rate. So if $\alpha=1$ and $t=1/2$, a quarter is lost for every dollar collected, but if $t=1$, the entire dollar is lost. In other words, tax increases generate increases in marginal cost. For $\alpha=1$, tax revenue increases as t is increased from 0 to $1/2$ and then falls. The Bolton and Roland model is one way to generate the Laffer curve promoted by supply-siders who claim that government revenue can be increased by cutting taxes.

With the quadratic loss model, the most preferred tax rate of a person decreases as her income rises—the rich want low taxes. In fact, the desired tax decreases linearly with the ratio of a citizen's pre-tax income to mean pre-tax income. If $\alpha=1/2$, the most preferred tax rate of a voter is simply

$$t_{preferred} = 1 - \frac{\text{voter's income}}{\text{mean income}}$$

Thus, as inequality increases—the ratio falls for the median voter—there should be higher taxes and more redistribution. Note further that the median voter always wants some redistribution but that the

Box 3.1
Voting over Alternative Tax Policies

Let the pretax income of a generic voter i be y_i. Let $\bar{y}$ denote average income. Bolton and Roland (1997) assume that the utility U_i of the voter is simply post-tax income. We can, without changing anything, divide through by $\bar{y}$ to get:

$$U_i = r_i + t(1 - r_i) - \alpha t^2$$

where $r_i = \dfrac{y_i}{\bar{y}}$.

If the political parties are polarized, the median voter is not decisive. Instead, voters must make the best of a bad situation and choose between the tax policies of the Republicans and Democrats, which we denote as t_R and t_D, with $t_D > t_R$. Some straightforward algebra then shows that the utility difference for the voters can be written as:

$$U_{iR} - U_{iD} = r_i(t_D - t_R) - (t_D - t_R)[1 - \alpha(t_D + t_R)].$$

The first term is positive, proportional to income, and independent of deadweight loss. The Republicans are favored because they tax less. The second term is negative (as long as α is not too large) and depends on the tax policies and deadweight loss but is independent of income. The Democrats are favored because they redistribute more. Voters trade off taxes and benefits, with higher-income voters tilting to the Republicans. If tax platforms are held constant, the Democrats benefit from increasing government efficiency.

desired tax rate will fall as government efficiency falls (α increases). For any level of efficiency, there will be more support for redistribution as the ratio of median to mean income falls. A shift in the ratio, say from 0.8 to 0.7, has important consequences for policy. These pressures for redistribution are likely to appear even if the median voter is not decisive for policy. In a responsive democracy, more inequality should typically lead to more redistribution. The ratio of median to mean income is a simple way of capturing the pressure to redistribute.

In box 3.1, we explain how voting decisions for a generic voter i will depend on the utility difference between Republican and Democratic tax policies. This difference works through the ratio of that voter's income to average income, the tax policies of the two parties t_D and t_R, and the extent of deadweight loss. The ratio is termed "relative income" and denoted r_i. Because a voter's party identification may depend on factors other than this income-based utility difference, let x_i be a vector of other factors that determine support for the

Republican Party and ε_i be individually idiosyncratic factors. For x_i variables we use standard demographics—race, gender, education, age, and region—and a behavioral variable—church attendance—that represent variables other studies have found to be related to partisanship.[12]

Our model of Republican Party ID is therefore

$$\text{Republican ID} = \tilde{\gamma} + \beta[r_i(t_D - t_R)] + \boldsymbol{\theta} x_i + \varepsilon_i$$

$$= \tilde{\gamma} + \tilde{\beta} r_i + \boldsymbol{\theta} x_i + \varepsilon_i \tag{3.1}$$

where

$\tilde{\beta} = \beta(t_D - t_R)$ and $\tilde{\gamma} = \gamma - \beta(t_D - t_R)[1 - \alpha(t_R + t_D)]$, with γ being a standard regression constant and the remaining term being a constant explained in box 3.1.

Given this model, we can identify several factors that in principle could account for the increased stratification of partisanship by income.

1. *Inequality.* Increases in economic inequality may have led to more extreme values of r_i. A standard measure of economic inequality is the ratio of the income of the top quintile to that of the bottom quintile. Thus increased inequality would raise the mean value of r for the upper quintile or reduce the mean value of r for the lowest quintile or both.

2. *Response polarization.* Party polarization on economic issues as reflected by $t_D - t_R$ has increased. From equation 3.1, this increases $\tilde{\beta}$.

3. *Differential economic success of partisan groups.* Other determinants of party identification such as race, gender, region, education, and age have become more related to income. Therefore income stratification may be a by-product of the differential economic success of the demographic groups that compose each party.

4. *Partisan demographic shifts.* Poorer demographic and social groups have moved toward the Democrats while wealthier groups have identified more with the Republicans.

Before assessing these different possibilities, we turn to some important data and estimation issues.

Data

We employ the National Election Study data from 1952 to 2002 to estimate equation 3.1. Our dependent variable is the seven-point scale of partisanship that ranges from Strong Democrat through Independent to Strong Republican, coded 0 to 6. Unfortunately, NES data pose a number of problems specific to the estimation of our model. Perhaps the biggest problem is that the NES does not report actual incomes but allows respondents to place themselves into various income categories. We use Census data on the distribution of household income to estimate the expected income within each category. These estimates provide an income measure that preserves cardinality and comparability over time. The details of our procedure are in the appendix.

In addition to the constructed income variable, we include control variables. These include race, region, gender, age, and education. We combine race and region to create two categorical variables, African Americans and southern non–African Americans.[13] The residual category is northern non–African Americans. We measure education by distinguishing between those respondents who have "Some College" or a "College Degree" from those who have a high school diploma or less. We also include the age of the respondent. To capture the effects of "moral" issues, we include a dummy variable for church/synagogue attendance (at least "once or twice a month"). Table 3.1 gives the average value of each of these variables for each election study.[14]

In fact, race, gender, age, education, and church attendance are the only demographics that are consistently available on all of the twenty-five National Election Study presidential and midterm year surveys from 1952 through 2002.

It is important to note that these additional variables are not only statistical controls but also variables that are not distributed randomly across income levels. Therefore, both changes in the joint distribution of these variables with income and changes in their relationship to partisanship may have effects on the extent to which partisanship is stratified by income.

To control for election-specific effects on partisanship, we include election fixed effects (year dummies) in the estimation.

Estimation

As just noted, we observe only placement on the seven-point partisan identification scale and not the continuous measure of Republican identification that is given in the linear equation 3.1. Our categorical data on partisan identification have, moreover, a bimodal distribution. Consequently, ordinary least squares regression is a highly inappropri-

Table 3.1
NES Sample Means of Variables

Year	Party ID	Relative income	Black	Female	Some college	College	Age	Southern non-African American	Church/ Synagogue attendance
1952	2.475	1.104	0.090	0.544	0.083	0.064	44.8	0.221	0.563
1956	2.660	1.099	0.083	0.553	0.108	0.080	44.8	0.237	0.608
1958	2.403	1.053	0.086	0.540	0.104	0.092	46.6	0.244	0.626
1960	2.546	1.075	0.074	0.539	0.114	0.096	48.4	0.263	0.590
1962	2.505	1.040	0.086	0.551	0.119	0.121	47.2	0.303	0.608
1964	2.060	1.002	0.230	0.561	0.121	0.109	45.9	0.191	0.595
1966	2.473	0.940	0.105	0.557	0.139	0.096	46.8	0.241	0.576
1968	2.333	0.969	0.158	0.567	0.136	0.130	46.7	0.227	0.546
1970	2.409	0.894	0.161	0.570	0.140	0.104	45.1	0.254	0.545
1972	2.605	0.968	0.099	0.568	0.161	0.132	44.4	0.240	0.490
1974	2.547	0.989	0.090	0.580	0.172	0.137	47.3	0.259	0.535
1976	2.606	0.975	0.100	0.580	0.181	0.152	45.6	0.235	0.525
1978	2.493	1.000	0.102	0.559	0.194	0.160	43.3	0.272	0.474
1980	2.518	1.017	0.116	0.569	0.206	0.162	44.3	0.271	0.480
1982	2.448	0.958	0.107	0.553	0.244	0.188	45.4	0.279	0.547
1984	2.768	0.918	0.111	0.562	0.247	0.167	44.4	0.227	0.489
1986	2.620	0.937	0.148	0.563	0.233	0.200	43.8	0.244	0.507
1988	2.823	0.861	0.132	0.573	0.225	0.198	45.1	0.243	0.504
1990	2.591	0.847	0.130	0.548	0.219	0.192	45.2	0.228	0.511
1992	2.705	0.909	0.128	0.534	0.236	0.235	45.8	0.241	0.515
1994	2.918	0.918	0.113	0.534	0.256	0.255	46.3	0.276	0.527
1996	2.678	0.909	0.121	0.555	0.271	0.275	47.6	0.242	0.529
1998	2.654	0.893	0.119	0.551	0.286	0.278	45.8	0.278	0.514
2000	2.726	0.937	0.118	0.563	0.303	0.309	47.2	0.268	0.533
2002	2.951	1.096	0.101	0.561	0.312	0.350	49.9	0.273	0.582

ate estimation method. A preferable alternative is to treat the partisanship variable as a set of ordered categories and estimate an ordered
probit model (McKelvey and Zavoina 1975). In box 3.2, we describe
how the ordered probit uses the data from the seven-category partisan
identification scale to estimate equation 3.1.

To capture changes in the relationship between income and other
variables to partisanship, we assume that the coefficients of equation
3.1 can change over time. For our relative income variable, we estimate
several different specifications that restrict the movement of $\tilde{\beta}$ in various ways. We report four sets of results corresponding to a constant income effect, an effect with a linear trend, an effect with a cubic trend,
and an income effect "dummied" for each of the five decades represented in our dataset. We also allow the effects of other variables to
change over time with linear trends. We assume that the category
thresholds estimated by the ordered probit are constant over time.
Therefore, the distribution of responses across categories changes only
with respect to changes in the substantive coefficients and the distribution of the independent variables.[15]

Results

Table 3.2 presents the estimates of our model for the four specifications
of the income effect. Not surprisingly, across all four specifications,
relative income is a statistically significant factor in the level of Republican partisanship. Model 1 has a constant income effect. Although it
is statistically significant, the estimate of the constant effect is rather
small. A person with twice the average income ($r_i=2$) has Republican partisanship that is only 0.127 larger than one with an average
income. This effect is less than one position on the partisanship scale,
as the distance between the category thresholds averages more than
0.3.

The small average effect of income masks a definite trend over the
entire period. Model 2 simplifies matters by assuming that the income
effect changes only linearly. This model produces a statistically significant growth rate in the income effect of 0.0018 per year. From 1952 to
2002, the income effect is estimated to have more than doubled, rising
from 0.081 to 0.171. These results are echoed by model 4, a specification with a separate income effect for each decade. Each subsequent decade has a higher estimated income effect. The estimated income effects
have grown substantially over time.

Box 3.2
Ordered Probit Model of Partisan Identification

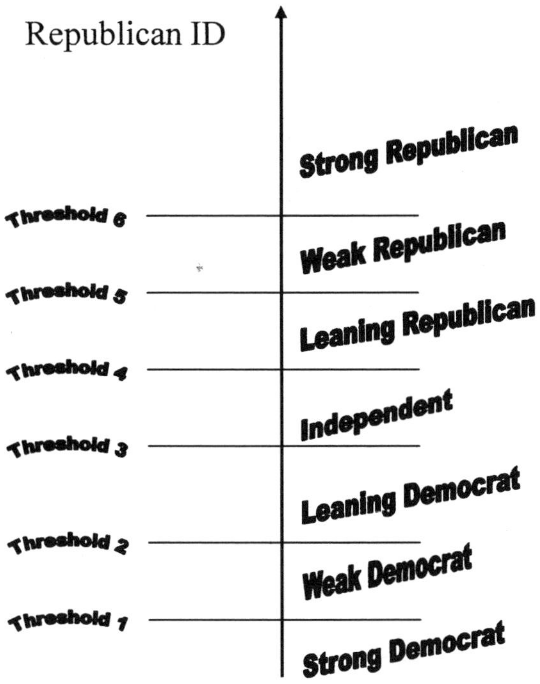

Republican ID

Strong Republican

Threshold 6 ─────────────

Weak Republican

Threshold 5 ─────────────

Leaning Republican

Threshold 4 ─────────────

Independent

Threshold 3 ─────────────

Leaning Democrat

Threshold 2 ─────────────

Weak Democrat

Threshold 1 ─────────────

Strong Democrat

The amount of Republican ID is given by equation 3.1. If the amount is below threshold 1, the respondent is a "Strong Democrat." If the amount is between threshold 1 and threshold 2, the respondent is a "Weak Democrat," and so on. Equation 3.1 contains a random error that follows the Unit Normal distribution (the "bell curve"). Because the error is not observed, estimates of equation 3.1 give only the probability that a person falls into each of the seven categories of party identification. Ordered probit chooses estimates of both the coefficients in equation 3.1 and the thresholds to maximize the likelihood of the observed responses.

Table 3.2
Effects of Relative Income on Republican Partisanship, Ordered Probit
(standard errors in parentheses)

	(1) Constant income effect	(2) Trended income effect	(3) Cubic income effect	(4) Step income effect
Relative income	0.127 (0.007)	0.079 (0.016)	0.126 (0.032)	
Relative income × [(Year − 1951)/10]		0.018 (0.005)	−0.091 (0.048)	
Relative income × [(Year − 1951)/10]^2			0.053 (0.021)	
Relative income × [(Year − 1951)/10]^3			−0.007 (0.003)	
Relative income × (1952–60)				0.085 (0.019)
Relative income × (1962–70)				0.102 (0.017)
Relative income × (1972–80)				0.112 (0.014)
Relative income × (1982–90)				0.156 (0.015)
Relative income × (1992–2002)				0.161 (0.015)
Log-likelihood	−72219.921	−72214.467	−72211.027	−72212.121
Likelihood ratio p-value (H0 = Constant Effect)		.001	.000	.004
Number of observations	39165	39165	39165	39165
African-American	−0.638 (0.041)	−0.657 (0.041)	−0.659 (0.041)	−0.660 (0.041)
African-Amer. × (Year − 1951)/10	−0.068 (0.013)	−0.062 (0.013)	−0.061 (0.013)	−0.061 (0.013)
Female	0.137 (0.023)	0.132 (0.023)	0.132 (0.023)	0.132 (0.023)
Female × (Year − 1951)/10	−0.055 (0.008)	−0.053 (0.008)	−0.053 (0.008)	−0.052 (0.008)
Southern nonblack	−0.600 (0.028)	−0.607 (0.028)	−0.607 (0.028)	−0.608 (0.028)
South nonblack × (Year − 1951)/10	0.149 (0.009)	0.152 (0.009)	0.152 (0.009)	0.152 (0.009)
Some college	0.298 (0.035)	0.314 (0.035)	0.315 (0.035)	0.316 (0.035)
Some college × (Year − 1951)/10	−0.044 (0.011)	−0.049 (0.011)	−0.050 (0.011)	−0.050 (0.011)

Table 3.2
(continued)

	(1) Constant income effect	(2) Trended income effect	(3) Cubic income effect	(4) Step income effect
College degree	0.407 (0.038)	0.443 (0.039)	0.443 (0.039)	0.447 (0.039)
College degree × (Year − 1951)/10	−0.074 (0.011)	−0.087 (0.012)	−0.087 (0.012)	−0.088 (0.012)
Age/10	0.076 (0.007)	0.073 (0.007)	0.073 (0.007)	0.073 (0.007)
Age/10 × (Year − 1951)/10	−0.029 (0.002)	−0.028 (0.002)	−0.028 (0.002)	−0.028 (0.002)
Attends church	−0.061 (0.024)	−0.060 (0.024)	−0.059 (0.024)	−0.059 (0.024)
Attends church × (Year − 1951)/10	0.051 (0.008)	0.051 (0.008)	0.050 (0.008)	0.051 (0.008)
μ_1	−0.469 (0.047)	−0.534 (0.051)	−0.494 (0.057)	−0.532 (0.052)
μ_2	0.230 (0.046)	0.165 (0.050)	0.206 (0.056)	0.168 (0.052)
μ_3	0.535 (0.046)	0.470 (0.050)	0.510 (0.056)	0.472 (0.052)
μ_4	0.830 (0.047)	0.765 (0.051)	0.805 (0.057)	0.767 (0.052)
μ_5	1.135 (0.047)	1.070 (0.051)	1.110 (0.057)	1.072 (0.052)
μ_6	1.721 (0.047)	1.656 (0.051)	1.696 (0.057)	1.658 (0.052)

The results on elite polarization in chapter 2 show a decline in polarization after World War II followed by a subsequent rise. In addition, figure 3.2 suggests that there may have been a leveling off or fall in income stratification at the end of the 1990s. To allow for both of these effects, we estimated model 3, where income effects follow a cubic trend. The results are displayed in figure 3.3.[16]

A first observation from figure 3.3 is that the confidence interval is always well above 0—income matters. The results, moreover, through the mid-1990s roughly match our earlier observations about elite polarization and income inequality. There is an initial (albeit imprecisely estimated) decline followed by an increase. The turning point, however, precedes the turning point in polarization by about a decade. At

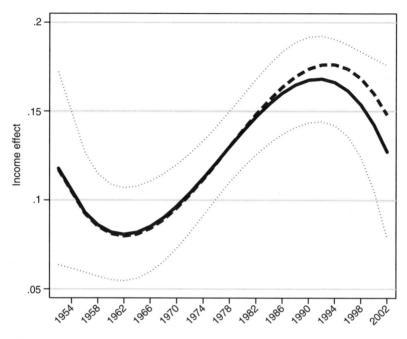

Figure 3.3
Income Effect on Party Identification Cubic Polynomial Estimates
Note: Dashed line is an estimate excluding responses to the 1998 NES. The dotted lines
represent the confidence interval.

the end of the 1990s, the income effect appears to decline, echoing popular claims that politics has now turned to abortion and other social
issues. The decline, however, is imprecisely estimated, as the width of
the confidence interval expands sharply in the 1990s. Caution is in
order about the import of recent changes.

The effect of income in the formal theory represented in equation 3.1
calls for the effect of income to be expressed as the product of an underlying behavioral parameter (β) and the difference in the party tax
rates or, more broadly, party platforms. The theory predicts that if we
include relative income and the product of the difference in party platforms and income, only the interacted variable should be significant.
To do an explicit test, we interacted relative income with the House
party polarization measures plotted in figure 1.1. Although the specification did not fit as well as the linear trend specification, the results
(not reported) are encouraging. The estimated coefficient of relative income, −0.0006, was smaller than its standard error, 0.046. In contrast,

the estimated coefficient on the interacted variable was 0.200 and was significant at p=0.005.

We now turn to the results for coefficients other than income. The constant in the formal model is contained in the (unreported) year fixed effects. If the term γ was constant in time, the measured fixed effects should, theoretically, be decreasing in time. Observe that the second term in $\tilde{\gamma} = \gamma - \beta(t_D - t_R)[1 - \alpha(t_R + t_D)]$ is negative if $\alpha(t_R + t_D)$ is less than 1.0. Average tax rates have always been less than 50 percent, and the deadweight loss is most likely much, much less than 1.0. So the second term is negative. In fact, if we assume, consistent with chapter 2, that polarization has taken the form of t_R falling faster than any possible increase in t_D, the entire second term should have become more negative over time, leading to a falling value for $\tilde{\gamma}$. That is, we should see a decreasing sequence of year fixed effects.

In fact, the reverse occurs. The result is illustrated by the step model, where the year fixed effects are less than 0.20 before 1964 and greater than 0.50 after 1992. The regression of the year fixed effects on time shows an R^2 of 0.90 and a t-statistic of 13.7. These results suggest, given our strong prior beliefs about the second term, that the behavioral parameter γ is growing even more sharply than the fixed effects. That is, there are trends favoring Republican identification that are not picked up in the effects of income and demographics, including trends in these effects. This increase in "valence advantage" is one reason that support for the Republican Party did not fall as a consequence of its shift to the right.

Turning to the effects of the other demographic variables, we find that the effect of each has changed dramatically over the period of our study. These changes should not be surprising to casual observers. African Americans and females have moved away from the Republican Party, just as nonblack southerners have flocked toward it. Older voters supported the Republicans in the mid–twentieth century, but by the twenty-first their allegiance deteriorated. The effects of education have diminished, in part because college attendance and graduation have skyrocketed.

The effect of income is very important compared to that of the demographics. Consider the estimates from column 4 of table 3.2. Table 3.3, based on the step model in 2000, shows how much the income of a respondent at half of the average income would need to increase to match the change of the other variables. Only in the case of race would

Table 3.3
Demographics and Income Shifts Compared

Demographic change	Pro-Republican party ID shift in 2000	Equivalent relative income shift is from one-half avg. income to:
Black to nonblack northern	0.955	6.483 avg.
85 to 25 years old	0.370	2.819 avg.
Female to male	0.128	1.299 avg.
Nonblack northern to nonblack southern	0.020	0.624 avg.
No college to college grad	0.136	1.351 avg.
No church attendance to church attendance	0.185	1.659 avg.

an extreme income change be needed to match the effect of the other demographics.

What Caused the Increase in Party/Income Stratification?

In this section, we attempt to assess the relative importance of the four hypotheses about the increase in party/income stratification. We use our estimates of equation 3.1 to compute implied levels of stratification under various scenarios. Consistent with testing hypotheses 1, 2, and 3, we can manipulate the coefficients of the model, the distribution of r_i, and the joint distribution of r_i and the other demographic variables. To assess the relative importance of each of these changes, we compute the levels of party/income stratification in 1960 and 2000 under different scenarios, using the results of the "cubic" specification in column 3 of table 3.2.

Before asking what accounts for the change in party/income stratification, we first consider the types of demographic changes that have occurred over this period. Table 3.4 gives the profiles of the lowest and highest income quintiles for the 1960 and 2000 surveys. A respondent is in the lowest quintile if his or her family income (or single income) is below the 20th percentile point of the March Current Population Survey household income distribution and in the highest quintile if above the 80th percentile point.

A comparison of the quintile ratio columns shows the magnitude by which the income distribution and the joint distribution of income

Table 3.4
Characteristics of Income Quintiles, 1960 and 2000

Variable	Top quintile, 2000	Bottom quintile, 2000	Ratio 2000	Top quintile, 1960	Bottom quintile, 1960	Ratio 1960
Average relative income	1.988	0.159	12.542	2.111	0.210	10.074
% African-American	4.8%	25.5%	0.190	1.6%	19.2%	0.085
% female	47.0%	70.6%	0.666	50.9%	64.4%	0.790
% southern	25.4%	31.6%	0.802	24.7%	32.8%	0.753
% some college	27.6%	25.5%	1.082	18.5%	4.0%	4.653
% college degree	57.5%	10.8%	5.318	23.4%	4.0%	5.911
% church attendance	52.6%	48.9%	1.075	67.1%	44.3%	1.514
Average age	44.9	50.3	0.895	45.1	62.7	0.719

and other attributes have changed over the past forty years. The top-bottom quintile ratio for average relative income has increased from around 10 to over 12.5. Beyond this striking change in the distribution of income, we find large changes in the placement of groups within the distribution.

Some changes have worked against the increased stratification of partisanship on income, for example in education. Both measures of education are distributed more equitably in 2000 than in 1960, whereas their correlation with Republican partisanship has diminished substantially. The changing distribution of age and its relation to partisanship also works against the increased overrepresentation of Republican identifiers in the top quintile. This change reflects the relatively lower age for the bottom quintile in 2000; age is negatively correlated with Republican identification in 2000, whereas it was positively correlated in 1960.

Changes in the income distribution of the other demographic categories, however, clearly work to increase stratification. With the increase in single females from 1960 to 2000, females have become a notably larger share of the lowest quintile respondents and a smaller share of the top quintile.[17] Because females have moved steadily toward the Democratic Party, the effects on party/income stratification are quite apparent.[18] Conversely, southerners have become better represented in the top quintile as they have moved into the Republican Party. This realignment also contributes to stratification.

The changes with respect to race are more ambiguous. Income inequality *among* African Americans has increased dramatically, so that blacks now compose a greater portion of *both* of the extreme income quintiles. African Americans as a group are largely Democratic identifiers. If the propensity to choose a Democratic identification were independent of income, the black increase at the top quintile would decrease stratification, and the increase at the bottom would increase it. If we control for income, however, we find that the propensity of African Americans to identify with the Democrats has increased. Because blacks remain substantially overrepresented at the bottom and underrepresented at the top, that they have become more Democratic increases stratification. This effect of increased African-American identification with the Democrats outweighs the effects arising from the changes in the income distribution of blacks.

To quantify the magnitude of some these effects, we simulate stratification scores for 1960 and 2000 using the results of the cubic income effect model. We manipulate the model and the profiles in order to assess which factors most contributed to the increased stratification. These results are shown in table 3.5.[19]

The first two rows of table 3.5 reflect the estimated stratification for each year using the actual model. That is, for each respondent in the top quintile, we use the estimated coefficients to compute the probability that the respondent is a Republican (strong and weak) identifier. We then sum these probabilities to estimate the fraction of the top quintile that are Republican identifiers. We do the same for the bottom

Table 3.5
Determinants of Party/Income Stratification

Scenario	Average Republican probability of lowest quintile	Average Republican probability of highest quintile	Party/Income stratification
1960	0.207	0.309	1.490
2000	0.201	0.349	1.736
2000 with 1960 sample	0.194	0.383	1.976
1960 with 2000 sample	0.208	0.345	1.660
1960 with 2000 income	0.206	0.305	1.481
2000 with 1960 income	0.203	0.356	1.751
2000 with 1960 income effect	0.199	0.308	1.549
1960 with 2000 income effect	0.211	0.352	1.673

Note: Probabilities are the estimated probabilities of weak or strong Republican identification from the model with the cubic specification of income effects.

quintile. The ratio of the two fractions is our stratification measure. These results are our benchmarks for comparison with other counterfactuals. They are somewhat greater for 1960 and somewhat less for 2000 than the actual stratifications reported in figure 3.2.

Our first exercise untangles whether the change in stratification is driven by changes in estimated model effects or by changes in demographics. In row 3, we estimate stratification using the estimated coefficients for 2000 applied to the 1960 sample respondents. The result is a stratification score of 1.976, which is significantly larger than the actual 2000 estimated score of 1.736. Alternatively, row 4 shows the estimated stratification applying the 1960 coefficients to the 2000 respondents to capture the effects of the demographic shifts. The resulting stratification of 1.666 is substantially closer to the estimated stratification for 1960 (row 1). These two results imply that the changes in the relationship between partisanship and demographic variables account for much more of the increase in stratification than do the changes in demographics. That is, although there have been important changes in the distribution of our demographic variables in the last half of the twentieth century—for example, more income inequality, higher levels of education, and a greater share of the population in the South— the effects of these changes on aggregate partisan identification have largely offset. In contrast, how demographic characteristics relate to identification—for example, the increasing effect of income, the flip in the gender gap—have had important net effects.

The remaining rows of table 3.5 deal specifically with the direct effects of relative income. Rows 5 and 6 correspond to counterfactual estimates of stratification in each year using the degree of income inequality in the other year. For row 5, we use the results in table 3.2 to multiply top 1960 quintile incomes by 1.988/2.111 (see table 3.4) and bottom quintile incomes by 0.159/0.210. Otherwise, we use the 1960 sample and coefficients. For row 6, we reverse the process to simulate 2000 stratification with the 1960 income distribution. These results show that the aggregate distribution of income has barely any effect on stratification. In both cases, the counterfactual stratification indices are almost identical to the actual ones. This finding suggests that increasing income inequality accounts for very little of the change in stratification. The change is largely one of increased "pocketbook" partisanship.

To see this link, we turn to the effects of the increased impact of relative income on partisanship. In row 7, we estimate 2000 stratification using the 2000 sample and all coefficients except for the one for relative

income, where we substitute the 1960 coefficient. In row 8, we reverse
the roles of 1960 and 2000. The two resulting stratifications are about
equal. That is, when we hold demographics and other effects constant,
the change in the income effect substantially increases stratification in
1960 and decreases it in 2000. The 2000 stratification in row 8, 1.673, is
nearly identical to that in row 4, 1.660, where all the coefficients were
changed. That is, just as the changes in demographic profiles offset,
the changes in demographic coefficients offset, except for the increased
effect of income.

These results suggest that the driving force behind the increased
stratification was the increased correlation between income and partisanship. If we interpret this increase as party polarization, these findings suggest that the changes in the bivariate relationship can be best
accounted for by the actions of the party elites and not the voters. In
other words, as the parties have become differentiated in fiscal and
other economic policies, they have cued the voters to vote more on the
basis of income.

Political Competition in a Richer Society

The 2000 presidential election ended in a dead heat, and the final outcome rested with a decision by the Supreme Court. This event reminds
us that the American political system has remained remarkably competitive. Indeed, the NES sample percentages of Republican partisans
from 1952 to 2002 have fluctuated, with no apparent trend (Green,
Palmquist, and Schickler 2002, p. 15). (There has been a decline for the
Democrats, to the benefit of Independents.)

Should such a balance have been maintained? Real median income
doubled between 1952 and 1996. Average income increased even more
sharply. Should not this change have benefited the Republicans?

If respondents computed their relative income not on the basis of average income in the year of the survey but on average income in 1960,
Republicans clearly would have been advantaged. Table 3.6 shows the
actual fraction of Republican identifiers in the sample, the estimated
fraction using the model coefficients, and the estimated fraction replacing average real income in the relevant year with average real income
in 1960 in computing relative income, r_i.

The results show that from 1988 onward, the increase in real incomes would have generated a gain of over 3 percent in Republican
identification had respondents compared their current incomes to 1960

Table 3.6
Republican Identification and the Change in Real Income

Year	Actual	Estimated from model	Estimated using 1960 mean income in computing relative income
1952	0.281	0.239	0.227
1956	0.303	0.260	0.257
1958	0.294	0.212	0.211
1960	0.297	0.250	0.250
1962	0.297	0.236	0.238
1964	0.220	0.173	0.176
1966	0.251	0.239	0.244
1968	0.231	0.216	0.224
1970	0.232	0.227	0.237
1972	0.238	0.266	0.278
1974	0.237	0.245	0.260
1976	0.242	0.262	0.276
1978	0.211	0.245	0.263
1980	0.230	0.257	0.276
1982	0.244	0.230	0.246
1984	0.276	0.284	0.303
1986	0.256	0.266	0.290
1988	0.280	0.300	0.327
1990	0.249	0.256	0.282
1992	0.255	0.275	0.301
1994	0.307	0.324	0.350
1996	0.278	0.274	0.301
1998	0.268	0.271	0.301
2000	0.254	0.277	0.310
2002	0.320	0.319	0.355

average incomes. Given that the actual system is very competitive, a gain of 3 percent would likely have swung many offices to Republicans. Arguably, the real incomes represented by the parties have increased in a way that preserves a competitive two-party system.

Did the South Do It?

In the period of our study, the last half of the twentieth century, the American South changed from a one-party system to a two-party

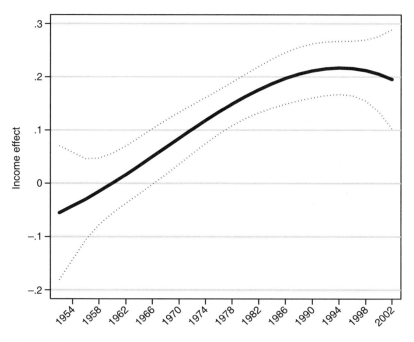

Figure 3.4
Income Effect on Party Identification Cubic Estimates for Southern Non–African
Americans
Note: The dotted lines represent the confidence interval.

system. In the results we have presented, we have seen how southern
nonblacks switched from being substantially more Democratic than
northern nonblacks to being substantially more Republican. This
change in partisan identification has already been examined by Green,
Schickler, and Palmquist (2002). Our contribution is to indicate that
pocketbook voting is an important part of the story of the dramatic
switch of partisan allegiances in the South.

What happened in the South with respect to income is vividly illustrated by figures 3.4 and 3.5. Figure 3.4 shows results for the cubic
polynomial estimation when the model is estimated with only nonblack respondents in the South. Figure 3.5 is the comparable figure for
northern nonblacks.

The South shows a sharply increasing income effect. Income had
essentially no effect on southern partisanship in the 1950s. The confidence interval shown in figure 3.4 includes 0 as late as 1966. A likelihood ratio test of the linear effect rejects the null hypothesis of a

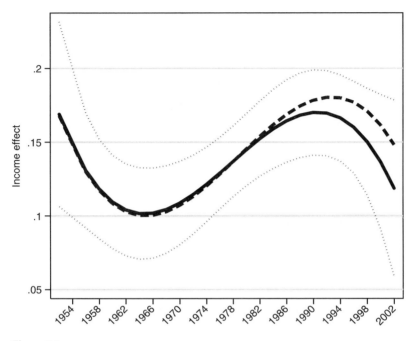

Figure 3.5
Income Effect on Party Identification Cubic Estimates for Northern Non–African Americans
Note: Dashed line is an estimate excluding responses to the 1998 NES. The dotted lines represent the confidence interval.

constant income effect. As the figure suggests, testing a cubic model against the linear does not lead to rejection of the null hypothesis that the increase is linear.

The results for the North form a stark contrast to the South. Although the confidence interval always lies above 0, the constant income effect model is not rejected for the linear model but is rejected for the cubic. The North went through a declining income effect in the 1950s, when elite polarization was low, and an increasing effect in the 1970s and 1980s, when elite polarization was increasing. But, intriguingly, the income effect in the North declined in the 1990s to a level no higher than it was in the mid-1970s. The decline is not nearly so precipitous, however, if we exclude the 1998 midterm elections. The estimated income effect excluding that election is indicated by the dotted line. In the next section, we examine whether 1998 is indeed anomalous and look at the extent of the recent decline in the income effect.

Table 3.7
Republican Identification by Quintile, 1996–2002

| | Income quintile | | | | |
Year	1	2	3	4	5
1996	0.187	0.184	0.282	0.290	0.411
1998	0.233	0.234	0.266	0.252	0.374
2000	0.144	0.222	0.215	0.294	0.324
2002	0.197	0.248	0.301	0.362	0.401

What Happened in the 1990s?

The income effect, especially for nonsouthern voters, has seemed to level off or decline over the last three elections. As we noted earlier, the decline was especially precipitous in 1998. There are several plausible stories behind this decline. The declines in 1998 and 2000 may have been due to the roaring economy and stock market, which may have increased the popularity of Bill Clinton's Democratic Party with higher-income voters. Cultural differences, especially those symbolized by the behavior leading to Clinton's impeachment, may have also narrowed the partisan income gap. This narrowing could have resulted either from adultery-repelled low-income voters or impeachment-repelled high-income voters. In any case, it is worth examining this period more closely.

We begin by looking at Republican identification broken out by income quintiles for the 1996–2002 elections.

Table 3.7 shows that the decline in income effect and stratification in 1998 resulted both from a pro-Republican swing among low-income voters and an anti-Republican swing by high-income voters. The income stratification rebounds in 2000, however, when low-income voters swing back to the Democrats. By 2002, the situation had returned to essentially where it was in 1996.

To determine whether views on impeachment were related to partisanship in the 1998 midterm election, we use questions about impeachment asked by the NES. Because the NES asked about impeachment well after asking the party identification question, impeachment is unlikely to have primed the party response or vice versa. In table 3.8, we rerun the party identification model for 1998 including a dummy variable indicating whether the respondent supported Bill Clinton's impeachment. Not surprisingly, views on impeachment had a large effect

Table 3.8
Impeachment and Republican Identification, 1998
(standard errors in parentheses)

	All	Impeachment supporter	Impeachment opponent
Relative income	0.083	0.189	0.040
	(0.040)	(0.074)	(0.049)
African-American	−0.799	−0.536	−0.853
	(0.105)	(0.324)	(0.112)
Female	−0.087	−0.044	−0.112
	(0.063)	(0.119)	(0.075)
South	0.053	−0.070	0.102
	(0.068)	(0.123)	(0.082)
Some college	0.121	0.276	0.072
	(0.077)	(0.145)	(0.092)
College graduate	0.168	0.422	0.068
	(0.082)	(0.152)	(0.098)
Age	−0.037	0.045	−0.071
	(0.019)	(0.035)	(0.022)
Church attendance	0.055	0.153	0.029
	(0.065)	(0.123)	(0.076)
Impeachment supporter	1.129		
	(0.074)		
N	1144	331	813
Log-likelihood	−2002.838	−559.746	−1417.633

on partisanship. Indeed, it is the single best predictor. When we estimate the model separately on impeachment supporters and opponents, we find something quite surprising. The income effect for
impeachment supporters is almost as large as the income effect in the
1996 elections, whereas there is no income effect for opponents. This
result is not a consequence of a stronger income effect in the South,
where impeachment support was high.[20] The same patterns hold even
if southern whites are dropped from the analysis.

The conventional wisdom holds that social conservatives do not vote
their economic interests (e.g., Frank 2004a). This viewpoint is at odds
with our comparison of impeachment supporters to impeachment
opponents. The "moralist" supporters of impeachment appeared to be
much more stratified by income than were the opponents. Perhaps
social liberals are the moralists who forsake economics for principle.

We can also take a closer look at recent years by using surveys conducted by the Pew Research Center for the People and the Press. Pew
has surveys in the field almost every month in both election and

nonelection years, and these generally include partisanship, income, and demographic variables compatible with our NES analysis. The advantages of the Pew surveys are that they take place at reasonably regular intervals and that large sample sizes can be obtained by pooling responses across studies. One important difference is that the Pew surveys allow for only five responses to the party identification question (Democrat, Leans Democrat, Independent, Leans Republican, and Republican). If we assume that Pew's Democrat and Republican responses are equivalent to collapsing the NES's weak and strong partisan categories, however, estimates of equation 3.1 are comparable across the NES and Pew samples. The other difference is that questions about the frequency of church attendance are asked only sporadically by Pew. Instead, we can use the perhaps more politically appropriate question: "Would you describe yourself as a 'born again' or evangelical Christian?"

The Pew studies are particularly valuable in determining whether there was a large drop in the income effect in 1998 and an overall decline over the past eight years. Unlike the NES, there is no drop in the income effect in 1998. This finding holds even in the Pew surveys taken closest to the election. Consequently, there is good reason to believe that the 1998 NES is quite unrepresentative of the broader trends.

The more important question, however, is whether there has been a general attenuation of the income effect during the past eight years. In figure 3.6 we show the income coefficient (and confidence interval) for each year since 1997 from the Pew studies.[21] With the exception of some temporary dips (all within the confidence interval of the 1997 effect), the attenuation in the income effect is rather mild. This finding also holds when we examine only nonblacks outside the South. For reasons that are not entirely clear, the NES seems to overstate both the attenuation of the income effect and regional differences in the effect.

The Moral Issue

As we mentioned at the beginning of the chapter, most popular analyses of recent elections have focused on moral and cultural issues.[22] These are certainly factors. Both NES and the Pew surveys indicate that regular churchgoers and evangelical Christians identify more strongly with the Republican Party than in the past. Nevertheless, it is hard to make the case that the emergence of these cleavages helps to explain the polarization of the past thirty years. First, moral and social

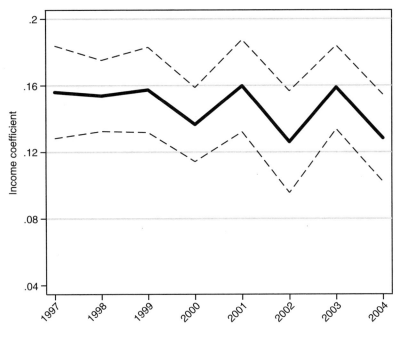

Figure 3.6
Annual Income Effect
Note: From PEW surveys conducted between 1997 and 2004 (N = 35,237). The dotted lines represent the confidence interval.

issues are not a large part of the congressional roll call agenda and thus cannot explain the divergence in NOMINATE scores between the two parties. Second, the rising effect of church attendance on Republican identification did not begin until the 1990s. If we estimate equation 3.1 just on the NES studies before 1992, the coefficient on church attendance is not significantly different from zero. The NES did not even ask about evangelical Christianity until 1984. This item, like church attendance, is insignificant in equation 3.1 until the 1990s. Even in the 2000 NES, church attendance is worth only about 1.5 units of relative income. If we replace church attendance with the NES's born-again variable,[23] the effect of being a born-again Christian in 2000 is also about the same as 1.5 units of relative income (about $50,000 in family income).

Perhaps the biggest fallacy about conservative Christian voters is that they systematically vote against their economic interests. There seem to be two reasons for this misunderstanding. The first has to do

with the observation that blue states have higher average incomes
than red states. This observation is true but misleading. It certainly
does not imply that richer people are more Democratic. The NES and
Pew studies show that this pattern is not true for party identification,
and we will show that it is not true for voting. The second misconcep-
tion is that conservative Christians are systematically poorer than other
groups. This pattern may be true, but the difference is much smaller
than the conventional wisdom would have it. Using the Pew studies,
we find that there is only about a $6,000 average difference between
the family incomes of born-again respondents and those of all other
respondents.[24] More that half of this difference can be accounted for
by demographic differences such as region, age, gender, and education.

Another reason that the "voting against economic interest" story is
not compelling is that income is an extraordinarily good predictor of
partisanship even among conservative Christians. Figure 3.7 shows

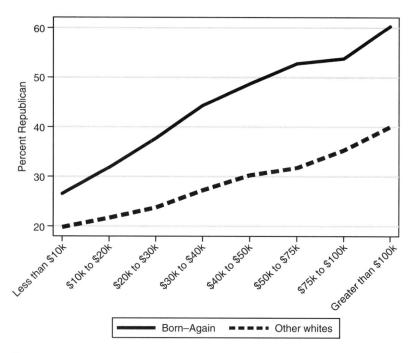

Figure 3.7
Republican Identification, Religion, and Income
Note: Computed from PEW surveys conducted between 1997 and 2004. The figures are
based solely on white, non-Hispanic respondents.

the percentage of born-again white Pew respondents who call themselves Republicans by income. For born-agains and evangelicals, the percentage Republican increases steeply with income. This income gradient is even larger than for non–born-again whites. The difference across groups is small for those with low incomes, about 8.5 percentage points, but grows to a difference of twenty percentage points. This bivariate finding holds up well in our econometric model. If we run equation 3.1 just on white born-again Christians, the estimated income effect is 0.199, 30 percent higher than the overall effect.

These results suggest that low-income conservative Christians do not completely ignore their economic interests (see also Bartels 2005). Certainly, they feel cross-pressures between their Bible and their pocketbook, and they do support the Republicans more than other low-income voters do. Nevertheless, support for Republicans is much lower than that of other conservative Christians with higher incomes whose Bible and pocketbook point in the same direction.

Presidential Voting

To this point, we have concentrated primarily on partisanship. There are good reasons to focus on partisanship, but elections are won and lost by voting, so we turn to an examination of vote choice.

Fortunately, our results for partisan identification replicate nicely in a dichotomous probit analysis of presidential vote choice. The dependent variable is coded 1 for Republican and 0 for Democrat. Our sample here is defined only by those respondents who expressed a choice for one of the major party candidates in the presidential year. Declared abstentions, votes for minor party candidates, and nonresponses resulted in our having only about two-thirds as many observations per year as for the partisan identification analysis. We use the same independent variable specifications as in our analysis of partisan identification. In table 3.9, we show the results.

For presidential voting, relative income continues to have a significant effect, as shown in column 1 of table 3.9. The result for the linear trend model in column 2 is very similar to that for partisan identification, particularly after we consider the effects of sample size on precision. Similarly, the pattern of the time polynomial coefficients for the cubic model is quite similar in comparing models 3 from table 3.2 and table 3.8.[25]

Table 3.9
Effects of Relative Income on Presidential Vote Choice, Probit
(standard errors in parentheses)

	(1) Constant income effect	(2) Trended income effect	(3) Cubic income effect	(4) Step income effect
Relative income	0.181 (0.015)	0.118 (0.029)	0.148 (0.050)	
Relative income × [(Year − 1951)/10]		0.025 (0.010)	−0.111 (0.089)	
Relative income × [(Year − 1951)/10]^2			0.086 (0.042)	
Relative income × [(Year − 1951)/10]^3			−0.013 (0.006)	
Relative income × (1952 + 1956)				0.116 (0.031)
Relative income × (1960 + 1964 + 1968)				0.127 (0.038)
Relative income × (1972 + 1976)				0.206 (0.029)
Relative income × (1980 + 1984 + 1988)				0.271 (0.037)
Relative income × (1992 + 1996 + 2000)				0.191 (0.030)
Log-likelihood	−8776.053	−8772.964	−8769.321	−8769.386
Likelihood ratio p-value (H0 = Constant Effect)		0.012	0.004	0.010
Number of observations	14329	14329	14329	14329
African-American	−1.135 (0.108)	−1.158 (0.109)	−1.161 (0.109)	−1.161 (0.109)
African-Amer. × (Year − 1951)/10	−0.139 (0.039)	−0.131 (0.040)	−0.129 (0.040)	−0.128 (0.039)
Female	0.141 (0.043)	0.134 (0.043)	0.135 (0.043)	0.134 (0.043)
Female × (Year − 1951)/10	−0.090 (0.015)	−0.087 (0.015)	−0.088 (0.015)	−0.087 (0.015)
Southern nonblack	−0.204 (0.053)	−0.213 (0.053)	−0.212 (0.053)	−0.212 (0.053)
South nonblack × (Year − 1951)/10	0.101 (0.018)	0.104 (0.018)	0.105 (0.018)	0.105 (0.018)
Some college	0.356 (0.064)	0.374 (0.065)	0.377 (0.065)	0.377 (0.065)
Some college × (Year − 1951)/10	−0.061 (0.021)	−0.068 (0.021)	−0.069 (0.021)	−0.070 (0.021)

Table 3.9
(continued)

	(1) Constant income effect	(2) Trended income effect	(3) Cubic income effect	(4) Step income effect
College degree	0.317	0.361	0.359	0.357
	(0.069)	(0.071)	(0.071)	(0.071)
College degree × (Year − 1951)/10	−0.078	−0.095	−0.094	−0.093
	(0.022)	(0.023)	(0.023)	(0.023)
Age/10	0.100	0.096	0.095	0.095
	(0.014)	(0.014)	(0.014)	(0.014)
Age/10 × (Year − 1951)/10	−0.023	−0.021	−0.021	−0.021
	(0.005)	(0.005)	(0.005)	(0.005)
Attends church	0.036	0.035	0.037	0.037
	(0.044)	(0.044)	(0.044)	(0.044)
Attends church × (Year − 1951)/10	0.086	0.087	0.087	0.086
	(0.015)	(0.015)	(0.015)	(0.015)
Constant	−0.530	−0.437	−0.456	−0.430
	(0.084)	(0.092)	(0.100)	(0.092)

The principal distinction between the partisan identification and vote choice estimates lies in column 4. Whereas we saw a steady increase in income-based voting for partisan identification, the vote choice coefficient for the last decade is smaller than that for the previous one. Nevertheless, the current income effect is still substantially larger than it was in the 1950s and 1960s. The reversal in the 1990s is caused by the extraordinarily high effect for 1984 and an extraordinarily low effect for 1992, the latter perhaps caused by the first Perot candidacy. If the model is run without these elections, the income effect is essentially flat from the 1980s.

Red and Blue

At this point, readers may wonder how our analysis jibes with the red and blue maps they saw on election nights 2000 and 2004. It is unmistakable from these maps that the Democratic candidates drew heavy support from the high-income coasts while Bush won the lower-income middle of the country. Nevertheless, suggesting that this pattern holds because Bush drew support from low-income voters is a classic example of the ecological fallacy of inferring individual behavior from aggregate statistics. If there is regional variation in support

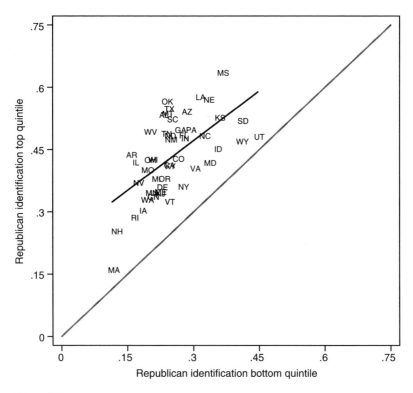

Figure 3.8
Party-Income Stratification by State: White Respondents to PEW Studies, 1997–2004

for Bush spuriously correlated to average income, the red-blue maps are entirely consistent with our results.

To demonstrate that there is indeed a strong income effect in partisanship within regions, we use the Pew studies from 1997–2004 to compute the partisan attachments of high- and low-income voters by state. Figure 3.8 shows the percentage of Republican identifiers in the top income quintile (based on the national income distribution) and the percentage of Republicans in the bottom quintile. To focus on cleavages among white voters, nonwhites and Hispanics have been eliminated from these calculations.

This figure reveals that there is at least some income stratification in each of the 48 states included in Pew's sample, as all the tokens lie above the 45-degree line.[26] Although a couple of states, such as Massachusetts and Utah, have very small income gaps in party identification, most states have cleavages on the order of that for the United States as a whole. Perhaps surprisingly, within-state income stratification does not seem to be a "red state" phenomenon. Many of the states that voted for Al Gore and John Kerry have large gaps in the party identification of rich and poor. Indeed, because the line produced by the regression of upper-income partisanship on lower-income partisanship is flatter than the 45-degree line (that is, a coefficient less than one), red states have lower values of our ratio measure of stratification than do blue states.

To show that the election maps provide incorrect inferences about the role of income in presidential voting, we examine county-level voting returns for president for each election from 1968 to 2000. Our main dependent variable is the Republican share of the two-party vote. We then use census data to construct an aggregate version of equation 3.1. For each election, we match each county to its demographic profile from the most proximate census. As an income variable, we use the natural log of median family income for each county. As the Census Bureau does not ask about religion, we use data on the number of churches per capita (Glenmary Research Center 2004).[27] We do not include the gender percentages because there is not much variation across counties.

We pool all of these election returns into one large panel. We allow linear trends in the demographic characteristics, but estimate a separate income coefficient for each year.[28] In model 1, we regress the Republican vote on just the annual income coefficients and year fixed effects. This model captures the annual bivariate relationship between county income and Republican voting. The income coefficients are given in column 1 of table 3.10.[29] According to the estimates, the income effect peaked in 1980 and has declined since. In 1996 and 2000, the effects are negative but statistically insignificant. This finding explains why the maps look the way they do. In column 2, the demographic characteristics (with time trends) are added to the model. The income effect still peaks in the 1980s, but it remains positive and is still borderline statistically significant in 2000. In comparison to column 1, this finding suggests that the perceived negative correlation between income and Republican voting in the maps is accounted for by geographical variation in other variables, notably the percentage of African Americans (and, to a much lesser extent, the number of churches). In column 3, we drop the demographic variables but use state-by-year fixed effects to capture regional variation in Republican support. Capturing regional variation through these fixed effects tends to boost the

Table 3.10
Republican Support by County, 1968–2000
(standard errors in parentheses)

Income measure	Model 1	Model 2	Model 3	Model 4
Log family income 1968	0.010	−0.012	0.072	0.019
	(0.019)	(0.025)	(0.022)	(0.022)
Log family income 1972	−0.120	−0.143	0.027	−0.028
	(0.018)	(0.021)	(0.020)	(0.018)
Log family income 1976	0.114	0.091	0.132	0.071
	(0.017)	(0.022)	(0.021)	(0.021)
Log family income 1980	0.129	0.102	0.148	0.077
	(0.028)	(0.031)	(0.024)	(0.025)
Log family income 1984	0.042	0.018	0.126	0.057
	(0.031)	(0.031)	(0.029)	(0.025)
Log family income 1988	0.040	0.108	0.155	0.171
	(0.020)	(0.028)	(0.021)	(0.022)
Log family income 1992	0.008	0.089	0.127	0.148
	(0.021)	(0.029)	(0.022)	(0.024)
Log family income 1996	−0.030	0.062	0.114	0.140
	(0.024)	(0.031)	(0.024)	(0.026)
Log family income 2000	−0.044	0.076	0.082	0.140
	(0.034)	(0.037)	(0.031)	(0.028)
N	28030	27734	28030	27734
R^2	0.207	0.456	0.456	0.721
Year fixed effects	yes	yes	no	no
Demographics	no	yes	no	yes
State × year fixed effects	no	no	yes	yes

income coefficients for each election. Column 4 contains the results from the model with demographics and state-by-year fixed effects. Now the pattern of income coefficients fits our survey results quite nicely. After 1988, the income coefficient is consistently double its level from the 1970s.

These results show that while Republicans have gained support in lower income *regions*, they have not lost support among higher-income *voters*. Within each state, the higher the income, the more Republican the outcome.

Conclusion

High-income Americans have consistently, over the second half of the twentieth century and into the twenty-first, been more prone to identify with and vote for the Republican Party than have low-income

Americans, who have sided with the Democrats. The impact of income persists when one controls for other demographics, and the magnitude is important. Moreover, there has been a rather substantial transformation in the economic basis of the American party system. Today, income is far more important than it was in the 1950s. American politics is certainly far from purely class-based, but the divergence in partisan identification and voting between high- and low-income Americans has been striking. This trend helps to explain the conflicts over taxation of estates and dividends in an era generally presumed to be dominated by "hot-button" social issues like abortion and guns.

In our simple theoretical model, we posited that relative, not absolute, income was important to voting behavior. As average incomes rose in the last half of the twentieth century, voters and political parties, we believe, made adjustments that maintained an extremely competitive two-party system, most strikingly in the 2000 presidential race. Indeed, a simulation suggested that the Republicans would have an additional advantage in partisan identification of more than three percentage points, if voters had compared their current incomes to the 1960 average income.

The fact that the political system has remained largely competitive because parties and voters have adapted to the large increases in real income should not mask some important observations about American politics and an important finding in this chapter. First, although the system is competitive, the system appears to have shifted from a slight advantage for Democrats to a slight advantage for Republicans. This shift is most notable in the Republican control of Congress, which began after the 1994 elections. Moreover, the Republicans have won five of the last seven presidential elections. Second, as we showed in chapter 2, the Republicans appear to have become more competitive while shifting to the right. As for taxes, the vigorous cuts of the Reagan and George W. Bush administrations were offset by relatively mild increases under Clinton. Third, we have seen an increase in year fixed effects in our estimates of partisan identification. Something has, at the least, compensated the Republicans for the shifts in the effects of relative income and demographics.

One possibility is that the Republicans have benefited from "moral values" shifts that are not captured in our church attendance variable. But other analysis in this chapter suggests that this possibility cannot be a complete explanation because born-again and evangelical Christians are particularly sensitive to income effects on political preferences. Another possibility is that the increase in real income has led a majority of the electorate to be less favorable to redistribution and social insurance than were the counterparts of these voters a half-century earlier. The diminished need for social insurance is perhaps marked by increases in net worth and wealth (Guiso, Haliassos, and Jappelli 2002), home ownership, and securities ownership. Home ownership rose from 63 percent in 1965 to 69 percent in 2004.[30] In particular, Duca and Saving (2002) have argued, using econometric analysis, that the increase in the Republican share of the popular vote for Congress can be attributed to the rise in securities ownership from 25 percent in 1964 to nearly 50 percent in 1998. In any event, the Republicans have prospered by moving strongly away from redistribution to the poor as income stratification of voters has intensified.

There are, of course, multiple sources for the increased political divergence between high- and low-income voters. But our evidence shows that changes in both overall income inequality and the incomes of various demographic groups have only marginally contributed to increased partisan stratification on income; the most important contributions seem to come from partisan polarization and the southern realignment. Consistent with our model, the coefficient of relative income roughly tracks patterns of elite polarization derived from congressional voting studies. That is, the basic pattern is a decline or leveling in the 1950s and 1960s followed by an increase in the 1970s and 1980s. In fact, we used both relative income and relative income interacted with our elite polarization measure in one variant of our statistical analysis. As called for by our theoretical model, only the interaction term was significant. Moreover, as our simulation results showed, the increased importance of the relative income variable seems to be primarily responsible for the increased connection between income and partisanship.

It is not terribly surprising that the southern realignment also plays an important role in our findings, because it is the most important change in the American party system during the twentieth century. Our results about the changes in southern politics, however, differ substantially from arguments stressing the role of race and social issues. We do not deny the importance of these factors, but we find that the political attachments of the contemporary South are driven by income and economic status to an extent even greater than in the rest of the country.

It is probably too early to tell whether recent declines in income-based partisanship and voting in the North are anything more than the effects of fat wallets produced by the economic boom of the 1990s. Even if this decline proves to be fundamental and enduring, the role of income in southern politics and the South's increasing share of the national electorate will likely prevent any significant depolarization of American politics in the near future.

Appendix 3.1: Approximating Incomes for NES Categories

Given categorical income data, there are two typical approaches to comparing income responses at different points in time. Let $x_t = \{x_{1t}, \ldots, x_{Kt} = \infty\}$ be the vector of upper bounds for the NES income categories at time t.[31] The first approach is to use the categories ordinally by converting them to income percentiles for each time period. This approach, however, throws away potentially useful cardinal information about income. Further, as it is unlikely that income categories will always coincide with a particular set of income percentiles, some respondents will have to be assigned *ad hoc* to percentile categories. A second approach is to assume that the true income is a weighted average of the income bounds. Formally, one might assume that the true income for response k at time t is $\alpha x_{k-1,t} + (1 - \alpha)x_{kt}$ for some $\alpha \in [0,1]$. The true weight will depend on the exact shape of the income distribution. When the income density is increasing in $[x_{k-1,t}, x_{kt}]$, the weight on x_{kt} should be higher than when the density is decreasing over the interval. The same weights cannot be used for each category at a particular point in time or even for the same category over time.

As neither of these two approaches can be used to generate the appropriate data, we use census data on the distribution of income to estimate the expected income within each category. These estimates provide an income measure that preserves cardinality and comparability over time.

To outline our procedure, let $y_t = \{y_{1t}, \ldots, y_{Mt}\}$ be the income levels reported by the census corresponding to a vector of percentiles $z_t = \{z_{1t}, \ldots, z_{Mt}\}$. We use family income quintiles and the top 5%. Therefore, for 1996, $y_{1996} = \{\$18485, \$33830, \$52565, \$81199, \$146500\}$ and $z_{1996} = \{.2, .4, .6, .8, .95\}$. We assume that the true distribution of income has a distribution function $F(\cdot|\Omega_t)$ where Ω_t is a vector of time-specific parameters. Therefore, $F(y_t|\Omega_t) = z_t$. In order to generate

Table 3.A1
Estimates of the Log-normal Income Distribution, by Election Year

Election	μ_t (Mean)	σ_t (Standard Deviation)
1952	7.894	0.817
1956	8.172	0.804
1958	8.269	0.798
1960	8.356	0.793
1962	8.419	0.822
1964	8.508	0.812
1966	8.607	0.796
1968	8.793	0.763
1970	8.959	0.756
1972	9.026	0.776
1974	9.179	0.786
1976	9.306	0.792
1978	9.455	0.803
1980	9.641	0.809
1982	9.794	0.822
1984	9.900	0.831
1986	10.016	0.839
1988	10.105	0.852
1990	10.215	0.848
1992	10.260	0.855
1994	10.300	0.877
1996	10.386	0.864
1998	10.470	0.881
2000	10.568	0.882
2002	10.613	0.888

Note: There was no NES study in 1954.

estimates $\hat{\Omega}_t$, let $w(\hat{\Omega}_t) = F(\mathbf{y}_t|\hat{\Omega}_t) - \mathbf{z}_t$. We then choose $\hat{\Omega}_t$ to minimize $w(\hat{\Omega}_t)'w(\hat{\Omega}_t)$. Given an estimate of $\hat{\Omega}_t$, we can compute the expected income within each NES category as

$$EI_{kt} = \begin{cases} [F(x_{1t}|\hat{\Omega}_t)]^{-1} \int_0^{x_{1t}} x \, dF(x|\hat{\Omega}_t) & k = 1 \\ [F(x_{kt}|\hat{\Omega}_t) - F(x_{k-1,t}|\hat{\Omega}_t)]^{-1} \int_{x_{k-1,t}}^{x_{kt}} x \, dF(x|\hat{\Omega}_t) & \text{otherwise.} \end{cases}$$

We assume $F(\cdot)$ log-normal with $\Omega_t = \{\mu_t, \sigma_t\}$. These parameters have very straightforward interpretations. The median income at time t is simply e^{μ_t}, and σ_t^2 is the variance of log income, which is a commonly used measure of inequality. Table 3.A1 gives the estimates of

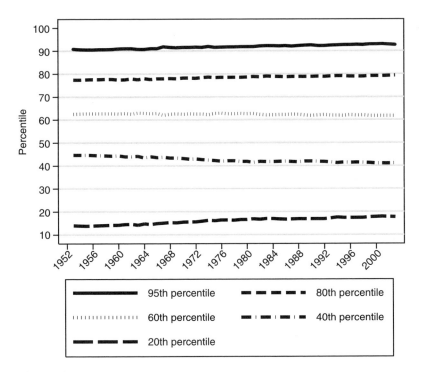

Figure 3.A1
Fit of Log-Normal Income Approximation

$\hat{\mathbf{\Omega}}_t$ for each presidential election year. These results underscore the extent to which the income distribution has become more unequal.

Figure 3.A1 plots $F(\mathbf{y}_t|\hat{\mathbf{\Omega}}_t)$ against $\mathbf{z}_t$ and shows how well the log-normal approximates the distribution of income—if it were a perfect fit, the lines would track 20, 40, 60, 80, and 95 exactly. Although the approximation is generally very good, the log-normal is a poor approximation of incomes at lower levels, as the lowest line is generally below 20, because the true distribution of income has a larger mass near zero and a larger tail than the log-normal. The effect is that EI_{kt} has a slight positive bias for low incomes and a slight negative bias for large incomes.

Appendix 3.2: Measuring Party/Income Stratification

Three complications arise in using the NES to measure the partisanship of the top and bottom income quintiles:

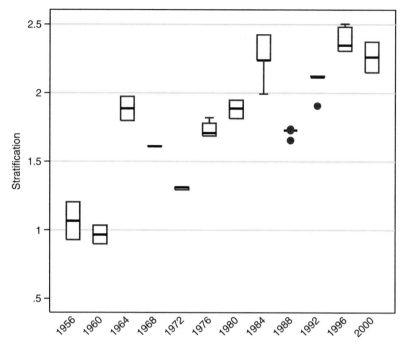

Figure 3.A2
Box Plot of Stratification Measures in Presidential Election Years
Note: The bottom of each box is the 75th percentile, the top is the 25th percentile, and the middle bar is the median.

1. *Some NES samples are unrepresentative.* In several years the distribution of respondents' income is very unrepresentative of the income distribution reported by the Census Bureau.

2. *NES sample matches neither the "Family" nor "Household" samples for which the Census Bureau reports income quintiles.* The NES asks respondents for the income of their family for the previous year. For single voters, the NES asks their individual income. Thus the NES sample includes families and single-person households. The census family sample, on the other hand, does not include single persons living alone, and the household sample aggregates multiple families living at the same household but does include single householders. Therefore, neither census sample matches the NES.

3. *Income quintile measures will often fall within NES income categories.* When a quintile measure falls within an income category, one must de-

cide how to allocate the respondents in that category into the adjoining quintiles.

It is very difficult to solve all three of these problems for the entire period from 1952 to 2000. Problem 1 necessitates matching the NES sample with the income distribution from the Current Population Survey, but problem 2 necessitates recomputing that distribution for units more closely resembling those of the NES. Nevertheless, even with appropriate measures of the income quintiles, problem 3 has no obvious solution. To compute figure 3.2, we used our log-normal approximation of the distribution of household income to compute expected income for each NES category. We then used these estimates to classify respondents into income quintiles on the basis of the Census Bureau's reported income limits for household income quintiles.

Given the limitations of these choices, we did a number of other calculations to see if the results in figure 3.2 are robust. To deal with problem 1, we recomputed the stratification measures using both household and family income distributions to classify respondents. We also use samples from the November Current Population Surveys from 1972 and 1996 that include single individuals and families so as to approximate the NES population and minimize problem 2.[32] Because the November CPS data are categorical, we use both linear and exponential extrapolation to compute the 20th and 80th percentiles. Thus, combining all of these data sources, we have four quintile estimates for 1972 to 2000 and two for each of the other years.

To deal with problem 3, we experiment with various ways of allocating respondents into quintiles. We do four computations for each quintile measure by including or excluding the relevant NES category in the top and bottom quintiles. Thus we have sixteen stratification measures for 1972–96 and eight for other years. Figure 3.A2 is a "box and whiskers" plot showing the variation across the different measures in each year. Fortunately, the variation is small, and the central pattern is close to that of figure 3.2.

Immigration, Income, and
the Voters' Incentive to
Redistribute

Economic inequality in the United States has increased sharply (chapter 1). At the same time, income differences have become more important in determining where a congressional district's representative is likely to fall on the liberal-conservative dimension (chapter 2) and how voters identify with parties and make voting decisions in presidential elections (chapter 3). Why has the increased importance of income not translated into policies that would curtail the sharp growth in inequality? At least in part, noncitizens who are ineligible to vote are concentrated at the bottom of the income distribution, so politicians feel little pressure to respond to their interests. Although economic inequality has increased, the relative income of the vast majority of *voters* has not markedly deteriorated.

In this chapter, we appear to shift gears by focusing on the median voter, whereas chapters 2 and 3 emphasized polarized parties that represented voters of different income characteristics. There is no contradiction. We simply use median incomes to focus the discussion. If, in contrast, redistributive policy reflected, for example, the 98th percentile voter under unified Republican government and the 40th when the Democrats are leading the dance, the conclusions of this chapter would most likely remain unchanged. An effect of immigration is that voter preferences as filtered through political parties and institutions are likely to have been tilted against redistribution.

In 1972, noncitizens were a small fraction of the United States population. They were also relatively well-to-do. In fact, the median income of a noncitizen was actually higher than that of citizens reporting themselves as having not voted in the presidential race between Nixon and McGovern. Noncitizens today are growing in number, and they tend to be at the bottom of the income distribution. In contrast, the relative economic position of voters and nonvoters shows little change since 1972.

The changing economic position of noncitizens is politically relevant. It is likely to contribute to the failure of the political process in the United States to generate redistribution that would eliminate growing disparities in wage and income inequality. As we said, the income of the median voter has *not* declined relatively over the past thirty years. How has the median voter's economic position been sustained, while that of the median family has declined? Part of the answer, as we show, is that lower-income people are increasingly likely to be noncitizens. The median income of noncitizens has shifted sharply downward, and the fraction of the population that is noncitizen has increased dramatically. From 1972 to 2000, the median family income of noncitizens fell from 82 percent of the median income of voters to 65 percent, while the fraction of the population that is noncitizen rose from 2.6 percent to 7.8 percent.[1]

One of the main reasons for the dramatic change in the number and poverty of noncitizens is federal legislation that has opened the doors to increased legal immigration while doing little to control illegal immigration. During the late nineteenth and early twentieth centuries, immigration was made more difficult for Europeans, and the Chinese and Japanese were excluded entirely. The immigration acts of 1921, 1924, and 1929 set up permanent quotas by national origin that both restricted total immigration and favored the relatively wealthy people of northwestern Europe. The barriers of the 1920s were only broken down by the 1965 amendments to the Immigration and Nationality Act of 1952. The amendments largely ended discrimination on the basis of national origin. Annual immigration quotas were greatly increased by the Immigration Act of 1990.

Economists have recognized that immigration, through low wage competition, has had an effect on inequality. But how big is the effect? Borjas, Freeman, and Katz (1997) argue that immigration accounts for only a small share of the increase in inequality. Studies by Borjas (1987), Altonji and Card (1989), and Lalonde and Topel (1989) also find only a small effect. Lerman (1999), on the other hand, finds that immigration explains 25–70 percent of the growth in the Gini coefficients presented in figure 1.1. More recent work by Borjas (2003) points to a substantial negative impact of immigration on wages for low-wage workers after controlling not only for education but also for work experience.

We stress that the direct economic effects must be combined with the indirect political effects. Changes in such public policies as minimum wages, income taxation, and estate taxation have, on balance, held the median voter's relative position in place. More redistributive policies would have occurred, we conjecture, had there been a sharp deterioration in the position of voters in the middle of the income distribution.

There is a large literature, including the references above, that focuses on immigration. In contrast, this chapter emphasizes citizenship because many immigrants eventually become naturalized citizens and are then eligible to vote. Our results suggest that naturalized immigrants are likely to look, in terms of income, much like native citizens. At least, it is clear that the relative income of the median voter has not greatly declined during the wave of poor, naturalized immigrants. In contrast, as some immigrants have become naturalized, they have more than been replaced by the continuing surge of poor immigrant noncitizens.

The analysis of this chapter is all in terms of relative incomes. Only these, and not the real levels, matter in the economic model of redistribution that we developed in chapter 3. We noted there, however, that over the period of our study real median income has in fact increased. To the extent that redistribution accomplished by the political process is social insurance (such things as unemployment benefits, old-age benefits, and medical benefits), the increase in real income should diminish support for redistribution, complementing the results of this chapter.[2] The effects of income inequality, however, are all on relative incomes.

We explore the relationship between income and voting in a way that differs from the standard approach taken by political scientists. (See Brady 2004 for a recent example.) The usual approach is to see if the rich in fact vote more than the poor. We take a different approach, comparing characteristics of the income distribution of voters to the same characteristics for nonvoters and noncitizens. We ask how the income characteristics have changed over time. In the standard approach, one is also concerned with verifying that income has an effect when one controls for other demographics. We are less concerned with this issue because public policy depends less on covariates than on income. A person's taxes are not lower because he or she is a college graduate, an African American, or an evangelical. (One's labor market experience may differ, however.) Taxes may be slightly less if a person is over 65, but the monthly social security check still depends on lifetime earnings and not race, education, or gender. So if we want to study redistribution, we should start with income, at least as a first cut.

In most political economy models, the income inequality that has arisen since the 1970s would have self-equilibrated. As inequality increased, there would be more pressure to redistribute. This prediction is apparent in the model of Bolton and Roland (1997) introduced in chapter 3. As inequality, defined as a decrease in the ratio of median voter income to mean income, went up, more redistribution should have occurred. In the United States, however, public policy veered in the opposite direction. As we detail in chapter 6, the real value of the minimum wage has been allowed to fall; taxes on income from capital have fallen, as have top marginal income tax rates and the estate tax.[3]

Other industrial nations have been exposed to the same technological change or opportunities as the United States. Although economic inequality might be driven by technological change, the responses elsewhere have not been the same. For example, Piketty and Saez (2003) show that during the last three decades of the twentieth century, the share of national income going to the top 0.1 percent of the population remained unchanged in France but sharply increased in the United States. We also note, in keeping with the theme of this chapter, that France has had a dramatically different experience with noncitizenship. From 1975 to 1999, roughly the period of our study, French government statistics show that the percentage of noncitizens decreased, falling from 6.5 percent of the population to 5.6 percent.[4] France and the United States, thus, have had contrasting trends in income inequality and in citizenship. How might these trends have been reflected in political processes?

To answer this question, we return to the Bolton and Roland (1997) model and focus on median/mean ratios. From the perspective of that model, noncitizenship has both a *disenfranchisement* effect and a *sharing* effect.[5]

The *disenfranchisement effect* can be viewed as a change in the numerator of the median/mean ratio. The median income of voters is higher than that of all families. This fact reflects not just that voters have higher incomes than eligible nonvoters, but also that voters have higher incomes than noncitizens. The effect of disenfranchising noncitizens will increase either if noncitizens become more numerous or if they become poorer.

If all citizens voted, the appropriate ratio would be median citizen income/mean family income. If all those over 18 voted, the appropriate ratio would be median family income/mean family income. By comparing these ratios to median voter income/mean family income, we can study how much "disenfranchisement" is due to nonvoting by citizens and how much to the ineligibility of noncitizens.

The presence of noncitizens in the population not only affects the numerator of the median/mean ratio, it also changes the denominator. Because noncitizens are poorer than citizens, mean family income is less than mean citizen income. Noncitizens thus increase the ratio, making redistribution less attractive to the median voter. Noncitizens shrink the per capita pie that has to be shared equally with all residents. The sharing of benefits with noncitizens has, of course, become a political hot potato. To assess the *sharing effect*, we will compare redistribution when mean family income for citizens is substituted for mean family income in the ratio. This counterfactual presumes that mean citizen income is unaffected by the presence of noncitizens. Although citizen income may well be affected by immigration, it is hard to argue that it would fall below realized mean family income. Some sharing effect must be present.

The sharing effect will drive all citizens to be less favorable to redistribution. The disenfranchisement effect decreases the political influence of relatively low-income families and increases the influence of higher-income families. We focus, for convenience, on median incomes, but our findings can be viewed as indicative of the incentives to redistribute that face a large segment of the electorate with incomes not very distant from the median. The main point of this chapter is that the relative income of the median income *voter* in the United States is in fact not worse today than it was thirty years ago. The disenfranchisement effect and the sharing effect have contributed to lessening voter support for redistribution despite increasing income inequality.

Although the ratio of family income of the median *individual* to mean family income has indeed fallen in the United States over the past thirty years, the ratio of the family income of the median *voter* to mean family income has been remarkably constant. The political process does appear to have equilibrated in the sense that the median voter is not worse off compared to the mean.

How has this distinction between the median voter and the median individual arisen?

First, not every eligible individual votes. United States citizens who do not vote have lower incomes than those who do. This income difference has always been the case, and it does not appear to have shifted much over the past thirty years.[6] An argument that it may have shifted originates in the observation that many states bar voting by convicted felons and that convictions and incarcerations have trended sharply upwards (Uggen and Manza 2002). Convicted felons—Bernie Ebbers, Michael Milken, and Martha Stewart aside—tend to be poor. Making felons ineligible might make nonvoters disproportionately poor. But we don't see such effects in our data. It is possible that the Census Bureau undersamples convicted felons and therefore consistently over-estimates the incomes of nonvoters. But it is also possible that people susceptible to felony convictions always had very low turnout, so changing conviction rates and eligibility would have minimal impact on the income distribution of nonvoters. In any event, the impact of in-eligible felons has to be small relative to that of noncitizens. McDonald and Popkin (2001), for example, estimate that, in 2000, noncitizens outnumbered ineligible felons by over five to one. Uggen and Manza (2002) estimate that 2.3 percent of the adult population was ineligible felons in 2000, in contrast to the 7.8 percent of the CPS sample that is noncitizen.

Second, and more important, the percentage of residents who are noncitizens has risen sharply, tripling between 1972 and 2000. More-over, as emphasized by Bean and Bell-Rose (1999) and Borjas (1999), noncitizens are increasingly low-wage and poor. Our most striking observation is the rapid decline of the median income of noncitizens relative to the median income of voters. In a nutshell, continuing immi-gration has created a large population of noncitizens. These non-citizens appear to be a leading cause of the fall of median family income relative to mean income. Voters are doing as well as they have ever done.

We have a second interesting finding. There is a midterm cycle in the income of nonvoters. The median income of nonvoters increases in off years and declines in presidential years. In other words, marginal voters who vote in presidential elections but not in off years have higher incomes than persistent nonvoters. The smaller set of citizens who vote in neither presidential nor off-year elections have particularly low incomes. In presidential elections, then, the median family income of a voter is sharply higher than that of the median income of a non-voter and much, much higher than that of a noncitizen.

Data and Methods

Our data are drawn from the November Current Population Survey (CPS) conducted by the Census Bureau. In even-numbered years, those with congressional or presidential elections, the CPS asks each respondent whether he or she is a citizen and whether he or she voted in the election held on the first Tuesday in November. The citizenship question has appeared every two years starting in 1972.[7] The CPS has long been used by political scientists and others interested in studying voter turnout, most notably by Raymond Wolfinger and Steven Rosenstone (1980) in their classic book *Who Votes?*

The CPS contains no information about voter behavior other than turnout. Its advantage is that the sample sizes are far larger than in surveys like the National Election Study. We analyze all respondents 18 and over who provide information about income and citizenship and who, if they are citizens, provide information about voting. Respondents with complete information on citizenship, voting, and income range from a low of 69,584 in 2000 to a high of 110,588 in 1980.

In figure 4.1, we show the 2000 distribution of respondents by citizenship and voting for each income category. The figure illustrates the strong relationship between income and voting. In the lowest income category used by the CPS, nearly two-thirds of the respondents are either noncitizens or nonvoters. In contrast, of those respondents who report themselves to be in the highest income category, over three-fourths also report having voted. The figure also indicates that noncitizens are far more likely to appear in the lower income categories than in the higher ones.

There are, however, many negatives that detract from using the CPS data despite the large N.

First, people lie. We know that voting is overreported. When we compare actual voter turnout data from the Federal Election Commission to self-reported turnout data in the CPS, we find that respondents overstate voter participation by 7 to 12 percentage points (see Rosenthal and Eibner 2005 for details). We suspect that citizenship is overreported as well. If the set of nonvoters who lie and claim to be voters had an income distribution identical to that of voters, we would still get correct estimates of the median and mean income of voters, but we would underestimate the median income of nonvoters. This effect would make the income contrast between voters and nonvoters less stark than the data indicate. If, on the other hand, the income distribution of nonvoters who lie is identical to that of honest nonvoters, we will underestimate the median and mean income of voters, implying that the true differences are even stronger than those we report. One hopes that lying nonvoters have an income distribution somewhat in

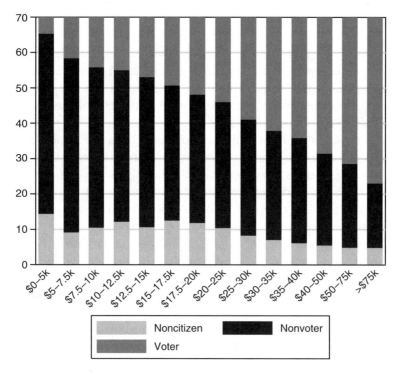

Figure 4.1
Citizenship and Voting in 2000
Source: November 2000 Current Population Survey.

between honest nonvoters and true voters, in which case the bias will not be severe.[8] An encouraging observation is that more voting is reported for presidential years than for off years, paralleling actual turnout. We also hope that there are no severe problems of bias generated by those who lie about their citizenship and, a fortiori, by noncitizens who claim to be voting citizens. People, of course, also lie about their incomes, a nasty problem swept under the rug by those who analyze census data.

Second, there are sampling problems with the census. The two tails, particularly the lower tail, of the income distribution are likely to be undercounted. We acknowledge the potential for bias here and move on.

Third, there is a top-coding problem. The Census Bureau adopted fourteen categories for reporting income in 1982 and has since left them unchanged. The top category is incomes of $75,000 and over. (For 1974–80, the top coding was at $50,000. In 1972, the top coding was at $25,000, and there were only eleven categories.) Economic growth and inflation have combined to increase sharply the fraction of the sample in that category. In 1982, only 2.41 percent of voters were in the top category: in 2000 and 2002, 28.2 and 31.3 percent were, respectively. The top coding reduces the accuracy of our estimation of the income distribution, particularly for voters. More detailed data on individual income can be found in the March CPS, but these data cannot be linked to the November survey.[9] It is regrettable that the federal government has both somewhat curtailed the size of the CPS and failed to adjust the income brackets in the November CPS, but we have to play the cards we are dealt.

In analyzing the CPS data, we first cross-tabulated income with citizenship and voting to obtain the income distributions of voters, nonvoting citizens, and noncitizens. These three categories are important to our purposes. For each of the three groups and for the entire sample, we estimate mean income and median income using the estimated mean and variance of a two-parameter log-normal distribution. The method is described in detail in the appendix of chapter 3. As there were at most fourteen categories in a given year, we chose parsimony and did not estimate a richer distribution with a larger number of parameters. The accuracy of the estimates is very likely to deteriorate with the top-coding problem that grows in more recent years. For centiles of the income distribution, we can, in contrast, obtain highly accurate estimates (except for centiles above the top code) by interpolation from category bounds.[10] The large N of the CPS makes interpolation accurate.

The 2002 data are particularly problematic. We exclude them from all centile comparisons because of the top coding. In addition, contrary to expectations, (1) the fraction of noncitizens fell slightly from 2000 to 2002 (see table 4.2) and (2) among noncitizens, the proportions of Hispanics and "Other" non-Hispanics fell slightly from 2000 to 2002 (see figure 4.6). These differences might be due to sampling variation, but they might also reflect more wary noncitizen respondents in the wake of 9/11. A change in overreporting citizenship of low-income noncitizens could explain the occurrence, once 2002 data are introduced, of a slight deterioration in our results based on median/mean comparisons.

Results

We begin, following the discussion in chapter 3 and earlier in this chapter, by examining ratios of median income to mean income. To re-cap: as this ratio falls, there should be more pressure to redistribute. Put simply, as the median voter's income falls relative to the mean, the voter's share of the initial pie falls and the voter will seek to get a larger piece. The pressure to redistribute persists even if the total pie shrinks somewhat as a result of changes in labor supply, deadweight loss from tax collection, and so on. We focus first on the disenfranchisement effect by making all families the baseline for comparison.

Using the ratio of the median to the mean as our measure of inequality, we find that income inequality significantly increased in the United States in the last three decades. The bottom line of figure 4.2 shows a decrease from 0.75 in 1972 to under 0.7 in 2000. A linear regression of the ratio on trend shows an estimated yearly decrease of 0.00189

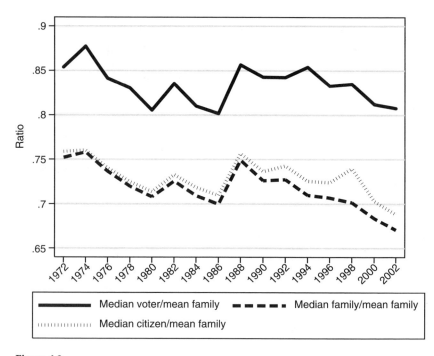

Figure 4.2
Median-Mean Ratios
Source: November Current Population Survey, various years.

(t=4.21, R^2=0.56, one-tail p-value=0.0004). Contrast the lower line with the upper one in figure 4.2, which shows the same ratio when we substitute the median income of *voters* for the median income of *all* families but still keep mean income as the denominator. Notice that this ratio is always substantially higher than that for the median individual in the entire sample. That is, the median voter has much less incentive to redistribute than the median individual. Moreover, there is no trend. There is no significant increase in inequality. The linear regression shows an estimated yearly decrease of only 0.00078 (t=1.37, R^2=0.12, p-value=0.10), less than half of the decrease that occurred in the entire population.

If we compare median *citizen* income to mean family income we find an intermediate situation, shown as the middle line in figure 4.2. The linear regression now shows a yearly decrease of 0.0012, only two-thirds of the decrease for the entire population. The decline has only borderline statistical significance (t=1.640, R^2=0.30, p-value=0.015). If median citizen income deteriorated, the deterioration has been minimal. The big drop is in median family income. The difference between citizens and all families is, of course, noncitizens.

We should point out that the contrasts are much sharper if we exclude the 2002 data. Moreover, the trend for voters is not even borderline significant. Although, conservatively, we give detailed results for the full time series, we are more inclined to believe the results without 2002, which show the decline in the ratio for families to be three times what it is for voters. In any case, what is clear is that the median voter's situation has deteriorated much less than has the median family's.

The information displayed in figure 4.2 permits us to calculate the disenfranchisement effect implied by the Bolton and Roland model (see chapter 3). We will work with $\alpha=\frac{1}{2}$. The preferred tax rates of the median voter calculated from this assumption average to 16.5 percent over the fifteen CPS biennial samples from 1972 to 2000. The federal income tax has averaged about 14 percent of total Adjusted Gross Income (AGI). But since most voters also pay state and local income taxes, the $\alpha=\frac{1}{2}$ assumption looks fairly reasonable. It is straightforward to explore the sensitivity of the results to variation in α.

Most of the disenfranchisement effect comes from the failure of all citizens to vote. Were the median citizen decisive, the tax rates would average 10.3 percentage points higher than in the median voter model, increasing from 16.4 to 26.7 percent. But as we have seen, this difference is fairly constant across time. In 1996, 1998, and 2000, the median citizen, relative to the median voter, would have raised taxes no more than in 1974. The additional increases brought about by the disenfranchisement of noncitizens, while smaller, show an important trend in time. From 1972 through 1988, the median family would have desired a tax less than 0.1 percentage points more than the tax desired by the median citizen. From 1992 through 2000, the increase would have been in excess of 1.5 percentage points.

Actual tax policy since 1972 has clearly headed in a direction opposite to that implied by these calculations but certainly is more akin to median voter preferences than to median citizen or median family preferences.

We are concerned, however, with the accuracy of our log-normal estimates of mean and median income.[11] Standard alternative measures used by economists compare ratios of centiles of the income distribution. We can compute centiles with reasonable accuracy by using log-linear interpolation from the categorical data.[12] A common ratio is 50-90, the ratio of the median to the 90th centile. We cannot use this ratio because of top coding. We can look at the 50-80 ratio for 1972–96. This ratio is shown in figure 4.3.

Figure 4.3 shows a more complex picture than figure 4.2. Overall, in terms of 50-80 ratios, income inequality does increase. But the damage here was done by 1980, before Reaganomics took hold in the United States. After 1980, all families and nonvoters basically have been treading water. Except for the aberrant data point represented by 1996, the relative situation of the median voter markedly improved after 1980.[13] As the median voter improved, the position of the median noncitizen continued to deteriorate. The presence of increasing numbers of relatively poor noncitizens bumped up voters in the overall income distribution.

The story told by the picture is echoed by the simple regression analysis shown in table 4.1. In each column, we regress the 50-80 ratio on a time trend and a dummy for presidential years. The first thing to note from the results is that, parallel to our results for mean/median comparisons, the median voter has much less incentive to redistribute than does the median family. This is shown by the regression constants reported in table 4.1. The median voter's income is 67 percent of that of the 80th percentile family, whereas the median family is at only 60 percent, even in 1972, before trend effects kick in. The median voter is also far better off than the median nonvoter and the median noncitizen.

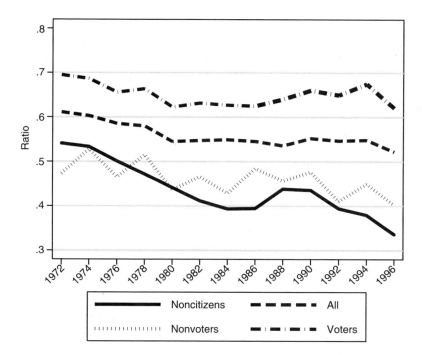

Figure 4.3
Ratio of Median Income in Categories to 80th Centile, All Families
Source: November Current Population Survey, various years.

Table 4.1
50–80 Comparisons
(*t*-statistics in parentheses)

Variable	Median noncitizen/ 80th family	Median nonvoter/ 80th family	Median voter/ 80th family	Median family/ 80th family
Constant	0.5219 (28.66)	0.5226 (56.79)	0.6742 (47.50)	0.5976 (65.99)
Presidential year	−0.0026 (−0.160)	−0.0477 (−5.63)	−0.0127 (−0.969)	−0.0063 (−0.750)
Year − 1972	−.00070 (−6.27)	−0.0030 (−5.32)	−0.0014 (−1.62)	−0.0029 (−5.25)
R^2	0.80	0.86	0.26	0.69

A second observation is that the median voter's position is not estimated to have deteriorated over time. The trend effect, albeit negative, is small and statistically insignificant. In contrast, there are significant negative trends for all families, nonvoters, and especially noncitizens, whose trend coefficient is more than twice the magnitude of nonvoters'. A third observation, one we return to later, is that there is a significant midterm cycle in the ratio for nonvoters. The cycle is captured in the sawtooth pattern for nonvoters shown by figure 4.3. Nonvoters are very significantly poorer in presidential election years. This income difference results from the fact that relatively rich nonvoters, who have income profiles much like those of midterm voters, turn out in presidential years. In contrast, there is no opposite midterm cycle for voters, partly because the additional voters in presidential years are small relative to the pool of midterm voters and partly because the additional voters, albeit well off relative to other midterm nonvoters, are not richer than midterm voters.

Very much the same story is told by figure 4.4. When we drop down from the 80th to the 72nd centile, we can cover all years through 2000. 1996 becomes a more normal data point, but now 2000 is aberrant.[14] A main theme carries over directly from figure 4.3—the relative position of noncitizens has deteriorated sharply over time. Similarly, the sawtooth pattern of the midterm cycle for nonvoters repeats in figure 4.4. In contrast to the 80th centile comparison, however, 50-72 ratios continued to decline after Reagan took office but then started to recover in the mid- to late 1980s. In fact, the ratio was best for voters in 1994, when they gave Newt Gingrich and the Republicans control of Congress. As a whole, putting aside 2000, citizen families look just a little worse off, in terms of 50-72 ratios, in the late 1990s than they did in the early 1970s.

The relative decline in median family income, shown most strongly by figures 4.2 and 4.3, has in large part been the result of the substantial immigration that has flowed into the United States every year since the passage of the Immigration Act amendments of 1965. As table 4.2 shows, noncitizens as a percentage of our sample have steadily increased, tripling from less than 3 percent in 1972 to nearly 8 percent in 2000.[15] Changes like these mean a lot in an electorate that is divided nearly 50-50. It is comforting to see that, whatever the bias in the reporting of citizenship, the bias appears to be fairly constant and unaffected by whether the year is presidential or not.

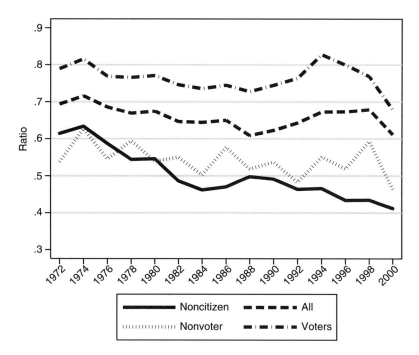

Figure 4.4
Ratio of Median Income in Categories to 72nd Centile, All Families
Source: November Current Population Survey, various years.

In contrast to the rapidly increasing noncitizen population, the percentage of the over-18 population that votes has been remarkably constant. Of course, turnout continues to be strongly affected by whether the election is midterm or presidential. A regression of the percentage of voters *among citizens* in table 4.2 on a time trend (1972=0) and a presidential year dummy gives (t-statistics in parentheses):

$$\text{Voters} = 51.18 + 0.052(\text{Year}-1972) + 14.27(\text{Pres. Year}), \quad R^2=.94$$
$$\qquad\quad (46.33) \quad (0.97) \qquad\qquad (14.42)$$

Thus, as first observed by McDonald and Popkin (2001), there has been no decline in turnout.[16] It is hard to blame increasing inequality on citizen apathy at the polls. Although it is not statistically significant, there is a small upward trend in the fraction of those respondents who claim citizenship who also claim to have voted. Reported citizen turnout in presidential years in fact peaked at over 70 percent of citizens in 1992, when Ross Perot enriched the choice set, and hit a low of 63

Table 4.2
Sample Percents by Voting and Citizenship

Year	Noncitizens	Nonvoters	Voters
1972	2.63	32.21	65.16
1974	2.86	49.82	47.32
1976	3.04	34.24	62.72
1978	3.38	47.43	49.18
1980	3.79	33.09	63.12
1982	3.96	43.35	52.70
1984	4.19	31.84	63.97
1986	4.40	45.79	49.81
1988	4.03	34.06	61.90
1990	5.47	44.87	49.66
1992	6.21	28.00	65.79
1994	6.36	44.22	49.42
1996	6.31	34.02	59.67
1998	6.82	45.86	47.33
2000	7.76	30.28	61.96
2002	6.89	43.31	49.79

percent in 1996, when Bob Dole produced about as much excitement as a Viagra ad. Similarly, midterm turnout hit a low of 48.7 percent in 1974, when Watergate drove away Republicans, and hit a high of 54.9 percent in 1978. In a nutshell, the rise in inequality and polarization in the last three decades of the twentieth century was not accompanied by a reduction in reported turnout of reported U.S. citizens.

So what sustained the ratio of the median income of voters to the mean income of the population? Certainly not that the voters had become a narrower slice of the eligible population. Figure 4.1, however, demonstrates that turnout is strongly correlated with income. Has voting just become more correlated with income, with apathetic poor citizens sitting out elections?

We can begin to answer this question by comparing the median incomes of voters to the median incomes of nonvoters and noncitizens. If low-income citizens had become apathetic and failed to vote, while overall citizen turnout remained roughly constant, we would expect to find the median income of nonvoters to have declined relative to voters. This decline didn't happen. What did happen is that the median income of noncitizens relative to the median income of voters

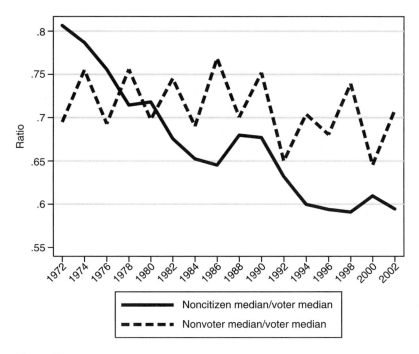

Figure 4.5
Income Ratios, 1972–2002
Source: November Current Population Survey, various years.

declined sharply. The evidence is in figure 4.5 and table 4.3, which use medians calculated by linear interpolation.[17]

As table 4.3 indicates, the income of the median noncitizen is falling sharply relative to that of the median voter. The ratio is unaffected by whether the year is a presidential one. The median income of non-voters has also fallen, but not nearly as sharply. The coefficient estimate of -0.0016 is less than one fourth the magnitude of the -0.0068 for noncitizens. Much of the negative trend for nonvoters results from the two high-turnout presidential election years of 1992 and 2000, years that were likely to have left the nonvoters poorer than usual. Moreover, if we drop the questionable 2002 data, the trend for non-voters is only borderline significant.

What happens systematically, in contrast, is that high-turnout elections draw the richest nonvoters into voting, tending to leave only the poorest as nonvoters. As we discussed earlier, we have a significant midterm cycle—the median nonvoter is relatively poorer in a presidential year than in the preceding or succeeding midterm elections.

Table 4.3
Comparisons of Median Noncitizen and Median Nonvoter Incomes to Median Voter
Income
(*t*-statistics in parentheses)

Variable	Median noncitizen/ median voter	Median nonvoter/ median voter
Constant	0.7660	0.7670
	(52.97)	(82.99)
Presidential year	0.0068	−0.0629
	(0.523)	(−7.60)
Year − 1972	−0.0068	−0.0016
	(−9.58)	(−3.60)
R^2	0.88	0.83

To show how the midterm effect operates, we compare the midterm election of 1998 to the high-turnout presidential year of 2000. If turnout in presidential years among off-year nonvoters were not correlated with income, we would expect to see a larger fraction of nonvoters with high nominal incomes in 2000 than in 1998. Inflation was low but positive and, moreover, there had been real economic growth between November 1998 and November 2000. Yet the percentage earning over $35,000 actually declined from 41.6 percent of nonvoters in 1998 to 39.0 percent in 2000. Therefore, the higher-income nonvoters in off years tend to vote in presidential years. A perhaps simpler way to see what underlies the midterm cycle is to note that while the nominal median income of voters increased in every two-year period through 2002, the nominal median income of nonvoters actually fell in 1988, 1992, and 2000.

There is an implication for the study of national elections in these results. The trend of Republican success in the three decades that inequality has increased (Duca and Saving 2002) can, as we argued in chapter 3, hardly be solely a matter of very poor social conservatives voting against their economic interests. A large segment of the truly poor does not have the right to vote. Whereas in 2000 noncitizens were 7.8 percent of the general population, they were 11.3 percent of families with less than $10,000 per year. (See figure 4.1.) Similarly, in 1996, noncitizens were 10.0 percent of families earning less than $10,000 but only 6.3 percent of the general population.

Our results comparing medians for nonvoters to the medians for voters do contrast with the earlier results where we compared medians for nonvoters to the 72nd or 80th percentiles of all families or families of citizens. There the result was a much more statistically significant decline for nonvoters. The results can be reconciled by observing that income growth has been increasing most in the higher centiles of the income distribution. When compared to the median income of voters, the median income of nonvoters has not deteriorated much. But because median income among nonvoters is much less than that for voters, the position of nonvoters has fallen more sharply in comparison to relatively high-income families.

The main thrust of our analysis, moreover, rests on the increase in economic differences between citizens and noncitizens. Our results bear out research by economists and demographers. As, for example, Borjas (1999) explains, in 1972 these immigrants came predominantly from first-world nations. Their median income was not far behind that of voters and in fact was higher than that of nonvoters. Over time, the immigrants came predominantly from the third world, in large part Mexico. By 1982, median noncitizen income had fallen permanently behind that of the median nonvoter.

The changing pattern of income of noncitizens, as indicated by the November CPS, is echoed by the changing racial-ethnic composition of this group. We graph the ethnic-racial composition of noncitizens in figure 4.6.[18] We break out Hispanics from non-Hispanics. Within non-Hispanics, we distinguish between white, black, and other. In 1974, noncitizens were slightly over 40 percent white.[19] The white percentage fell to just over 20 percent by 2000. The decrease among whites was made up by an increase in the "Other" category in the 1970s and by Hispanics in the 1980s and, increasingly, in the 1990s. Our results are likely to overestimate the income of noncitizens if illegal immigrants are less likely to be sampled and more likely to be Hispanic. We will also overestimate the income of noncitizens if illegal immigrants with low incomes overreport citizenship more frequently than legal immigrants.[20]

Up to this point, our analysis has focused on the disenfranchisement effect. We have shown a steep and increasing difference in the tax rates that the Bolton-Roland model associates, with the median voter, as opposed to the median family, being pivotal. Taxes would be higher, however, were it not for the sharing effect. Our analysis of the sharing effect presumes that there would not have been major changes in relative income had there been a closing of the immigration floodgates. This assumption is perhaps not outrageous. Cutting off immigration

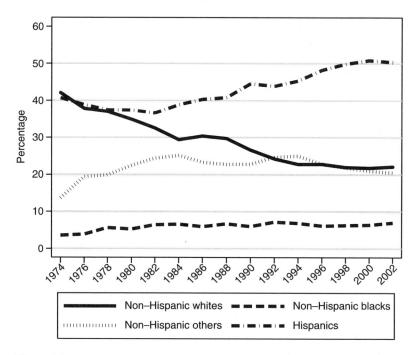

Figure 4.6
Noncitizens by Race and Ethnicity
Source: November Current Population Survey, various years.

might have raised wages of citizens at the very low end. It might also have, for example, eliminated the supply of nannies that permits two spouses to work and obtain very high incomes. Here the impact is likely to be greatest at very high incomes. The impact at the median would have been lower. So the comparisons we make have some credibility, especially 50-72 and 50-80.

We begin the comparisons, however, with the median/mean ratios first seen in figure 4.2. In figure 4.7, we compare the previously plotted ratio of median voter income to mean *family* income and the ratio of median voter income to mean income for all *citizen* families. As can be seen, there is little difference between the two series until 1990, when the gap widens. The breach eventually widens to a point where, in terms of the Bolton-Roland model, the median voter would want substantially higher taxes if the income distribution were that of citizens rather than all families. In the benchmark Bolton-Roland scenario with $\alpha=1/2$, the tax rate for a ratio of 0.79 would be 21 percent; it falls

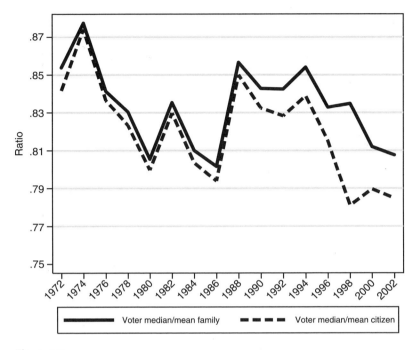

Figure 4.7
Ratio Median Voter Income to Mean Income
Source: November Current Population Survey, various years.

to 17 percent if the ratio increases to 0.83, the type of difference between citizens and families seen in figure 4.7. Note that in this range,
we have not chosen an unreasonable value for government ineffi-
ciency. The cost, $\frac{1}{2}t^2$, would only be about two cents on the dollar.
The magnitude of the trend for citizens over time, 0.00163, is over
twice the 0.00078 ratio estimated for families. The decline is statistically
significant ($t=-2.76$, $R^2=0.353$). (Again, the contrast between the two
series is somewhat greater if the 2002 data are excluded.)

The results for the median/mean ratios are confirmed by analysis of
the 50-80 and 50-72 ratios. In figure 4.8, we produce the 50-80 comparisons of medians of voters and nonvoters to the 80th percentiles of all
citizen families. In the same figure, we include the previous comparisons to the 80th percentiles of all families. The curve for citizens lies
below that for all families. In the 1970s, however, the curves are indistinguishable, reflecting that noncitizens were few and of relatively similar income to citizens. As noncitizens become both more numerous
and relatively poorer, a gap opens up, small but increasing.

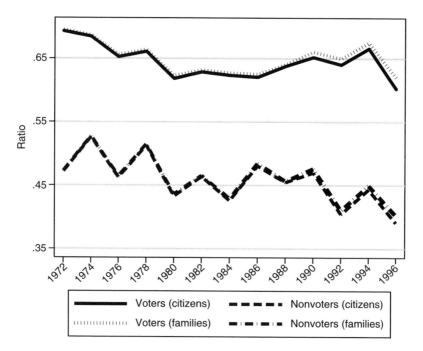

Figure 4.8
Ratio of Median to 80th Centile Income Citizens and Families Compared
Source: November Current Population Survey, various years.

In table 4.4, we report regressions similar to those in table 4.1, replacing families with citizens. The pattern for nonvoters changes little from table 4.1. Voters do show a statistically significant negative trend (at the 0.05 level, one-tail) when compared to citizens, unlike the comparison to families. That is, noncitizens are bumping voters up a bit in the income distribution, compensating in part for the rise in income inequality.

In figure 4.9, we show a similar comparison for 50-72 ratios. This figure shows a larger gap between the citizen and the family comparison than does figure 4.8. Regression results (not reported) again show a significant decline of median voters within the citizen population.

Conclusion

The median income *voter*'s incentive to redistribute has not increased as overall economic inequality has risen in the United States. The reason is partly that the rise in inequality has been offset by immigration,

Table 4.4
50–80 Comparisons of Median Voter Income to 80th Centiles Income of All Families
(t-statistics in parentheses)

Variable	Median nonvoter/ 80th family, citizens	Median voter/ 80th family, citizens
Constant	0.5225	0.6747
	(55.32)	(48.05)
Presidential year	−0.0481	−0.0138
	(−5.69)	(−0.969)
Year − 1972	−0.0033	−0.0019
	(−5.53)	(−2.17)
R^2	0.86	0.37

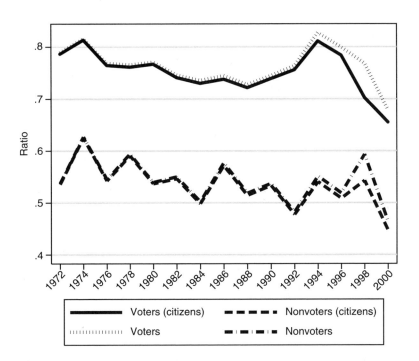

Figure 4.9
Ratio of Median to 72nd Centile Income Citizens and Families Compared
Source: November Current Population Survey, various years.

which has changed the location of citizens in the income distribution. Those ineligible to vote are substantially poorer than the eligible. Moreover, poorer citizens have not become increasingly apathetic, at least as measured by the tendency to vote. Most citizens, and voters in particular, have been "bumped up" by the disenfranchisement of poorer noncitizens. At the same time, a voter of a given income is less eager to redistribute if that redistribution has to be shared with the noncitizen poor.

In any event, immigration cannot have been a driving force in the onset of the increase in income inequality and political polarization. In the early 1970s, noncitizens were quite a small share of the population of the United States, and their income profiles were close to those of citizens. Increasingly, however, noncitizens became a larger, poorer share of the population. From 1990 on, this change placed a number of ineligibles at the bottom of the income distribution, sufficient to make a substantial impact on the redistributive preferences of the median income voter. Even if immigration occurred too late to have produced the increases in inequality and polarization, it may well be contributing to the blocking of efforts to redress these trends.

Our results argue against the claim of Lijphart (1997) in his American Political Science Association presidential address that low voter participation is responsible for the much greater inequality in the United States than in Europe. Lijphart's claim may make sense in terms of contemporary cross-national comparisons, but it does not hold up in the time series. Piketty and Saez (2003) present evidence that inequality fell in the United States just as much as in France and Britain from the First World War until 1970. During this period, there was considerably lower turnout in the United States than in France. Since 1970, the three nations have diverged in inequality, but turnout of eligible citizens in the United States has not fallen. Turnout in France fell, but inequality has remained in check. It is true that turnout of *residents* of the United States over 18 has fallen, but few would be prepared to extend the right to vote to noncitizens. Compulsory voting for citizens, proposed by Lijphart, might indeed lead to more redistribution, but the absence of compulsory voting cannot by itself explain the rise in inequality in the United States in the past thirty years. The explanation is likely to be more closely related to the rise in noncitizenship. The increase reflects two political outcomes. First, immigration reforms in the 1960s and 1990s permitted a large increase in legal immigration. Second, the United States did little to contain illegal immigration. The two outcomes have changed the relationship of income to voting.

Campaign Finance and Polarization

Cryogenically preserved in the 1960s, Austin Powers's nemesis Dr. Evil emerged in the 1990s to continue his quest for world domination. As a first step toward his goal, Dr. Evil and his minions plot to extort vast sums of money from the United Nations by hijacking a nuclear weapon from Kerpla-chistan. His initial proposal to his followers is to demand a hefty ransom of one million dollars. After an uncomfortable pause, Evil's second-in-command, Number Two, responds, "Don't you think we should maybe ask for more than a million dollars? A million dollars isn't exactly a lot of money these days."

Indeed, even a *billion* dollars isn't that much money these days. In 1982, the *Forbes* 400 list of the wealthiest Americans identified seventeen fortunes exceeding a billion dollars. The 2004 list contains the names of 313 billionaires. A fortune of $750 million was required just to make the list.

America's megarich have a problem that many of us wish that we had—figuring out what to do with all of that money. For many on the Forbes 400 list and the exploding numbers of the merely rich, politics has been the answer. They have entered politics through two routes. Some have used their fortunes to jump-start their own careers in electoral politics, and others have become generous patrons of other candidates and causes.

The most spectacular examples of the first path are former presidential candidate Ross Perot (Forbes 400 #40, with assets of $4.2 billion) and New York City Mayor Michael Bloomberg (#34, with $5 billion). During two runs for the presidency, Perot spent in excess of $70 million, and Bloomberg spent $69 million to win the mayoralty. These are enormous sums, but they only represent about 1.5% of each man's net worth.[1] Although no other Forbes listees have made the jump to electoral politics,[2] such not-quite-so-super-rich Americans as Jon Corzine (D-NJ) and Maria Cantwell (D-WA) have entered politics by self-financing expensive Senate campaigns.[3] According to opensecrets.org, twenty congressional candidates spent more than $1 million of their own money on their own campaigns in 2002, although all but three lost.[4] Despite the seemingly low returns of self-financing, the number of millionaires in the U.S. Senate has reached forty.[5] If Austin Powers had not foiled his plot, Senator Evil might now be serving on Capitol Hill.

Entering politics through the purely financial route has become even more common these days. In the 2004 election, new campaign finance regulations sent the big money into "527 groups," such as MoveOn.org and the Club for Growth.[6] Twenty-five individual donors contributed more than $2 million apiece to these, led by George Soros at $23.5 million.[7] It is not surprising that fifteen of the twenty-five belong to the Forbes 400. The contributions as a percentage of the respective contributor's wealth remain small, but the pocket change of billionaires is a lot more valuable than the sofa cushions of millionaires.[8]

One striking aspect of the big money in politics is how partisan it is. One might expect the wealthy to support pragmatically powerful incumbents regardless of party. If this behavioral pattern was ever dominant, it is certainly no longer the case. Of the one hundred largest individual contributors in 2002, ninety-five split their contributions less evenly than 85 to 15 percent between the major parties.[9] Only one of the donors split his contributions in half. Perhaps more surprisingly, despite its control of the presidency and the House, the Republican Party was not the primary beneficiary of this new largess. Of the ninety-five partisan contributors on the list of the top one hundred, sixty-three gave disproportionately to Democrats.

Reformers have not failed to notice the rise of big money or its partisan nature. In 2002, Congress passed and the president signed the Bipartisan Campaign Finance Reform Act of 2002 (BCFRA), popularly known as McCain-Feingold. For many of its supporters, BCFRA was essential to mitigate the disproportionate political influence of large donors. Though less often articulated, a second motivation was the belief that effective reform could lower the temperature of national politics. As we shall see, however, the early returns suggest that campaign finance reform has done little to achieve either of these goals.

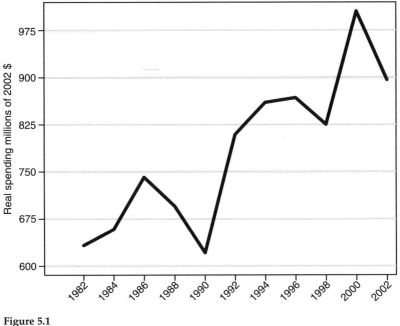

Figure 5.1
Real Spending on House and Senate Campaigns
Source: http://www.fec.gov
Note: Spending deflated to year 2000 using the CPI-U series.

The Escalation in Campaign Spending

The contemporary period of polarized politics has also been one of rapidly escalating campaign expenditure. Figure 5.1 shows the total spending by House and Senate candidates in year 2000 dollars.[10] Real spending has increased roughly 50% over twenty years, peaking at just over a billion dollars for the 2000 election.[11]

There are two obvious hypotheses about the link between campaign spending and polarization. The first is that increased financial demands make congressional candidates more responsive to the positions of extreme interest groups. If this scenario is true, we would expect to observe financial rewards for more extreme members of Congress. A second hypothesis reverses causality. Perhaps campaign spending increased because polarization increased the stakes of winning elections to such a degree that ideological contributors became willing to contribute ever greater sums. Both hypotheses can, of course, be rejected. The correlation of polarization and campaign spending could be entirely spurious. Television, in particular, may have increased both polarization and campaign costs.

Legal developments also appear to have spurred the acceleration of campaign contributions. The "soft money" loophole and the so-called 527 groups have dramatically enhanced the role of very wealthy contributors by allowing unlimited contributions. As we will see, the Democrats have become just as dependent as the Republicans, if not more so, on the largess of multimillionaire contributors. Such dependence is obviously consistent with the Democrats not moving further to the left on economic issues in response to increasing inequality. In this chapter, we examine these hypotheses more closely.

The Legal Environment of Campaign Finance

From early in the twentieth century, direct electoral contributions from corporations and labor unions have been illegal. The Tillman Act (1907) banned direct campaign contributions from corporations, and the Labor-Management Relations (Taft-Hartley) Act of 1947 banned them from labor unions. Consequently, campaigns were financed primarily by unregulated individual contributions. These restrictions, however, were a far bigger hindrance for organized labor than for businesses, which could count on wealthy individuals to contribute on their behalf. To level the playing field, labor unions devised the political action committee (PAC), an independent organization that would raise money from union members for disbursement to political campaigns. The first such organization was the AFL-CIO's Committee on Political Education (COPE). PACs, however, had an uncertain legal status. Numerous legal challenges argued that these PACs violated the provisions of Taft-Hartley. A favorable decision in the 1972 case of *Pipefitters Local #562 v. U.S.* and the passage of the Federal Election Campaign Act (FECA) of 1971 secured the legal status of political action committees. Amendments to FECA in 1974 put limits on the contributions individuals could make to PACs and the contributions that PACs could make to candidates.[12] Subsequently, the Federal Elections Commission ruled that organizations could pay the administrative costs of their PACs (Sorauf 1992, p. 15).

With new legal and statutory protections, the number of PACs proliferated, increasing almost fourfold by the early 1990s. Corporations and single-issue interest groups were especially active in creating new PACs. Correspondingly, candidates became increasingly reliant on PACs for campaign funds.

The campaign finance system that emerged was predicated on a set of tradeoffs. Interest groups could play a greater role in campaign finance, but there were limits on contributions and provisions for disclosure and transparency. Nevertheless, there were plenty of loopholes, the biggest of which led directly to "soft money." No provisions under FECA regulated campaign contributions to state and local affiliates of the national political parties. Individuals, corporations, and unions could make unlimited contributions to these organizations. Subsequent court decisions held that even the national parties could set up "non-federal" accounts to pay for "party building" expenditures. By the time the Supreme Court ruled that parties could spend these funds to make "independent expenditures" on behalf of its candidates, the soft money loophole had become the central feature of campaign finance.

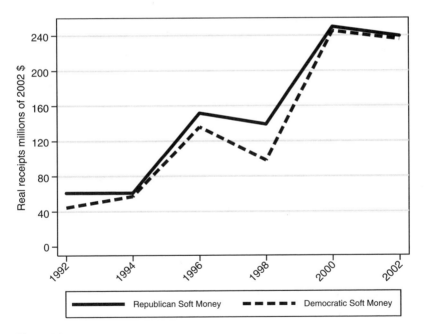

Figure 5.2
Real Soft Money Receipts by Party
Source: http://www.fec.gov
Note: Spending deflated to year 2000 using the CPI-U series.

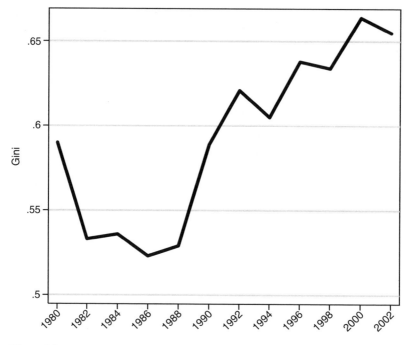

Figure 5.3
The Gini Coefficient for Individual Campaign Contributions
Note: Gini coefficients based on the inequality of contributions sizes for all individual
contributions over $200.

As figure 5.2 shows, soft money contributions to the national parties
went from $100 million to almost $500 million in real terms in just ten
years.

Soft money has exacerbated unequal access to the political process.
As soft money has proliferated, inequality of financial participation in
elections has increased dramatically. To measure the extent to which
the sources of campaign funds have become more concentrated, figure
5.3 presents the Gini index for the size of total contributions, hard and
soft money, by individuals from the Federal Election Commission
itemized contribution file.[13] If all individuals made equal total contributions, the index would be zero. If there were a single contributor,
the index would be one. A very important initial observation is that
the distribution of campaign contributions is much less equal than the
distribution of income, as can be seen by comparing figure 5.3 to figure
1.1. Because our Gini index for contributions is biased downward (see

note 13), the difference between contribution inequality and income inequality is even greater than the difference indicated by the comparison of the two figures. A very small number of people account for most of the financial participation in politics.

Contribution totals, nonetheless, were clearly becoming more equalized through much of the 1980s. Presumably this equalization is a reflection of the strict and non-indexed limits on individual contributions. The soft money loophole greatly exacerbated inequality in contributions in the 1990s because a few wealthy people began making six- and seven-figure donations to political parties.[14]

Unease with the escalating prominence of soft money contributed to the passage of McCain-Feingold. This act banned all soft money contributions to the national political parties and made it harder for state parties to funnel soft money to the national committees. In an attempt to reduce the influence of PACs, it also increased the amount that individuals could give in "hard money" to campaigns but maintained the current limits on PACs, which have not been adjusted for inflation since 1974. In addition, the act restricts the ability of corporations, nonprofit organizations, and labor unions to run "electioneering" ads featuring the names or likenesses of candidates close to an election.

If one of the goals of McCain-Feingold was to depolarize American politics, the early evidence suggests that it will fail. Money that had flowed into the soft money accounts of the national parties now goes to the 527 groups, which spend it freely on campaign advertisements. In the 2004 presidential campaign, groups ranging from Swift Boat Veterans for Truth to MoveOn.org ran numerous attack ads against John Kerry and George Bush. So just two years after a reform designed to minimize the effect of large donors, billionaires like George Soros could spend tens of millions of dollars directed at influencing the presidential election.

Contributor Motives: Ideology or Access?

Although the institutional changes and the increased demands of campaign funding are clearly important, these developments exacerbate polarization only if contributors are primarily motivated by ideological concerns and have extreme preferences. If contributors behaved in such a way, we would expect to see them concentrating their money on the legislators who agree with them most.

Contributors, however, might have any number of motivations. Political scientists and economists have often assumed that most contributors seek to use their money to buy access to critical decisionmakers. Accordingly, campaign money should flow to key legislators such as committee chairs, party leaders, or the pivotal voter on an important roll call.[15] Because policymaking is generally bipartisan, such contributors may wish to contribute to members of both parties. If contributors are access-oriented, we would expect some concentration of contributions in the middle of the spectrum but also a broad dispersal to obtain crucial support on both sides of the aisle. If most individual contributions are in fact widely dispersed, it would be hard to argue that the increased campaign spending and fundraising has contributed to the polarization of Congress.

Identifying Ideological Motivations in PAC Contributions

Clearly, any assessment of the role of campaign finance on party polarization hinges on our ability to identify the motives of contributors. We have developed a simple, yet powerful, tool for identifying ideological contribution behavior.[16] Our method is based on two summary statistics for each individual contributor. The first is the *ideological mean contribution*, M. This measure is just the money-weighted average of the NOMINATE scores of a contributor's recipients.[17] The second measure is the *ideological standard deviation of contributions*, S. This measure is simply the standard error of the ideological position of the recipients, again weighted by contribution amounts.[18]

In order to minimize distortions in standard deviation S caused by the bimodal distribution of candidate ideal points, we use the rank orderings of the NOMINATE scores and normalize them from -1 to 1, combining the House and Senate for each term. Thus, the ideal points are approximated by the uniform distribution on the interval $[-1, 1]$.

To see how these measures relate to ideological contribution behavior, consider the contributions of a purely ideological group that spends a total of $\$B$. An ideological group should concentrate its money on the candidates closest to its ideal point. To be precise, if C is the maximum legal contribution to any candidate, the group should contribute to the $N=\text{int}(B/C)$ nearest candidates and $B - CN$ to the next closest. Let y be the x_i closest to the group's ideal point and K be the number of legislators. Then it is straightforward to show that (approximately)

$$M = \begin{cases} y & \text{if } -1 + N/K < y < 1 - N/K \\ -1 + N/K & \text{if } -1 + N/K \geq y \\ 1 - N/K & \text{if } 1 - N/K \leq y \end{cases}$$

and

$$S = \frac{N}{\sqrt{3}K}.$$

Now consider a group that uses criteria other than the candidate's policy positions in making contribution decisions. The extreme case is a group that contributes randomly with respect to ideology. Then the expected value of M is 0 and $S = 1/\sqrt{3} \cong .577$. Because $N < K$, the ideological contributor has lower S than the nonideological contributor. Furthermore, we can identify ideological contributors as those who have the lowest value of S given a particular number of contributions.

When S is low, indicating highly ideological contributions, M serves as a rough measure of the group's ideal point (although the measure is truncated at $-1 + N/K$ and $1 - N/K$). This observation allows us to locate the policy preferences of ideological contributors.

We begin our analysis by examining M and S for political action committees. To work with reasonably large samples, we study only PACs making at least thirty contributions to legislators within an electoral cycle. Table 5.1 provides some important summary statistics on PAC contributions from the 2002 election. We break the data down

Table 5.1
Summary Statistics for PACs, 2002 Elections, House and Senate

FEC PAC classification	Number	Mean number of contributions	Mean size of contribution	Mean M	Mean S
Corporate	381	81	$2032	0.127	0.477
Labor unions	59	148	$3481	−0.390	0.366
Nonconnected PACs	38	80	$2285	−0.012	0.459
Trade, membership, and professional associations	215	100	$2112	0.118	0.471
Cooperatives	11	106	$1468	0.061	0.511
Corporations without stock	13	97	$2019	−0.012	0.505
Unclassified	50	60	$3547	0.095	0.364

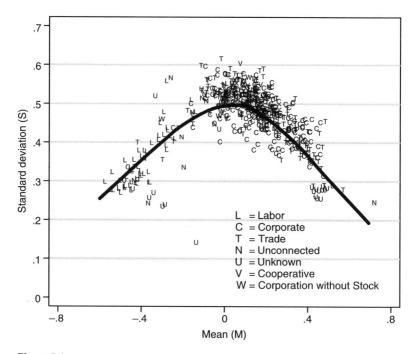

Figure 5.4a
PAC Contribution Patterns, 2002
Note: Includes committees making more than thirty contributions.

by the Federal Election Commission's classification of interest group affiliations.[19]

The FEC groupings show some noticeable differences in contribution behavior. In particular, labor unions appear to engage in more ideological behavior than the other groups. Most groups have values of M close to 0 (the median legislator), labor unions concentrate their contributions at $-.39$. Labor also has the most concentrated contributions with an average $S = .37$. Although corporate and trade groups shade to the right, their contributions are spread more evenly across the spectrum. As the nonconnected and unclassified categories tend to contain the ideological and issue-oriented PACs, it is not surprising that their average values of S are lower than those of the trade and corporate groups. In addition, it is worth noting that all the group classifications have lower values of S than .577, the theoretical benchmark for random contributions.

Although informative, table 5.1 masks considerable heterogeneity in behavior within the FEC classifications. Thus, in figures 5.4a–c, we plot

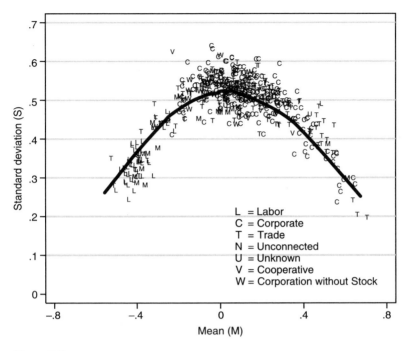

Figure 5.4b
PAC Contribution Patterns, 1992
Note: Includes committees making more than thirty contributions.

S versus *M* for the 1982, 1992, and 2002 elections for all political action committees making more than thirty contributions.[20] The type of political action committee is denoted by its token—Corporate (*C*), Labor (*L*), Trade (*T*), Nonconnected (*N*), Unaffiliated (*U*), Cooperative (*V*), and Corporation without Stock (*W*). The fitted values from a locally weighted (lowess) regression of *S* on *M* are included in the figure.[21] Plots for other elections since 1980 are similar.

Each of these plots reveals an inverted-U relationship in which some groups are concentrating on liberal or conservative members while others are spreading their largess across the spectrum. Few groups, if any, concentrate their money on the middle of the ideological spectrum. Very few moderate groups have values of *S* as low as those for extreme groups. Indeed, many moderate groups have values of *S* very near or above the theoretical value (*S*=0.577) for purely random contributions.[22]

These figures reveal substantial ideological contribution behavior, but they suggest that any increase in such behavior over time is quite

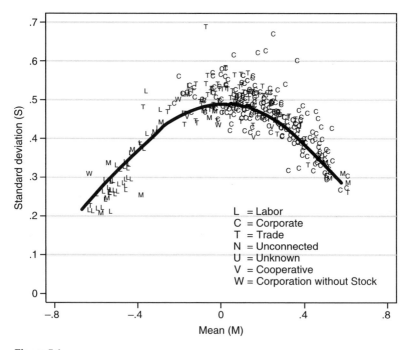

Figure 5.4c
PAC Contribution Patterns, 1982
Note: Includes committees making more than thirty contributions.

modest. In particular, there seems to be no trend toward more groups concentrating at edges of the spectrum. Nevertheless, there does seem to be some movement toward greater ideological concentration overall. Although most of the lowess curves for elections since 1980 peak at higher than $S=.5$, the peak for the last three elections is closer to .48.

One of the problems with evaluating these figures is that they do not control for the relationship between S and N (K is the same across all groups). Perhaps moderate ideological groups make more contributions and therefore have higher values for S. To control for this possibility, we estimated the following model:

$$S = \beta_0 + \beta_1 M + \beta_2 M^2 + \beta_3 N$$

In this specification, the relationship between M and S is assumed to be quadratic. Given the results of the nonparametric lowess results in figure 5.4, this assumption seems reasonable. The estimates of the model for each year are given in the appendix of this chapter. More important

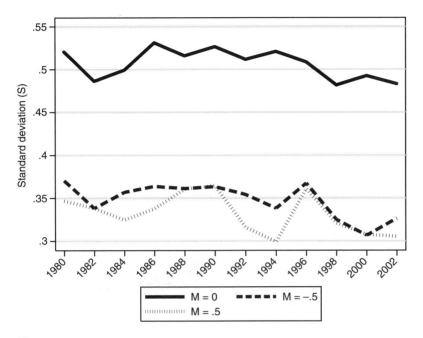

Figure 5.5
Estimated Standard Deviations as a Function of *M*
Note: M and *S* defined in text.

than raw coefficient estimates are the implications of the model for the change in ideological contributions over time. As we mentioned above, if we hold *M* constant, a decline in *S* represents greater ideological consistency in contributions. Such an effect would be polarizing if the decline in *S* were greater for extreme values of *M* than for moderate values. In figure 5.5, we plot the biennial estimate of the expected value of *S* for *M*=0, *M*=−.5, and *M*=.5. Clearly, *S* has declined for all values of *M*, reflecting an increase in ideological consistency. The declines at *M*=−.5 and *M*=.5 are larger in magnitude, suggesting more polarization. Although the differences seem modest, it is important to note that they surely underestimate the polarization of PAC contributions. Recall that the estimates of *M* are based on the normalized rank ordered NOMINATE scores. Because the distribution of actual scores has become increasingly bimodal, *M*=−.5 and *M*=.5 have moved much farther apart. Despite this divergence, contributions became more, not less, concentrated.

It is important to note that the increasing ideological consistency of campaign contributions does not necessarily imply that extreme

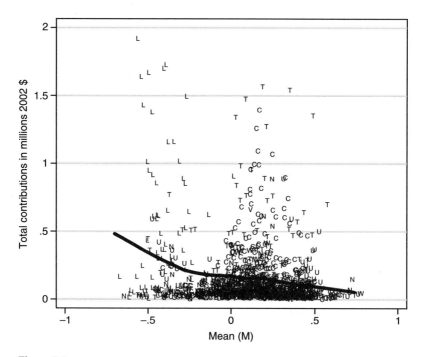

Figure 5.6
Contribution Levels by M in 2002
Note: Groups contributing more than two million dollars are excluded from figure.

legislators receive a contribution windfall. First, as is obvious from figure 5.4, there continue to be far more "access" contributors than ideological contributors. Nor is it the case that ideological contributors are larger and contribute more to legislators. Figure 5.6 shows the total hard money contributions to legislators as a function of M for PACs making at least eight contributions. There is only a slight liberal bias as labor unions tend to be more ideological and larger on average than corporate or trade access PACs.

One might suspect that figure 5.4 suggests an extremist advantage, given that members of Congress receive the largess of ideological groups and are not harshly penalized by access groups. Nevertheless, the data show that they are penalized enough by the access groups (at least those with $S < .577$) to eliminate a financial advantage. Figures 5.7a–c plot candidate receipts from PACs as a function of ideal point for House candidates for the 1982, 1992, and 2002 elections. These figures reveal that there seems to be no ideological advantage with

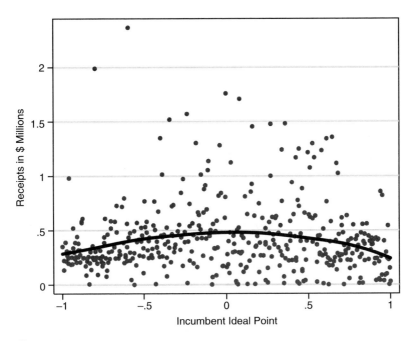

Figure 5.7a
Candidate Receipts from PACs 2002 House Elections
Note: Ideal points are from common-space NOMINATE scores at pooleandrosenthal
.com.

respect to PAC receipts and that in the 2002 election extremists suffered a small financial penalty.[23]

Of course, as shown by figure 5.4, without the ideological groups the penalty would have been more severe. Nevertheless, there is not a large amount of support for the hypothesis that PACs have contributed greatly to polarization.

Ideology and Contributions by Individuals

PACs often receive the lion's share of the scrutiny, but it would be a mistake to ignore the role of individual contributors. After all, contributions from individuals typically constitute more than one-half of all monies raised by congressional candidates in each election cycle. Individuals have also donated hundreds of millions of dollars in soft money. The increasing restrictions on PAC giving, especially in real terms, has increased the importance of individual expenditures.

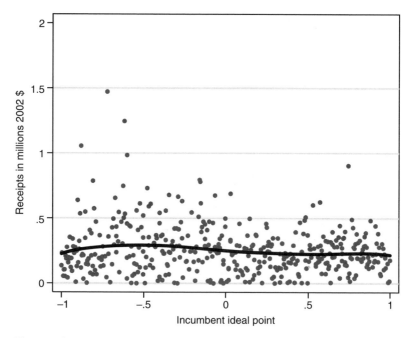

Figure 5.7b
Candidate Receipts from PACs 1992 House Elections
Note: Ideal points are from common space NOMINATE scores at pooleandrosenthal
.com.

We can analyze individual contributions in a manner very similar
to the way we did PACs. For each contributor, we can compute the
average ideal point of its recipients M and the standard deviation S.
Figures 5.8a–c show the scatterplots and lowess curves for individual
contributors making more than eight contributions for three congressional elections. Notice that once again the relationship appears as an
inverted U. The relationship is not as tight, and there are a few ideologically moderate contributors, but there appears to be a far smaller concentration of access contributors.[24]

Another development revealed in figure 5.8 is the proliferation of
individuals who make numerous contributions to legislators. In 1982,
there were just 179 such contributors, whereas by 2002 there were
1,874. It is clear from figure 5.8 that much of the proliferation corresponds to donors who concentrate on the extreme parts of the spectrum, especially on the right.

Despite this growth, just as we found for PAC contributions, there
does not seem to be a financial advantage in being extreme. Figures

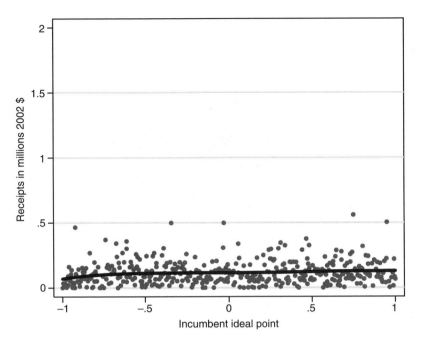

Figure 5.7c
Candidate Receipts from PACs 1982 House Elections
Note: Ideal points are from common space NOMINATE scores at pooleandrosenthal
.com.

5.9a–c plot the total individual contributions as a function of the recipient's ideal point for House members. Center-left members do a bit better, but the differences are not large. The extreme right never does particularly well.

Soft Money

The polarizing effects of hard money contributions are modest; a much bigger effect can be found if we turn to so-called soft money. Figure 5.10 plots the soft money contributions in the 2001–02 election cycle for all individual contributors for whom we were able to estimate M. Clearly, most of the very large soft money contributors have extreme values of M.

In fact, the four largest contributors for whom we can estimate M are omitted from Figure 5.10 because they are such huge outliers that they distort the scale. They are Haim Saban (television producer, $11,680,000, $M = -.472$), Fred Eychaner (media mogul, $6,040,000,

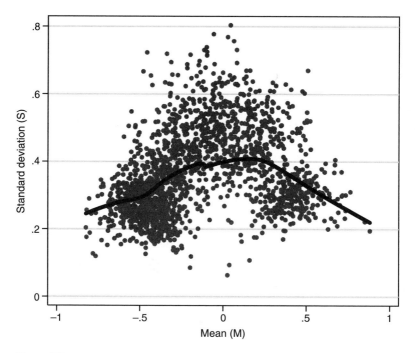

Figure 5.8a
Individual Contributions to Legislators, 2002
Note: Includes individuals making more than eight contributions.

$M = -.399$), Bren Simon (wife of the owner of the Indiana Pacers, $1,550,000, $M = -.388$), and Steven Kirsch (high tech mogul, $2,030,250, $M = -.557$).[25] The results from previous elections tell exactly the same story as figure 5.10.

Almost all the large contributors are extremists. Of the twenty-one individual donors in our data set who contributed more than $250,000, none has a value of M closer to zero (the median) than .321. To take a closer look at the role of extreme views in individual soft money contributions, we estimate two econometric models. In the first, we estimate a probit model of the decision to make a soft money contribution as a function of M, M^2, and S. The results of this model are presented in column 1 of table 5.2. The large and statistically significant coefficient on M^2 confirms that extreme contributors are the most likely to make soft money contributions. Minimizing the estimated probabilities with respect to M, we find that the least likely to make these contributions are those located at $M=-.074$. The independent effect of contribution dispersion S is negative and consistent with ideological soft money

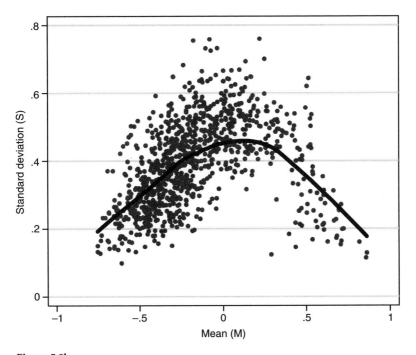

Figure 5.8b
Individual Contributions to Legislators, 1992
Note: Includes individuals making more than eight contributions.

but just short of statistical significance.[26] Assuming a value of $S=.3$, contributors located at $M=.5$ donate soft money at a probability greater than .2. Those at $M=0$ are about .06 less likely to make a soft money contribution. In the second model, we use ordinary least squares regression to estimate how the size of contribution relates to M and S for those who do contribute.[27] Here our dependent variable is the natural log of contributions because of the skew in the distribution of contribution sizes. These results are reported in column 2 of table 5.2. Here we find significant effects for both M^2 and S.[28] Estimated contributions are minimized at $M=.25$, reflecting the leftward bias in the really large contributions. Contributions for $M=-.5$ are about twice as large as those at $M=0$. The estimated effect of S is substantial as well. A person whose hard money contributions match the random benchmark of $S=.577$ contributes about 75 percent less soft money than one at $S=.3$.

Of course, it is hard to estimate the effect of the extreme soft money contributions directly. Presumably the parties have an incentive to use these contributions for the electoral benefit of all their candidates, not

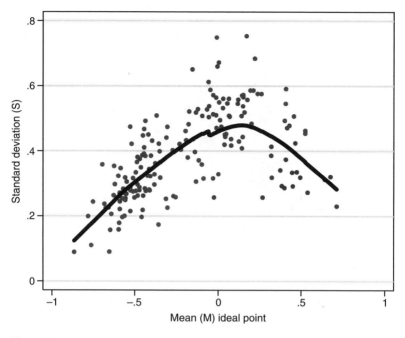

Figure 5.8c
Individual Contributions to Legislators, 1982
Note: Includes individuals making more than eight contributions.

just those who share the donor's views. But if the parties prove to be poor agents of the donors, contributions might dry up. Therefore, even if the parties do not use these soft money contributions exclusively for the benefit of their extreme members, such large sums from ideological contributors must make the parties more responsive to the extreme ideological views.[29]

Campaign Finance and the 527s

McCain-Feingold sought to diminish the influence of large soft money contributors by eliminating soft money contributions to the federal parties. The legislation, however, did not prevent the emergence of the 527 groups. It is too early to engage in a systematic analysis of the effects of this transition, but the early evidence suggests that matters have only gotten worse. The major contributors to the 527s are exactly the same people who made large soft money contributions. According to opensecrets.org, eighteen individual donors gave $3 million or more

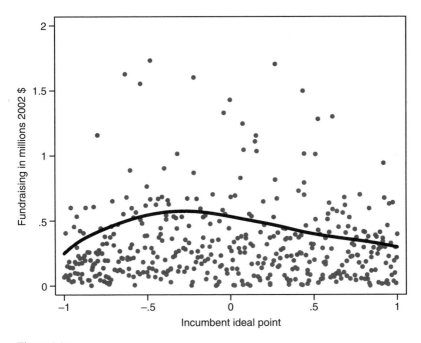

Figure 5.9a
House Fundraising from Individuals, 2002
Source: Derived from Federal Election Commission data and computations by authors
Note: In millions of 2002 dollars.

to various 527 groups. To make matters worse, as the parties cannot
control these expenditures, the groups can better target the money in
ways that support extreme candidates, in both general and primary
elections. Consider the Club for Growth, a libertarian-conservative 527
group. An important goal for the group is the defeat of RINOs (Republicans in name only) in the primaries. In 2004, the Club spent $2.3 mil-
lion in a failed attempt to defeat Republican moderate Arlen Specter in
Pennsylvania's Senate primary.[30] On the left, groups like MoveOn.org
have moved on from trying to defeat Bush to trying to push the Democratic Party to the left. Of course there are groups dedicated to a more
centrist politics such as the New Democrat Network, but they are
dwarfed financially by their more ideological rivals. In addition to the
New Democrat Network, the remaining fifteen largest 527s are ten
groups pursuing an explicitly liberal or conservative agenda, two labor
unions, and the Swift Boat Veterans for Truth, whose only agenda was
beating John Kerry.

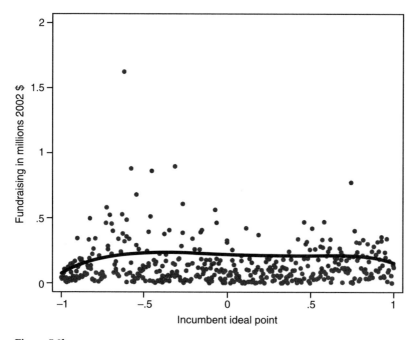

Figure 5.9b
House Fundraising from Individuals, 1992
Source: Derived from Federal Election Commission data and computations by authors
Note: In millions of 2002 dollars.

Conclusion: The Big Soft Money Comes from Ideological Extremists

The past thirty years have been a period not only of political polarization but also of rapidly increasing campaign spending, which has led many to speculate that the two are linked. Our analysis shows no simple causal link leading from the demand for more campaign cash to polarization. Extreme candidates are not better funded than moderates, so there is little evidence that candidates have an incentive to move to the extremes to please their donors. This finding is especially true of our analysis of organized groups. The evidence seems more consistent with a causal arrow pointed in the other direction. Over the past twenty years, the numbers of individual donors contributing large sums have gone up enormously. Many of them are concentrating their largess on the most extreme legislators. As we show, it is the most ideological of these contributors who most exploited the soft money loopholes and will continue to be active in the 527 groups. It is not

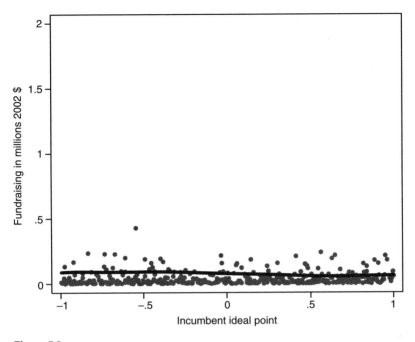

Figure 5.9c
House Fundraising from Individuals, 1982
Source: Derived from Federal Election Commission data and computations by authors
Note: In millions of 2002 dollars.

unreasonable to speculate that the impetus for the greater financial involvement was the increase in polarization and the increased ideological stakes of who wins elections.

Despite the large increases in campaign spending, Ansolabehere, Snyder, and de Figueredo (2003) puzzle over "why there is so little money in politics." Most Americans can afford only relatively small contributions. They can be expected to free ride while others contribute. From the perspective of free riding, it is not surprising that inequality in campaign contributions is far greater than inequality in income. Campaign finance is not the result of significant participation by millions of citizens. The American economy, however, has created thousands of not-so-typical American multimillionaires and -billionaires who have the resources to make contributions substantial enough to have a major effect on electoral outcomes. That many of these wealthy Americans have ideological agendas, while perhaps not the cause of polarization, certainly provides its sustenance.

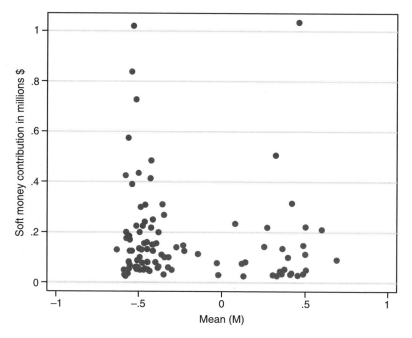

Figure 5.10
Soft Money Contributions, 2002
Source: Derived from Federal Election Commission data and computations by authors
Note: Figure includes only contributions exceeding $25,000. In millions of current dollars.

Table 5.2
Soft Money Contributions
(standard errors in parentheses)

	Probit	OLS on contributions
M	0.138	−1.034
	(0.100)	(0.326)
M^2	0.932	2.230
	(0.319)	(1.242)
S	−0.492	−2.817
	(0.339)	(1.267)
Constant	0.954	9.843
	(0.154)	(0.592)
N	1874	296
log-likelihood	−808.734	
R^2		0.117

Appendix

Table 5.A1
Estimates of Equation 5.1 for 1992–2002
(standard errors in parentheses)

Election	2002	2000	1998	1996	1994	1992
M	−0.004	−0.011	−0.011	−0.007	0.015	−0.001
	(0.009)	(0.015)	(0.009)	(0.009)	(0.008)	(0.008)
M^2	−0.584	−0.723	−0.614	−0.573	−0.770	−0.648
	(0.026)	(0.040)	(0.023)	(0.020)	(0.024)	(0.021)
N	0.02	0.031	0.031	0.029	0.021	0.027
	(0.006)	(0.010)	(0.005)	(0.006)	(0.005)	(0.005)
Labor	−0.045	−0.022	−0.033	−0.035	−0.045	−0.069
	(0.011)	(0.016)	(0.011)	(0.013)	(0.010)	(0.010)
Nonconnected	−0.028	0.001	−0.018	−0.002	−0.046	−0.051
	(0.009)	(0.013)	(0.008)	(0.009)	(0.007)	(0.007)
Trade	0.004	−0.003	−0.005	−0.005	−0.006	0.007
	(0.005)	(0.006)	(0.005)	(0.005)	(0.005)	(0.004)
Unassigned	−0.078	−0.050	−0.049	−0.050	−0.028	−0.054
	(0.007)	(0.013)	(0.008)	(0.009)	(0.012)	(0.014)
Cooperatives	0.002	0.013	−0.004	0.012	−0.015	−0.004
	(0.017)	(0.021)	(0.014)	(0.015)	(0.013)	(0.014)
Corporations without stock	0.016	0.034	0.029	0.042	0.005	−0.006
	(0.014)	(0.017)	(0.013)	(0.013)	(0.011)	(0.011)
Constant	0.489	0.493	0.485	0.510	0.523	0.513
	(0.004)	(0.005)	(0.004)	(0.004)	(0.003)	(0.003)
N	1273	721	1264	1236	1172	1202
R^2	0.482	0.464	0.512	0.537	0.594	0.590

Table 5.A2
Estimates of Equation 5.1 for 1980–1990
(standard errors in parentheses)

Election	1990	1988	1986	1984	1982	1980
M	−0.026	−0.013	0.001	0.009	−0.025	−0.002
	(0.008)	(0.009)	(0.009)	(0.010)	(0.010)	(0.012)
M^2	−0.596	−0.598	−0.673	−0.604	−0.554	−0.592
	(0.021)	(0.021)	(0.022)	(0.022)	(0.024)	(0.027)
N	0.013	0.018	0.010	0.019	0.023	0.018
	(0.005)	(0.006)	(0.007)	(0.006)	(0.009)	(0.010)
Labor	−0.064	−0.040	−0.040	−0.036	−0.043	−0.048
	(0.010)	(0.011)	(0.011)	(0.012)	(0.014)	(0.014)
Nonconnected	−0.016	−0.003	−0.034	−0.033	−0.037	−0.024
	(0.007)	(0.007)	(0.008)	(0.008)	(0.010)	(0.014)
Trade	0.007	0.009	0.006	0.002	0.005	0.007
	(0.005)	(0.005)	(0.005)	(0.005)	(0.006)	(0.006)
Unassigned	−0.006	0.020	0.006	−0.025	—	—
	(0.021)	(0.025)	(0.024)	(0.029)		
Cooperatives	−0.033	0.001	0.009	0.016	0.001	0.030
	(0.014)	(0.015)	(0.017)	(0.016)	(0.019)	(0.020)
Corporations without stock	−0.001	0.006	0.024	0.017	0.049	0.080
	(0.012)	(0.012)	(0.012)	(0.013)	(0.018)	(0.021)
Constant	0.523	0.511	0.531	0.500	0.485	0.515
	(0.003)	(0.004)	(0.004)	(0.004)	(0.005)	(0.005)
N	1182	1257	1187	1169	970	787
R^2	0.543	0.505	0.603	0.534	0.541	0.575

Polarization and Public Policy

Politicians have become more polarized, and the rightward move and electoral success of the Republicans have moved the political system away from public policy that might alleviate income inequality. We have shown that repolarization started in the 1970s. Since then, voters have increasingly aligned their incomes and their voting behavior, more ineligible adults have become concentrated at the bottom of the income distribution, and soft money campaign contributions have emerged as a polarizing force.

These political changes can directly exacerbate income inequality. Redistributive policies such as income tax rates, estate tax rates, and minimum wages evolve in a similar fashion to polarization, income inequality, and immigration. As we argued earlier, the rise in real income and the absence of a severe economic downturn since World War II should make the median voter less favorable to policies like unemployment insurance and welfare, which smooth current consumption of people of working age. At the same time, support for social insurance for the elderly has been strong. In contrast to taxes on income and wealth and to minimum wages, taxes for social security and Medicare programs have increased as polarization has grown.

In politics, change is difficult and punctuated. There is no market to fine-tune allocations to demand and supply. An example highly pertinent to our story is that estate tax rates and exemptions were fixed in nominal dollars in 1940 and received no adjustment until 1977. With inflation, smaller and smaller estates in real value were subject to tax. Taxable estates of a given inflation-adjusted size were subject to increasing rates. The example illustrates what social scientists term the status quo bias of American politics. Polarization accentuates *gridlock*, that is, *status quo bias*. Major legislation is produced less frequently as polarization increases, and polarization may produce gridlock that affects governmental capacity to reduce inequality.

Polarized politics is not the only source of income inequality. There are abundant alternative hypotheses about the rise of inequality. The list includes greater trade liberalization, increased levels of immigration, declining rates of trade unionization, the fall in the real minimum wage, the decline in progressive taxation, technological change increasing the returns to education, the increased rates of family dissolution and female-headed households, the aging of the population, pure racism, America's federal political system, gridlocked national politics, and the absence of proportional representation in elections. (See Atkinson 1997 for an overview of some of these topics; see also Alesina and Glaeser 2004.)

Most of the factors listed above are either directly political or potentially affected by public policy. Technological change, however, would appear to respond to many forces that are independent of government policy. Similarly, the decline of marriage is universal throughout the western world. The roots of the decline may lie just as much in technological changes that affect work in the household and in changes in lifestyle as in changes in incentives produced through welfare and other public policies. Similarly, immigration is driven not just by the American economy and public policy but also by the economies and policies of the source nations. We acknowledge these "exogenous" factors but keep our focus on the public policies produced in the American political system.

The Turnaround in Public Policies Affecting Inequality

Let us look at time trends in public policy. We focus on minimum wages, estate taxes, and income taxes, largely because we can report long time series of these policies. The policies reverse in a manner that parallels the reversals in inequality and politics.

Federal minimum wages were introduced in 1938.[1] The real value of the minimum wage follows a sawtooth pattern, as demonstrated in figure 6.1. The teeth reflect the fact that the wage is not indexed to inflation. Without new legislation, the real wage will decline. The Democrats attempted to index minimum wages in the 1960s and the 1970s. On September 15, 1977, an amendment sponsored by Congressman Phil Burton of California to index the wage for five years failed by the relatively narrow margin of 232 to 191.[2] The vote was strongly along

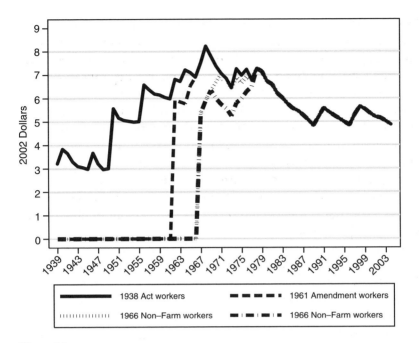

Figure 6.1
Real Minimum Wages
Source: Department of Labor, at http://www.dol.gov/esa/minwage/chart.pdf. Deflator:
CPI-U.

liberal-conservative lines, with moderate Democrats joining Republicans to defeat the amendment. Had Burton succeeded, the minimum wage might be far higher today. It might have been as difficult to remove indexation as it now is to pass meaningful increases.

The sawteeth, however, were only temporary interruptions in an upward trend that persisted until 1968, at the very end of Lyndon Johnson's Great Society. Minimum wages have always engendered liberal support and conservative opposition. Both because of their desire to redistribute income to low-wage workers and to avoid competition with non-unionized labor, liberals have favored a high minimum wage covering large segments of the workforce. Conversely, conservatives have sought to keep the minimum wage low and to limit its scope, as they believe that it creates unemployment by artificially inflating the cost of labor and that it imposes too great a burden on small businesses. Minimum wages initially failed to cover large categories of workers, largely as a matter of concessions to southern Democrats.

Despite these general differences, increases in the minimum wage and expansions of coverage historically generated a fair amount of bipartisan support. For example, in 1949, Republicans overwhelmingly supported a near-doubling of the wage. Moreover, Republican support was pivotal in the 1961 and 1966 amendments that increased the wage and extended it to new groups of voters. That is, as long as polarization was falling, liberals were able to overcome the status quo bias in the non-indexed policy. This relationship is shown in figure 6.1. The figure also shows that coverage was expanded at the same time that the basic minimum wage was increasing. The postwar period was indeed one of generous increases. Although the largest increase occurred in the Truman years, there was a real increase even under Eisenhower, a Republican president.

This bipartisanship disappeared, as it did on so many other issues, as polarization rose in the 1970s. When Congress passed increases in 1977, it did so with a majority of Republicans in each chamber voting in opposition. Subsequently, Reagan's election and the Republican takeover of the Senate blocked further increases until 1989. Although Republicans did support the 1989 bill on final passage, the three-step increase was so modest that it failed to reverse the long decline of the 1980s. In 1996, the minority Democrats were able to force a minimum wage bill onto the agenda with a deft combination of obstruction of the Republican agenda and symbolic election-year politics. Nevertheless, the result was again a very modest increase, at the cost of $20 billon in new business tax breaks. Minimum wages have not been increased in the presidency of George W. Bush.

The consequence of increasing Republican opposition in the period of polarization is a dramatic decline in the real value of the minimum wage. The decline began when Richard Nixon took office. Even though there was some increase after Watergate, minimum wages did not recover even half of the losses of the first six Nixon years. Increases in minimum wages were passed under President Carter, but they were quickly eroded by the high inflation at the end of his four years. In Carter's last year in office, 1980, real minimum wages were actually less than in Ford's last year, 1976. The Reagan years saw much further erosion of the minimum wage. The "kinder, gentler" increase accepted by George H. W. Bush restored very little of the losses. Bill Clinton was then barely able to better the Bush restoration.

Politically, the reversal in the minimum wage chart is consistent with the end of Democratic dominance in American politics, which can probably be dated from the Nixon election in 1968. But it is also possible that preferences on minimum wages have changed for individual legislators. We (Poole and Rosenthal 1991) did an admittedly crude calculation of preference shifts by comparing the votes of senators who had voted on minimum wages in both 1977 and 1989. We found that the real wage these senators would support had fallen by about 15 to 20 percent from 1977 to 1989. The decline in this support might reflect the academic debate over the employment effects of minimum wages, but it might also reflect a shift in preferences of increasingly better-off citizens in the upper half of the income distribution. Both a shift in these preferences and an overall shift to Republicans would be consistent with a shift in an electorate that immigration has increasingly tilted toward the well-to-do.

The real minimum wage today is no higher than it was in the 1950s. But because real wages have generally risen, this wage is less and less a binding constraint on employers. It should be noted that twelve states currently have higher minimum wages than the federal minimum of $5.15. The highest of these wages, $7.35 in Washington, is still substantially below the real value of the federal minimum in 1968. The minimum wage in California, the most populous state, is $6.75.[3] Lee (1999) exploits the cross-sectional variation induced by state minimum wage laws to conclude that the fall in real minimum wages in the 1980s was a leading source of wage inequality. He estimated that declining minimum wages accounted for about half of the increase in the ratio of median wages to wages at the 10th percentile. The reduction in inequality in the 1950s and 1960s could, conversely, reflect the increase in real minimum wages during this period. But changes in the minimum wage obviously cannot account for all of the long-term trends in inequality; there was no minimum wage in the United States before 1938, yet, as we showed in chapter 1, inequality fell during this period.

We should also consider taxation. The story is clearest for the estate tax, cleverly relabeled the "death tax" by its Republican detractors. Because it is difficult to reduce complex tax codes to single numbers, we focus on two series for the estate tax. The first is the maximum estate tax rate—how much the taxpayer would have to pay without giving away or sheltering wealth. The second is the maximum estate without tax liability, that is, the minimum taxable estate. Both series are shown in figure 6.2. To make the series comparable with each other and with the various inequality graphs, we have graphed 1.0 − the maximum tax rate.

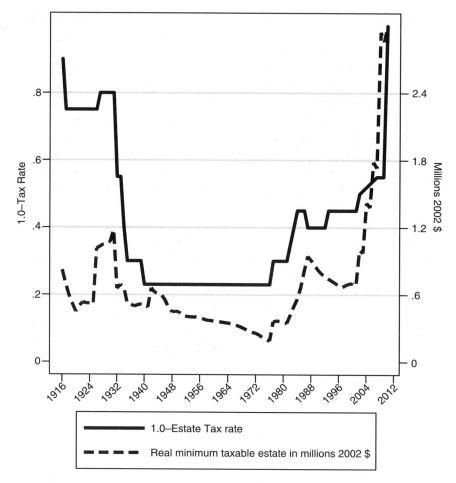

Figure 6.2
Estate Tax, 1916–2010
Source: Miller, Monson, Peshel, Polacek & Hoshaw, San Diego, California. See http://
www.estate-plan.com/pdf/Art_History_Tax.pdf, 2002. Deflator: CPI-U
Note: The estate tax is abolished for 2010, so the minimum taxable estate has been set at
the maximum value of the figure ($3 million).

The influence of partisan politics is even clearer for estate taxes than for minimum wages. The first estate taxes were introduced under unified Democratic government during World War I. More estates were subject to tax until a unified Republican government in 1926 both lowered the tax and increased the minimum estate subject to tax from around $500,000 to $1,000,000 (in year 2002 dollars). Taxes were increased and the minimum decreased when the Democrats took control of the House in the 1930 elections. Taxation of the wealthy increased in the Roosevelt years until the maximum estate tax rate reached 77 percent in 1940. Rates then remained unchanged for thirty-seven years, until 1977. During this time, inflation eroded the minimum until, by 1976, estates under $250,000 were subject to tax. The failure to increase the minimum for so many years resembles the failure of California to adjust real estate taxes during the real estate price boom that preceded the passage of Proposition 13 in 1978. The lack of adjustment meant a broader base for an antitax movement.

Estate taxes then reversed with legislation in 1976 (effective for 1977) passed under the Ford presidency. The reduction in rates and the increase in the minimum were minor. The phased-in minimum adjustments failed to outstrip inflation in the Carter years. Reagan did lower taxes on large estates substantially. His bill, which would have eventually lowered the top rate to 50 percent, was replaced by the Tax Reform Act of 1986. The 1986 act, enacted in a time of large deficits, temporarily increased the rate from 55 percent to 60 percent. Clinton's legislation in 1993 made 55 percent, not 50 percent, permanent. Moreover, the minimum again decreased as the result of inflation. The minimum was stabilized, but not substantially increased, after the Republicans took control of Congress in the 1994 elections. Finally, a unified Republican government made drastic changes in 2001.

The picture just given, of gradual change from Ford through Reagan followed by a "big bang" with Bush 43, is to some degree misleading. A generous exclusion, of about $1,000,000 (year 1998 dollars), for a closely held business was introduced in 1977.[4] In 1986, the marital deduction was increased from 50 to 100 percent (see Carroll 2002, p. 393). "Family Limited Partnerships" for limiting estate taxes began to be mass-marketed, apparently in the late 1980s.[5] In other words, when one considers features of the tax other than maximum rates and minimum taxable estates, the changes in the 1970s and 1980s were more substantial.

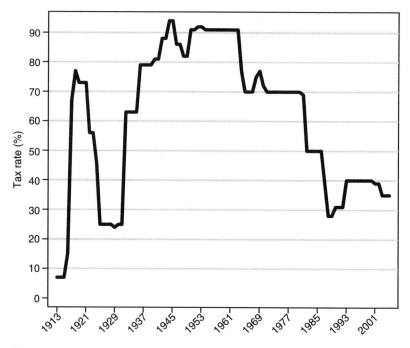

Figure 6.3
Top Federal Income Tax Rate, 1913–2005
Sources: "Historical Top Tax Rate" downloaded October 21, 2005, at http://www
.taxpolicycenter.org/TaxFacts/TFDB/TFTemplate.cfm?Docid=213
Note: This table contains a number of simplifications and ignores a number of factors,
such as a maximum tax on earned income of 50 percent when the top rate was 70 percent
and the current increase in rates due to income-related reductions in the value of itemized deductions. Perhaps most importantly, it ignores the large increase in the percentage
of returns that were subject to this top rate.

A somewhat different story holds for top minimum federal income
tax rates, shown in figure 6.3. Marginal tax rates increased in the
period of decreasing inequality. The Kennedy tax cuts, however, led to
a decrease in marginal tax rates before the turnaround in inequality.
While inequality has grown, however, top marginal tax rates have continued to fall.

Wolff (2002, p. 28) provides marginal rates on the real incomes of
$135,000, $67,000, and $33,000 from 1947 to 2000 (year 2000 dollars).
His data provide a pattern more in accord with what we found for
estate taxes. These marginal rates were fairly steady throughout the
period of declining inequality after World War II. In 1980, the marginal
rate was 59 percent on $135,000, 49 percent on $67,000, and 28 percent

on \$33,000, consistent with strong progressivity in taxation. By 1991, the three marginal rates were nearly equal, 31 percent, 28 percent, and 28 percent, respectively.

The picture of income taxes drawn from marginal rates is echoed by the effective rate on the top one percent by income. The effective rate adjusts for shelters and other gimmicks used to reduce taxes. Carroll (2002, p. 393) presents data for various years from 1963 to 1995. The effective rates on the rich rose from 24.6 percent in 1963 to 27.8 percent in 1977 and then declined to 19.2 percent in 1985. Pressures to reduce the deficit thereafter led to an upward trend, but after the Clinton bill of 1993, the effective rate reached only 23.8 percent in 1995, still slightly below the 23.9 percent during 1980, Carter's last year in office. Phillips (2002, p. 96) presents effective rates for those earning more than \$1 million from 1948 to 1970, which peaked in the 1955–60 period at 85.5 percent and then declined to 66.9 percent in 1965. Phillips also shows rates with FICA tax included for 1977 onward. These declined during the Carter years from 35.5 percent in 1977 to 31.7 percent in 1980. Under Reagan, the rate dropped further, to 24.9 percent in 1985, before rebounding to 26.9 percent in 1988.

We can summarize the three public policies of minimum wages, estate taxes, and income taxes:

• Consistent with the trend in inequality in the twentieth century, redistributive policies were first strengthened and then relaxed.

• The dates of a move away from redistribution are somewhat different—early 1960s for marginal tax rates, late 1960s for minimum wages, and mid-1970s for estate taxes and effective tax rates on the rich. It is important to note that, like the tax revolts at the state level, all of these preceded the election of Ronald Reagan. One might say that, by analogy to Andrew Jackson riding a wave of democratization to the presidency, Reagan rode a wave of antigovernment sentiment.

Social security, an extremely important public expenditure, has not suffered the same fate (as of late-2005) as minimum wages for the poor or taxes on the rich. The data are presented in figure 6.4. Social security is financed by a tax that, unlike the estate tax and the income tax, is openly regressive. Earnings above the cap are untaxed. Moreover, the tax is just a payroll tax; income from capital is untaxed. This tax, however, has grown. In an antitax era, as we see in the figure, Congress has supported an increase in the maximum real amount that a wage earner can pay into the system. This increase has been accomplished

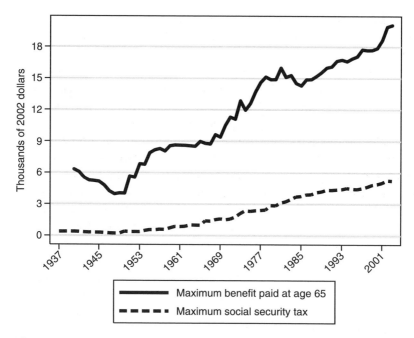

Figure 6.4
Social Security Benefits and Taxes
Source (except CPI-U): Social Security Administration, Annual Statistical Supplement 2003, released July 2004. Available online at http://www.ssa.gov/policy/docs/statcomps/supplement/2003/
Note: In thousands of 2002 dollars. In 2003, the full retirement age was increased from 65 to 65 and 2 months. But benefits are still calculated for someone who retires exactly at 65.

by raising both the tax rate and the cap (the cap for 2006 is $92,400). At the same time, notwithstanding the perpetual "crisis" in social security, the maximum real amount a worker gets out of social security has risen dramatically. In part, the rise reflects a generous indexing of benefits to wages rather than prices, thus promising retirees the living standard of the current working generation rather than their own.

Social security is formally called Old Age Insurance and was, misleadingly, sold to the public in that guise. Although the payments are mildly redistributive to lower-wage earners, it is largely a middle-class program that is not supported by taxes on high incomes or capital. So far, in distinction to high taxes on the rich, social security taxes are being maintained. In a nutshell, social security insures old age consumption via a regressive tax. Barry Goldwater's electoral fiasco in 1964 is likely to have been accentuated by his opposition to social security. In Ronald Reagan's time, Republicans were still running away from this hot potato. Has the increase in real income since 1980 convinced George W. Bush to take on the traditional program because a large portion of the population can now self-insure for old age consumption?

Like social security, Medicare has grown as inequality has grown. Again, we see demand for a government program that offers broad insurance in old age rather than earlier in the life cycle. Medicare taxes, originally capped at the same earnings level as social security taxes, had higher caps instituted in 1991 and became totally uncapped in 1994. Because of the great variance in health care outcomes, health care consumption is far riskier than the rest of old age consumption. This risk, we argue, makes Medicare taxes far less vulnerable than estate taxes or income taxes. Indeed, although George W. Bush has pushed tax cuts, the Medicare tax has not been on the table. Indeed, over the opposition of many House conservatives, Bush pushed through a very expensive prescription drug program.[6]

In summary, we would argue that as polarization increased through the last quarter of the twentieth century, policies moved in a less redistributive way when it was a matter of either taxing the income or the estates of the top brackets or improving the wages of the bottom brackets. In contrast, other policies maintained the status quo on some old age consumption financed by a regressive tax and expanded, in part via moving from regressive to proportional taxation, insurance for the risky component of old age consumption represented by health care. All of these changes in policy would appear to meet the demands of middle-income voters with rising real incomes and wealth.

Polarization and Gridlock in Public Policy

Having shown how the time series of polarization tracks policy changes with regard to minimum wages and taxes, we now turn to a more detailed discussion of how polarization might influence policy formation. We can then see how polarization relates to the ability of Congress to pass major legislation. Finally, we return to a specific policy, welfare benefits, to illustrate how polarization produces gridlock.

Theories of Majoritarian and Partisan Politics
Some well-known models in political economy have the feature that polarization should have a limited influence on policymaking. The

median voter model, which we used in chapter 4, asserts that two-party competition will always lead to policies that enact the preferences of the median voter. If the median voter's preferences change, there should be a swift policy response and no gridlock.

Similarly, the model of partisan, ideological politics in which the winning party enacts its preferences rather than those of the median voter (Wittman 1983, Calvert 1985, Alesina 1988) leaves no gridlock. Polarization should simply lead to wider policy swings after changes in power. (We implicitly used this model in chapter 3 in modeling the tax policies of the two major parties.)

The formal theory of partisan politics sees policy as flowing directly from an election. As in the median voter model, there is no role for a legislature. Nonetheless, the formal theories resonate with views expressed by legislative scholars.

Many legislative scholars (for example, Cox and McCubbins 1993, 2005) argue that legislators have strong electoral incentives to delegate substantial powers to partisan leaders to shape the legislative agenda and to discipline wayward members. To the extent that parties can successfully pursue such strategies, policymaking becomes the interaction of parties.

In such a world, polarization becomes something of a mixed bag. American political scientists have long suggested that more cohesive, distinct, and programmatic political parties would offer a corrective to the failures of policymaking in the United States. Enamored of the "party responsibility" model of Westminster-style parliaments, they have argued that a system where a cohesive majority party governs encumbered only by the need to win elections would provide more accountability and rationality in policymaking. As formulated by the American Political Science Association's Report on the Committee for Parties (1950): "An effective party system requires, first, that the parties are able to bring forth programs to which they commit themselves and, second, that the parties possess sufficient internal cohesion to carry out these programs."

Implicit in this statement is that policy will, as in the formal theories, be firmly in the control of one of the two parties. Any benefits of polarization, however, are offset when control of the executive and legislative branches is split between cohesive parties. Unfortunately for the Responsible Party model, political polarization has occurred in an era of increasing frequency of divided government. Before World War II, there was no positive association between divided government and polarization, whereas the two phenomena have frequently occurred together in the postwar period.[7]

In situations of divided government with cohesive parties, party theories predict that policymaking will represent bilateral bargaining between the parties. The moderating elections version of the partisan model (Alesina and Rosenthal 1995) assumes that a bargain is struck, thus eliminating wide policy swings. Indeed, it calls, like the median voter model, for immediate enactment of the preferences of a pivotal, albeit nonmedian, voter.

Polarization, however, may affect whether a bargain can be struck. Just as a house cannot be sold when the buyer values it at less than the seller's reservation price, increased policy differences shrink the set of compromises that both parties are willing to entertain. The increased policy differences have a second effect on bargaining that endangers even feasible compromises. Returning to the analogy of a home buyer, consider the case of a buyer who is willing to pay only slightly more than the seller is willing to accept. Under such circumstances, the buyer may be more willing to make a "low-ball" offer, as her only risk is losing out on a transaction in which she stands to gain little. Returning to the political context, increased policy differences exacerbate the incentives to engage in brinksmanship so that even feasible policy compromises might not be reached.[8] Thus, this perspective predicts that polarization should lead to more gridlock and less policy innovation during periods of divided government. The prediction for unified government would be a positive effect of polarization attributable to increased party responsibility.

Although theories of majoritarian and partisan politics are important benchmarks for the study of legislative politics, their predictions about the consequences for polarization depend heavily on assumptions that eliminate the frictions inherent in American institutions. A very different picture emerges from a more realistic approach that incorporates the internal procedures of each house of Congress and the interactions of the two houses. It is precisely these features of the American political system that give polarization its bite.

Pivot Theories

In contrast to majoritarian and partisan models of the political process, pivot theories model the implications of various supermajoritarian institutions such as the presidential veto and the Senate filibuster.[9] In these theories, policymaking is not driven directly by pivotal *voters* but by those elected politicians whose support is *pivotal* in overcoming vetoes and filibusters.

A pivot is an agent in the policy process whose support is necessary for the passage of a new law. The possible pivots are the president and critical members of the House and Senate. Consider, for example, the effects of the Senate's rules for debate and cloture. Currently, debate on most legislation cannot be terminated without a vote on cloture, which must be supported by three-fifths of the senators present and voting.[10] It is easy to see the effect of the cloture rule within our unidimensional liberal-conservative perspective. If all one hundred senators vote according to their ideal points, the senators located at the 41st and the 60th most leftward positions must support any new legislation, as no coalition can contain three-fifths of the votes without including these legislators. Therefore any policy located between these pivotal senators cannot be altered or is *gridlocked*. After Alaska and Hawaii were admitted in 1959 (increasing the number of states to fifty) but before reforms in 1975, the requirement for cloture was a two-thirds vote so the *filibuster pivots* were located at either the 34th or 67th positions.

Additionally, pivot models take account of the presidential veto. Either the president must support new legislation or a coalition of two-thirds of each chamber must vote to override. Suppose the president is located toward the left of the policy spectrum. Then he or both the legislator at the 145th (one-third of 435) position in the House and the legislator at the 34th position in the Senate must support any policy change. These legislators are dubbed the *veto pivots*. If the president is on the right, similarly placed legislators on the right become the veto pivots.

Putting these institutional requirements together, a rough measure of the propensity for legislative gridlock is the preference distance between the 34th senator and the 60th senator when the president is on the left and the distance between the 41st senator and the 67th senator when the president is on the right.[11] When these distances are large, new legislation should be harder to achieve.

We have computed the gridlock interval using the NOMINATE scores. Results from a time series regression of the size of the interval against polarization and a dummy variable for the 1975 reforms are shown in table 6.1. The width of the gridlock interval and party polarization are conceptually distinct, but we can see empirically that they

Table 6.1
Polarization and the Gridlock Interval, 1945–2002
(standard errors in parentheses)

Senate polarization	0.992
	(0.158)
1975 reforms	−0.123
	(0.035)
Constant	−0.160
	(0.087)
N	29
R^2	0.616

go hand in hand. These two measures are closely related because the filibuster and veto pivots are almost always members of different parties. As the preferences of the parties diverged, so did those of the pivots. In fact, more than 60 percent of the variation in the width of the gridlock interval in the postwar period is accounted for by polarization and the 1975 cloture reforms. Thus, the pivotal politics approach suggests that polarization will be a serious legislation retardant.

This perspective also underscores why the Senate's cloture rules have come under scrutiny and have elicited calls for reform. Once an infrequently used tool reserved for the most important legislation, with the rise of polarization the filibuster has become a central feature of American politics. Filibusters, both threatened and realized, have been used to kill a number of important pieces of legislation. Perhaps even more consequentially, the filibuster has led the Senate to greater reliance on legislative tricks to avoid its effects. One such gimmick is using the budget reconciliation process to pass new legislation because reconciliation bills cannot be filibustered. This procedure was used to pass the large income and estate tax cuts in 2001. To avoid points of order under the so-called Byrd Rule, however, such legislation can have only deficit-increasing fiscal effects for the term of the budget resolution (five to ten years).[12] Many important pieces of fiscal policy have become temporary artifices built on a foundation of budgetary gimmicks.

Strategic Disagreement
Another mechanism that might help transform polarization into legislative paralysis is the increased incentive for politicians to engage in strategic disagreement. Strategic disagreement occurs when a president,

party, or other political actor refuses compromise with the other side in an attempt to gain an electoral advantage by transferring blame for the stalemate to the other side. Classical instances include attempts to bring up controversial legislation near an election in the hopes that a president will cast an unpopular veto, as was done with the Family and Medical Leave Act in 1992 and the partial-birth abortion ban before the 2000 election. Such electoral grandstanding not only lowers legislative capacity by diverting resources into an unproductive endeavor but it also makes both sides less willing to engage in the compromises necessary for successful legislation.[13]

There are several reasons to believe that polarization may exacerbate these incentives. As the parties have become more extreme relative to voters, making the other side appear to be the more extreme becomes more valuable. If a veto of a family leave bill can make the president look like a heartless panderer to the probusiness lobby, why exclude small firms from its provisions to get it passed? If a veto of a partial-birth abortion ban can make the president look like a heartless panderer to NARAL Pro-Choice America, why make an exemption for women's health to get it passed? Strategic disagreement leads to the erosion of the remaining strands of common ground.

Exacerbating such grandstanding is contemporary media coverage of politics. Especially since Watergate and Vietnam, the media cover policymaking much as they would a heavyweight boxing match, scoring the winner and loser round by round. In such an environment, both sides are loath to make any compromises for fear of being scored the round's loser. The result is policy stagnation.

Citizen Trust

Another potential pathway from polarization to gridlock lies in how voters respond to polarized elites. David King (1997) and Marc Hetherington (2004) have separately argued that a primary consequence of polarization is that it undermines citizens' trust in the capacity of government to solve problems. Such claims are bolstered by the fact that the polarization measures in chapter 2 track survey evidence of citizen trust in government fairly closely.[14]

It is not hard to speculate how declining trust can lead to policy stalemate. If the two parties cannot agree how to solve a problem, it is hard to mobilize the public around any policy response. It is even worse when one side says a proposed policy ameliorates the problem while the other says it exacerbates it.

Polarization and Legislative Productivity

As discussed in the last section, many approaches to the study of policymaking predict that polarization should make it more difficult for Congress to pass important new legislation. Despite this prediction, there have been few attempts to document such a relationship. For example, in his seminal analysis of post–World War II lawmaking, David Mayhew (1991) studies whether divided party control of the executive and legislative branches produces legislative gridlock, but he does not consider the effects of polarization and declining bipartisanship. Indeed, he attributes his "negative" findings about divided government to the fact that during the postwar period, bipartisanship was the norm.

Despite Mayhew's oversight on the issues of polarization, his data on landmark legislative enactments can be used to assess polarization's effects on the legislative process. Figure 6.5 plots the number of significant legislative enactments by congressional term against the NOMI-NATE polarization measure.[15] It reveals a striking pattern. Congress enacted the vast majority of its significant measures during the least polarized period. The ten least polarized congressional terms produced almost sixteen significant enactments per term, whereas the ten most polarized terms produced slightly more than ten. The gap would be even bigger except for the enormous legislative output following the September 11 terrorist attacks during the most polarized congressional term of the era.

To control for other factors that might explain these differences, McCarty (forthcoming) developed a multivariate model of legislative output. In this model, he attempted to isolate the effect of polarization by controlling for unified party control, the election cycle (congressional terms preceding presidential elections aren't very productive), changes in party control of the presidency, and secular trends. These models produce a variety of estimates for the effect of polarization—these depend on how a number of data issues are handled—but McCarty consistently finds substantively large and statistically significant effects. At the upper end of the range, the least polarized congressional term produces a whopping 166 percent more legislation than the most polarized. For the lower estimate, the figure is still a large 60 percent increase in legislative output.

To get at the magnitude of these differences, figure 6.6 presents a counterfactual analysis of Congress's output if polarization had

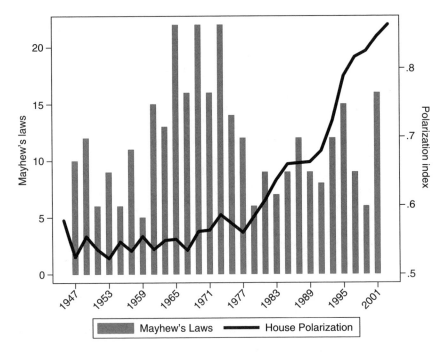

Figure 6.5
Polarization and Legislative Production
Note: Data on significant legislation is from Mayhew (1991). The figure combines
the Sweep I and Sweep II laws from his original analysis supplemented by his subsequent list of significant laws from 1990–2002, available at http://pantheon.yale.edu/
~dmayhew/datasets.html.

remained the level of the 1960s, using the estimates of the multivariate
model.

Even though this figure uses the lowest estimate of the effect of polarization, the effect is substantial. Without polarization, a substantial
secular trend in legislative output would likely have continued. Polarization did not just dampen the trend, it reversed it.

One potential objection to these findings is that Mayhew's enactments are only the tip of the legislative iceberg. Perhaps polarization
affects the landmark bills but not the merely important ones. Data collected by William Howell and his colleagues can help address this
issue (Howell et al. 2000). They coded thousands of postwar statutes
according to their "legislative significance," grouping them into four
levels. Their *A*-level statutes roughly correspond to Mayhew's enact-

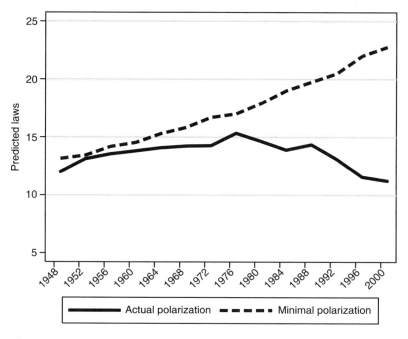

Figure 6.6
What If There Were No Polarization? The Effect of Polarization on Producing Major
Legislation
Note: Based on the estimates of Model 1 in Table A1 of McCarty (forthcoming).

ments. Their *B*-level statutes are statutes with significant policy
changes that do not quite reach "landmark" status, and *C*-statutes are
the remaining broad and substantive enactments. The lowest level, *D*,
contains the remainder—trivial and narrow legislation. McCarty estimated a separate multivariate model for each of these sets of statutes
identical to the one run on Mayhew's data. The results show that polarization has very large effects for the top three categories of legislation, with the largest effect on type *B*. Polarization appears to reduce
output across a broad spectrum of possible legislation.

One might nonetheless object that the findings reported above are
just for the postwar period and are solely the consequence of the historical coincidence of the Great Society with polarization's nadir. To
alleviate these concerns, McCarty marshaled data collected by a number of scholars on the legislative output of the late 19th and early 20th
century.[16] Estimates based on these data also confirm the negative
effects of polarization on legislative output.

Effects of Polarization on Social Policy

Given the evidence that polarization has reduced Congress's capacity to legislate, we now ask how this gridlock has affected public policy outcomes. The most direct effect of polarization-induced gridlock is that public policy does not adjust to changing economic and demographic circumstances.

There are a number of reasons to believe that these effects would be most pronounced in the arena of social policy. Given that one of the aims of social policy is to insure citizens against the economic risks inherent in a market system, it must be responsive to shifts in economic forces. If polarization inhibits these responses, it may leave citizens open to the new risks created by economic shifts brought on by deindustrialization and globalization. For example, consider the political response in the United States to increasing economic inequality. Inequality can be attributed to a variety of economic forces described at the outset of this chapter. Nevertheless, many West European countries faced with many of the same forces developed policies to mitigate the consequences so that the level of inequality changed only marginally.[17] Similarly, Jacob Hacker (2004) has recently argued that polarization was an important factor in impeding the modernization of many of the policies designed to ameliorate social risks.

A second issue concerns the ways in which social policies in the United States are designed. Many policies, especially those aimed at the poor or near poor, are not indexed with respect to their benefits.[18] Therefore these programs require continuous legislative adjustment to achieve a constant level of social protection. We have seen that the non-indexed minimum wage has withered away in the current era of polarization. We now provide evidence that polarization has had a conservative effect on the Temporary Assistance to Needy Families program.

Temporary Assistance to Needy Families

The Temporary Assistance for Needy Families (TANF) program was created by the 1996 welfare reform act. This program was designed to replace the Aid to Families with Dependent Children (AFDC) program with a series of block grants to states to implement their own welfare programs. Under TANF, benefits are no longer an entitlement, and it was left up to the states to determine the various aspects of eligibility

Table 6.2
Polarization Measures from Various States

State	Normalized polarization measure
Utah	1.018
Rhode Island	.996
Missouri	.996
Texas	.981
South Carolina	.959

and the level of benefits. Given that no state has indexed the level of TANF benefits, this program seems to be one in which polarization-induced gridlock might be expected to allow the real level of benefits to deteriorate.[19] To support this claim, we look at data on real benefit levels for a family of four for each state from 1996 through 2000.

Unfortunately, good measures of polarization for state legislatures are available for only a handful of states. But the existing evidence seems to show that state legislatures are at least as polarized as the U.S. Congress. Table 6.2 presents NOMINATE polarization measures for a handful of states from various regions. These measures have been normalized against the 2001–02 U.S. House so that a score of 1 equals the polarization level of the House and scores greater than 1 imply more polarization. By way of comparison, the normalized measure for the 1973–74 U.S. House was only 0.698.

As the available evidence seems to show that most contemporary state legislatures are quite polarized, we will simply focus on the effect of divided party government on TANF benefit levels. Given that most states are quite polarized, divided government will represent cases where the preferences of the governor and the legislature diverge sharply. In those states, gridlock should be more likely than in states with unified governments.[20]

Our main hypothesis follows directly from the fact that TANF benefits are not indexed. The real value of TANF benefits should fall more sharply over time when there is divided government in the state. Table 6.3 provides evidence on this point by showing the annual percentage change in real benefits for a family of four for each form of party control.

Clearly, the declines in real benefits are larger for the two forms of divided government than for the two forms of unified government. The drops are especially large in states where Democratic governors

Table 6.3
Percentage Real Changes in TANF Benefits

Year	Unified Republican	Unified Democrat	Divided, Dem Governor	Divided, Rep Governor
1997	−.025	−.023	−.296	−.237
1998	−.041	.092	−.079	.016
1999	−.015	−.012	−.098	−.015
2000	−.028	−.027	−.018	−.022

Note: Computed from data in Urban Institute (2005).

face Republican legislatures. Most important, the declines for divided governments exceed those of Republican unified government.

In the appendix to this chapter, we show that these differences hold up when we control for other factors such as the racial and ethnic composition, income level, and economic inequality. The average declines in unified governments and divided governments with Republican governors are statistically indistinguishable, but benefits have dropped 13 percent more per year in divided governments with Democratic governors. This finding is quite remarkable in that, on ideological grounds, one might have expected the biggest declines to come under unified Republican state governments. The automatic declines in real benefits imposed by non-indexation, when combined with gridlock on policy change, have proven to be a stronger influence than conservative ideological preferences.

The evidence about the effects of polarization on the minimum wage and TANF benefits is far from conclusive, but it does seem to point strongly in the direction of a conservative effect of polarization on social policy.

Other Policy Consequences of Polarization

Perhaps one of the most important long-term consequences of the decline in legislative capacity caused by polarization is that Congress's power will decline relative to the other branches of government. Several recent studies have shown that presidents facing strong partisan and ideological opposition from Congress are more likely to take unilateral actions rather than pursuing their goals through legislation.[21] This effect is perhaps best exemplified by the large number of executive orders issued by Bill Clinton at the end of his second term. Many of these had no chance of passage through Congress. The consequence of not getting statutory authorization, however, was that George W. Bush was able to reverse many of them even though the reversals would have been filibustered in the Senate.

Not only are presidents likely to become more powerful, polarization may also increase the opportunities of courts and regulatory agencies to pursue their policy goals since such activism is unlikely to be checked by legislative statute.[22] The courts and regulators have become the dominant arena for a wide swath of policy, from tobacco regulation to firearms to social policy. A much-publicized recent example is the new policy change of the Federal Communications Commission, led by Bush appointee Michael Powell, that banishes "racy" material from broadcast television and radio. Such a policy would have been unlikely to arise via legislation in a polarized Congress. It is also unlikely to be overturned.

We have concentrated on the effects of polarization within the legislative process, but contemporary work in bureaucratic and judicial politics suggests that polarization may also have detrimental effects at the implementation stage. The first effect concerns Congress's willingness to delegate substantial authority to administrative agencies. One of the most systematic studies to date shows that Congress is far less willing to delegate policymaking authority to agencies when there are large ideological disagreements between the president and congressional majorities.[23] Given that party polarization has exacerbated these disagreements (especially during divided government), it has caused Congress to rely far less on the expertise of the bureaucracy in the implementation and enforcement of statutes. In many cases, the results are excessive statutory constraints; in others, Congress chooses to delegate enforcement to private actors and courts rather than agencies (Farhang 2003). This effect further weakens the executive and legislative branches vis à vis the judiciary.

The second effect of polarization on policy implementation comes through its distortion of the confirmation process of judges and executive branch officials. In studies of all major executive branch appointments over the past century, McCarty and Razaghian (1999) find that increased partisan polarization is a primary culprit in the increasing delays in Senate confirmation. As a consequence, long-term vacancies in the political leadership of many departments and agencies have become the norm. As these problems are exacerbated at the beginning of new administrations, presidential transitions have become considerably less smooth.[24] Polarization has also clearly contributed to the well-documented conflicts over judicial appointments which have similarly led to an understaffing of the federal bench.

Polarization and Policy Paralysis

We have shown that polarization tracked, for much of the twentieth century, the evolution of redistribution through taxation and minimum wages. In many respects, this tracking reflects the ability of polarization to paralyze policy formation. Public policies are sticky. The stickiness is exacerbated by polarization.

The pattern of change thus appears to respond to the "pivot" theories we discussed in the second part of this chapter. Real minimum wages have fallen because they are not indexed to inflation. Proposals to lower their nominal value are not even on the table, but proposals for meaningful increases can't pass either. High estate taxes prevailed for the thirty-seven years between 1940 and 1977 largely because, we conjecture, pivots among Democrats blocked change. The adjustments passed under President Ford returned the real value of the minimum taxable estate only to what it had been in the 1960s, and the maximum rates were rolled back only to the levels found in the early Roosevelt administrations. Major changes required the Republican dominance of the 1980s and 2000s. Income taxes began to fall from the levels used to finance the Second World War only during Kennedy's presidency.

There are many other striking examples of legislative failure to respond to changes in voter preferences or to changes in economic circumstances. Here are three:

1. In the previous period of great polarization at the turn of the twentieth century, presidential vetoes forestalled restrictive immigration legislation until the 1920s, even though congressional majorities had favored it for several decades (Goldin 1994). The restrictive immigration laws of the 1920s remained largely intact for more than forty years, until the reforms enacted in 1965. Although Congress subsequently passed compromise immigration bills, the liberal 1965 policy was extended in 1990 and prevailed for the rest of the century.

2. Economic regulations adopted in the New Deal remained in effect for decades. Transportation and telecommunications were deregulated only in the late 1970s and 1980s. The separation of commercial and investment banking and other aspects of the Glass-Steagall Act remained in effect from 1933 until the passage of the Gramm-Leach-Bliley Act in

1999. (At the same time, many changes in financial services were produced by the Treasury and the Federal Reserve. These changes illustrate our point about polarization increasing discretion outside the legislature.)

3. Welfare as an entitlement, known as AFDC, was initiated by the Social Security Act of 1935. The basic system remained in place and was extended until more than sixty years later, with the passage of the Personal Responsibility and Work Opportunity Reconciliation Act (PRWORA) of 1996.

Inactivity, we have argued, is more likely to occur in periods of polarization. In addition to its consequences for redistribution, the increasing polarization of the past twenty-five years may have produced a number of less than desirable outcomes. There is considerable evidence that it has weakened the ability of legislatures to engage in policymaking and has reduced their responsiveness to new economic and social problems. At the same time, it has shifted influence to less representative and accountable institutions, such as the president and the courts. Given the evidence that polarization is a problem, what can be done about it? We turn to this problem in our concluding chapter.

Appendix. State-Level TANF Benefits

To test for the effects of divided government on TANF benefits, we regress the percentage change in the benefits for a family of four on the current level of benefits, indicators for each pattern of party control, indicators for each year, and economic and demographic factors within each state. The monthly benefit levels for a family of four by state from 1996 through 2000 were obtained from the Urban Institute's *Welfare Rules Database*. We converted nominal values to real values using CPI-U series. The average real benefit levels were $828, and the average annual real change in benefits was −$38. The economic and demographic controls include data on the racial and ethic composition of the state as well as its per capita income. These are all obtained from the U.S. Census. Finally, we use a measure of economic inequality, the Gini Index of Family Income, estimated by Western, Guetzkow, and Rosenfeld (2004) from the Current Population Survey.

7   Where Have You Gone, Mr. Sam?

Sam Rayburn once upon a time ran the House of Representatives on a relatively genteel and bipartisan basis, and the country seemed destined to have but one class, the middle class. We now live in an era where political elites literally hate each other and CEOs live on a different planet than their lowest-wage employees. We are not so presumptuous to assert that we can identify any one causal factor that explains the conjunction of high levels of political polarization and economic inequality. Instead, we have taken a much more modest approach and identified some causal pathways that would explain the strong set of empirical regularities reported in this book.

The commonality of these micro-level relationships is that American political institutions are ill-suited to mitigating the economic pressures that lead to greater levels of inequality. Two features of the American system are especially important in this regard. The first is an electoral system that relies on plurality rule to elect senators and representatives. A well-known implication of such a system is a tendency toward the development of two major political parties (see Duverger 1954, Palfrey 1989, and Fey 1997).[1] A two-party system might hold economic inequality in check if the policy positions of the parties converged on the preferences of the median (income) voter, as suggested by Anthony Downs (1957). If convergence were the result of electoral competition, an increase in inequality that generated a fall in the median income relative to the average income in the economy would produce a majority in favor of increasing taxes and transfers resulting in a reduction of inequality.

As we thoroughly documented in chapter 2, however, the Republican and Democratic parties have *diverged*, not converged. The political science literature on party competition has generated dozens of explanations as to why political parties might not converge. In relation to our arguments, several stand out as especially important. First, if there is sufficient uncertainty about voter preferences, the distinct ideological preferences of politicians and the activist bases of each party will produce divergence in platforms.[2] In such situations, rational parties make tradeoffs between satisfying ideological preferences and choosing more moderate policies in order to win elections. Consequently, the position of each party will partially reflect the views of its activist base.

The movement of the base has been most profound in the Republican Party where the modern conservative movement that emerged from the ashes of 1964, shifted the party sharply to the right (Perlstein 2001; Micklethwait and Wooldridge 2004). Nevertheless, this conservative movement would have failed to obtain power had electoral conditions not moved in its favor; in particular, the rising overall affluence produced by the long periods of economic growth after World War II. As we demonstrated in chapter 3, the underlying Democratic advantage in presidential voting and identification began to give way to the Republicans during the 1970s. This increase in the electoral fortunes of the Republican Party allowed it to shift to the right and still win elections because its message of lower taxes and more limited government resonated with the increasing population of affluent voters.[3]

The second factor leading to platform divergence is that American parties are reasonably undisciplined coalitions of politicians who seek to win election in a heterogeneous collection of constituencies. Thus, politicians will have strong incentives to defect from a party platform at the national median toward the position of the district median. In an innovative model, Snyder and Ting (2002) show that this lack of discipline produces polarized parties (in a world where disciplined ones would converge). In a related paper, Callander (2004) shows that parties that compete in multiple elections will diverge when heterogeneity across districts increases. Thus, during periods of increasing inequality when the fortunes of different economic groups are diverging, the policies preferred by each will diverge as well. In the current context, the Democratic Party will continue to support policies that redistribute to the poor and collectivize social risks, while the Republicans represent the interests of those whose incomes are growing rapidly and hence support policies to cut taxes and privatize risk. Of course, we do not argue that everyone who votes for the Democratic or Republican Party is in complete sympathy with their positions on these economic issues. But the essence of a two-party system is that these are the only choices

voters have.[4] As a result, electoral behavior is considerably better predicted by a voter's income than before the parties polarized, as we
showed in chapter 3.

Another implication of America's electoral system is that it does
little to stimulate high voter turnout, especially among the lower
income-classes. As we demonstrated in chapter 4, however, the social-
economic biases in turnout among *citizens* have been relatively constant
since 1972. The real economic biases in turnout come from the dramatically increased numbers of resident noncitizens as well as the decline
in the economic status of this group. While overall inequality has increased, the pressure for redistributive policies has been sharply miti-
gated by the fact that the income inequality of *voters* did not increase.

Once the voters have spoken, the politicians enact policies in a very
unique institutional setting. Specifically, the American government is
not majoritarian. The separation of powers and bicameralism require
that very large majority coalitions, typically bipartisan, must be formed
to pass new laws and revise old ones. Thus any policy response to the
economic and social factors that lead to inequitable economic growth
will be muted by the gridlock of our institutions. Take one of the more
important policy areas in our story, immigration. The Immigration Act
of 1965 was passed by bipartisan majorities during the nadir of polarization. An unanticipated consequence of the legislation, however,
was a large influx of less-skilled labor. This influx contributed to
economic growth (and was driven in part by that growth) but also
contributed to competition in low-wage labor markets. Congress has
attempted to reform immigration laws several times over the past
thirty years, but partisan divisions over the distributive consequences
of reform have precluded major reform. As we demonstrated in chapter 6, in addition to immigration policy, social welfare and tax policies
have been especially affected by the gridlock produced by polarization.

When gridlock can be broken, policy must reflect a bargaining "compromise" within and between the chambers and the president. The
nonmajoritarian institutions of policy formation can feed back into polarization in party electoral platforms. The very system of "checks and
balances," where power is shared between the executive and the legislature, affords the voters an opportunity to "moderate" the parties by
splitting their tickets (Alesina and Rosenthal 1995). If the parties know
that there is moderation in the policy process, they will "posture" and
take more extreme platform positions than would be the case if only
the president made policy (Alesina and Rosenthal 2000). Moreover,

the tendency to polarize will increase as the power of Congress is increased relative to that of the president. Political scientists have argued that Congress became more assertive post-Watergate (Sundquist 1981) and documented (Fiorina 1996) that voter ticket-splitting has increased. To put the argument slightly differently, the possibility of divided government with increased congressional powers contributes to polarization.

Polarization also contributes to gridlock by enhancing the incentives to engage in strategic disagreement or "blame game" politics (Gilmour 1995; Groseclose and McCarty 2000). In a world of polarized parties and moderate voters, each party will attempt to portray the other as the real extremists. Such a strategy often involves distortions of the other party's proposals and an increased recalcitrance in negotiation.

While the basic electoral system and legislative institutions are an important part of our story, other institutions, although seen by some scholars as sources of polarization, seem in retrospect to not be so important. Consider partisan gerrymandering. It cannot explain the polarization of the Senate. Consequently, we are reluctant to see gerrymandering as a major source of the overall polarization of American politics. Furthermore, we find that its effects on polarization in the House of Representatives are likely highly overrated. Polarization does not grow significantly more following reapportionment, and the distribution of partisanship across congressional districts does not differ much from the overall geographic distribution of partisanship. Yes, districting has gotten more sophisticated and politicized, but that seems to be as much a consequence of the current electoral and ideological divides as the cause. Similarly, we are not terribly persuaded that primary elections play a role in our dance either. Primary elections for Congress have been nearly universal for more than half a century, so it is hard to explain a change with a constant. Further, the evidence shows that it is unlikely that opening up primaries to less partisan voters would have much of an effect on who is elected to office.

The link between polarization and the American campaign finance system is somewhat more complex. We do not find much evidence that the evolution of campaign finance since the 1970s caused polarization. Giving by interest groups through PACs has not become more polarized. Contributions by individuals, especially soft money, have tilted the scales towards the extremes. The biggest effect, however, seems to have been to increase the reliance of the Democratic Party on very wealthy contributors and it is this reliance, we conjecture, that has tempered its demands for more redistribution.

Extending Invitations

We conceded at the outset that we were going to focus primarily on the link between political polarization and income distribution. Given the evidence we presented about long-term trends in these variables, we felt that this focus was the most fruitful. Nevertheless, there are clearly other macrosocial trends that have also moved with polarization over the last half-century. Perhaps the most prominent of these are trends in social capital (see Putnam 2000). Many measures of social capital, such as rates of volunteering and membership in organizations, began declining in the 1970s after increases following World War II. These trends in social capital complement our story in a number of ways. The first is that the declines in social capital are clearly related to the changes in income inequality and the increases in ethnic diversity brought about by relaxed immigration policies. Costa and Kahn (2003a, 2003b) find that a very large proportion of the declines in volunteering, membership, and social trust among 25- to 54-year-olds are due to the increased economic and ethnic heterogeneity of metropolitan areas. These results complement the cross-sectional findings of Alesina and La Ferrara (2000, 2002).

Second, declining social capital may play a role in the declining support for redistribution and the increase in income voting. In theory, both declining trust and cross-class bonds may make higher-income citizens less likely to tax themselves for redistribution to lower classes. This disincentive to redistribute may be especially large in diverse communities where the upper and lower classes may be separated not only by income but by race or ethnicity (Alesina, Baqir, and Easterly 1999; Luttmer 2001).

While the time series evidence and the theoretical logic of a social capital story are compelling, the cross-sectional evidence linking social capital to our story is weak. Blue states do score higher than red states on Putnam's state-level social capital index, but the difference is only significant at the .108 level. Social capital, measured again at the state level, does have a very weak correlation with the partisanship of high-income white voters ($r=-.25$ for Republican partisanship).[5] Controlling for partisanship of lower-income voters, an increase of one standard deviation in the social capital index decreases the Republican partisanship of the top quintile voters by a modest 2.7 percentage points. To isolate the effects of social capital, we added control variables, including state median household income, racial and ethic composition, church attendance, the percentage of noncitizens, and urbanization. When we control for these factors, however, the effect of social capital on the partisanship of high-income voters is no longer statistically significant. The effects of racial composition, however, are quite significant. The greater a state's nonwhite population, the more Republican the upper quintile of white voters.

Thus, while inequality and perhaps immigration have played a very important role in undermining social capital, there is little evidence of a strong link to income-based voting or polarization.

The 2004 Election and Beyond

We completed the first draft of this book for the Eric M. Mindich Encounter with Authors Symposium at Harvard in January 2005. Thus, the 2004 presidential election had been fully interpreted by the pundits, but the data wasn't readily available to determine the extent to which our arguments held up in its aftermath.

The headlines on Wednesday, November 3, 2004, were telling a story very different from ours. The interpretations of the partisans were not terribly surprising. The winning party struck a triumphant pose. Although the election was as close as a 50,000-vote swing in Ohio, Republicans reveled in their new mandate, with George W. Bush proclaiming that he had some political capital and was going to spend it. The losing party was characteristically dejected. The Democrats engaged in the time-worn debate of losing parties about how poor their candidate was, how their message didn't get across, or how the party is too liberal (or moderate or conservative or something else).

The pundits' approach to the election was also predictable. They needed to find *the* cause of the election outcome. The most prominent explanation in the week following the election was the role of "moral values." Journalists seemed to converge on this explanation when it was revealed that 22 percent of respondents in the national voter exit poll listed "moral values" as their top issue concern, by far the modal response. The power of this explanation, however, was undercut by the fact that the survey listed no other social issues for the voters to select. When all responses listing a social issue (abortion, gay rights, and so on) as the number one issue in previous exit polls were added up, the number of "morals" voters was actually down a bit in 2004. Proponents of the morals explanation also pointed to the role of the so-called Defense of Marriage voter initiatives in several states. It was widely speculated that these initiatives stimulated the turnout of social conservative voters and allowed the Republicans to make important inroads into the African-American and Hispanic electorates. But closer analysis reveals that these effects were more illusory than real. George W. Bush's popular vote gains from 2000 to 2004 were smaller in states that had anti–gay marriage initiatives on the ballot than in states that did not.[6] Republican gains with African Americans were trivial, and exit polls dramatically overestimated the gains among Hispanics.[7] Other analyses focused on the strategic brilliance of Karl Rove, especially in identifying Republican votes in fast-growing exurban counties. While it is true that the Republican ticket ran very well in the fastest-growing counties, it is hard to evaluate how well the Republicans would have performed absent Rove's visible hand. Indeed, the Republican success in these economically vibrant communities—and in moving the state of Florida, tied in 2000, into a solid Bush state in 2004—is entirely consistent with our arguments.

Finally, there were the "terror" voters. Yes, those that said fighting international terror was a "very important" foreign policy goal voted disproportionately for Bush (56–44). But those who said fighting terrorism was important are also whiter, richer, more male, and more Republican than those who did not. Consequently, some of the difference can be accounted for by the fact that Republican voters were especially attuned to terrorism rather than the proposition that terrorist fears led voters to Bush.

In contrast to the direction of the leaps of the pundit ballet chorus, the noneconomic issues may well have worked against President Bush. At least this is the view that comes from well-tested and accepted social science models that predict presidential elections based on aggregate economic conditions and incumbent advantage. These all showed the president winning in a near-landslide, with a popular vote share somewhere around 55 percent.

With some hindsight and the release of systematic data on the election, moreover, we can provide a more serious evaluation of the election in light of our thesis. The results of the 2004 National Election Study provide little evidence that our basic picture of the American political system was altered very much by the campaign or the events of George W. Bush's first term. There is very little evidence that the electorate is less defined by income. The measure of income stratification of party identification that we introduced in chapter 3 remains well above 2.0, at 2.26. In comparison to the 2000 election, the top three income quintiles are about 6% more Republican, while the second quintile is a bit less Republican and the bottom only a bit more. Income was less powerful in predicting who voted for Bush, however. Stratification in presidential voting dipped a little bit, to 1.45. Closer analysis reveals that much of this drop is due to the increase in support of Bush in the bottom quintile. It is also reflected in the fact that Bush was unable to gain more support at the top. Much of this weakness can be attributed to a very poor showing among the most educated voters. Since these changes in the top and bottom quintile are not reflected in partisan identification, it is not clear that the changes represent a longer-term shift in voter behavior or transient responses to Bush.

That the 2004 election was an extension of the status quo is also reflected in a multivariate analysis of party identification and voting. When we estimate the model of partisan identification from chapter 3, we find that the coefficient on relative income remains at levels typical of the past decade, with the same regional difference in magnitude between northern and southern voters. The income effect in party identification also remains larger for church attendees. Finally, extending the analysis of voting patterns across U.S. counties reveals that within each state, Republican support is highest in those counties with the highest household incomes.

Not only did income continue to play a role in the elections, the post-election legislative agenda also looks much as we would have forecast. While much media attention focused on President Bush returning to Washington from a Texas vacation to sign a congressional intervention in the Terri Schiavo case, the more consequent legislative maneuverings concerned highly distributive economic policies. Shortly after the election, President Bush decided to use his new political capital to reform the Social Security system. The centerpiece of his plan was to allow younger workers the opportunity to divert a portion of their payroll taxes into private retirement accounts. The plan had a certain appeal to higher-income voters, who have become much more receptive to the idea of privatizing risk, but was quickly challenged by the Democrats, who felt that the diversion into private accounts would undermine the system's guarantees to lower-income citizens as well as balloon the federal budget deficit. To make sure that his appeal to higher-income voters did not get lost in translation, the president refused to put on the table increases in social security taxes either by raising the rate or the income caps. The Democrats, for their part, were unwilling to provide their own plan to restructure the Social Security finance system, which is expected to begin running large deficits in little more than a decade. Not surprisingly, given our discussion in chapter 6, gridlock was the outcome.

In choosing to go first with Social Security, President Bush has not abandoned several other controversial economic proposals. First, the president wants to make the tax cuts of 2001 and 2002 permanent, including the repeal of the estate tax. By pressing for full repeal of the estate tax rather than the much higher exemption offered by Democrats, the Republicans have narrowed the debate to the tax liability of only America's richest families. The next pillar of Bush's second term agenda is tax reform, where he and the Republicans are expected to push for a much flatter tax system with fewer deductions and a much lower top marginal rate. While there may be some economic merit in such reforms, the reduction of the income taxes paid by those at the top would be large. Finally and perhaps most important, given our findings in chapter 4, Bush's immigration proposals, centered on a more extensive guest worker program and limited amnesty, remain gridlocked between the Republican paleo-conservatives, who want to curtail both legal and illegal immigration, and the Democratic left, who wants more protections for guest workers as well as more guarantees that guest workers do not compete in the same labor markets as citizens.

While many of these proposals seem almost destined for gridlock's dustbin, it should not be forgotten that the 109th Congress's first important enactment (leaving aside the Terri Schiavo case) was a bankruptcy bill that makes it substantially harder for middle-income Americans to obtain the more generous protections of chapter 7 of the bankruptcy code and forces them into chapter 13 filings. Although proponents of the bill point out that it does not affect the lowest-income families,[8] the bill does little to reign in the abuses of the bankruptcy code by high-income earners through sheltering their assets in trusts or in real estate in unlimited household exemption states.

How Will It End?

In this book, we have outlined a very stable political system. Partisan polarization and economic inequality have proven to be durable features of our political economy for almost three decades. Thus, it is very doubtful that a simple fine-tuning of institutional arrangements will have much of an effect. We do not doubt that compelling cases could be made for opening up primaries, ending partisan gerrymandering, and making it easier to vote. We feel, however, that the data show that these problems are second- and third-order contributors to our current problems. In any case, partisan polarization is likely to place real limits on how far these reforms will be carried.

A reordering of the current system will require major changes in the loyalties of various groups to the political parties. This dynamic has clearly been important in the fall of prior political regimes. The problems of the Democratic-Whig system resulted in the emergence of slavery as the dominant political cleavage. Slavery temporarily replaced economics as the central issue defining the first NOMINATE dimension. This political realignment led to the complete demise of the Whig party and, most horrifically, the Civil War. The New Deal realignment replaced a Republican-dominated system following the stock market crash and the Great Depression. Finally, as we have documented, the current system was established only after the rapid economic growth of the postwar period seemed to undermine the logic of the New Deal system.

So what factors might lead to a new realignment? In answering this question, it is important to keep in mind the current coalitional structure of the political system we outlined in chapter 3. The Republican Party, we argued, is primarily supported by high-income secular voters along with middle- and higher-income social conservatives. There are a number of things that could cause such a coalition to unravel. First, Republican actions on social issues might begin to match their rhetoric in such a way that further drives secular voters from the party. Such a scenario seemed more than plausible following the passage of a law allowing the federal courts to intervene in the decision to remove Terri Schiavo's feeding tube. While the conflict between Schiavo's family and her husband as well as the lack of a living will complicated the issue, public opinion was decidedly against the Republican role in the legislation. Not only were secular voters who support the "right to die" alienated, but the issue intensified middle-class insecurities about the cost of providing care to a family member in such a state. While we argue that a religious cleavage has not supplanted the economic one, we do not suggest that it cannot happen.

The second scenario under which the current alignments might change is if the Republicans push so far to the right with libertarian economics that even middle-class social conservatives abandon them. The debate over social security reform might lead to such an outcome. Because of the association that many older voters perceive between the Republicans and the retrenchment of social security, the party has done fairly poorly with seniors, apart from those that are conservative in religion. According to the Pew studies, the NES studies, and the 2004 National Exit Poll, born-again Christians and regular churchgoers are significantly older than the rest of the population on average. If reform raises the salience of Social Security above that of religion, such voters may return to the Democrats. The Bush administration, aware of this problem, has flatly refused to ask current retirees to share in resolving the financial crisis of Social Security by reducing their benefits, even by changing future indexing for current retirees from wages to prices.

While we stress the negative consequences of gridlock to low-income families, it is also quite possible that the system will be strained when gridlock begins to hit the middle and upper-middle classes. The looming possibility here is the Alternative Minimum Tax. The AMT was created in the early 1970s after it was realized that a couple of dozen millionaires failed to pay any income taxes. The system was structured with a very large income exemption but very few deductions. Taxpayers must pay the higher of the regular income tax and the AMT. Because the exemption level was not indexed for inflation, each year more and more Americans pay their taxes under the AMT. Thus, despite the cuts in marginal rates under the regular tax code, many Americans have seen their income tax liabilities increase (especially those in "blue" states where the filers lose large property and state income tax deductions under the AMT). Recognizing that the Republicans might take the brunt of the blame if the AMT is not reformed, Democrats have (uncharacteristically) taken the lead in arguing for an increase in the AMT exemption or exempting deductions for state and property taxes from the AMT.[9] Thus, if Republicans fail to reform the tax, the Democrats may gain among higher-income voters.

It also seems plausible that the Democratic Party need not wait for the Republicans to mess up in order to change the alignment of American politics. Beginning in the 1990s, the apparent strategy of the Democratic Party was to expand by appealing to high-income secular and socially liberal voters. As we show in chapter 5, the party has done quite well indeed in attracting money from this group. Despite the importance of money in American politics, however, money is not the same as votes, and the party needs more votes. Our results suggest that the votes up for grabs are those of socially conservative middle-class voters so long as the party can temper its secular message. According to the 2004 National Election Study, the Republican gains were the greatest not among those who go to church every week or almost every week but among those who go to church once a month. One interpretation of this result is that the Democrats do not need to reach out to the most pro-life or antigay segments of the electorate but only to those individuals that are Christian more by culture than by practice and have moderate views on many social issues. Democratic politicians like Joseph Lieberman and Hillary Clinton seem to recognize this possibility, but it is yet to be seen whether the rest of the party will follow.

Finally, though no one wishes for any of these scenarios, the system is vulnerable to an economic or domestic security calamity. As we write, federal budget deficits are soaring, the U.S. dollar is declining, and real estate prices are precariously high. The necessary macroeconomic correction of rising interest rates will hit highly leveraged Republican constituents hard and hit the party even harder at the ballot box. Another terrorist attack on American soil could erase the Republicans' electoral advantage on security and foreign policy and thereby expose its weakness on economic policies toward the middle class.

Whether a shift from Republican dominance would end polarization depends on whether the Democrats sit on their heels or occupy the middle. When the Great Depression discredited the Republicans, the Democrats adopted policies they had long advocated that moved *away* from a market economy to a highly regulated state. A large part of the ensuing decrease in polarization was due to Republican moderating and accommodating in an effort to rebuild their electoral fortunes. Moderation was a slow process. The end of polarization and, as well, economic inequality, should be a process measured not in months or years but in decades.

A quite different route to moderation may in fact pass through Republican dominance. One should not rule out long-term success of the coalition of the affluent and the "moral." After all, the Roosevelt coalition of ethnics in the North and racists in the South held for many years. In the absence of a Great Depression–like shock, the Democrats would have to move to acceptance of an economy with highly unequal outcomes.

The reader who has stuck with us to this point may be feeling a bit gloomy. We have painted mostly negative scenarios and have not offered the reader a happy solution to the problem of polarization. Nevertheless, we end on a positive note. Two of us grew up in the 1950s with Depression-era parents.[10] We know all too well from our parents and our extended families how hard things were during the Depression and how surprised people were when the country did not slide back into depression after World War II. The spread of mass affluence beginning in the 1950s is real. It is a tremendous achievement of millions of hard-working Americans like our extended families. Prosperity also reflects sixty years without a major war. Trade has vastly augmented the goods available to American consumers. Young people today simply have no idea how rich and diverse the cornucopia of goods in the big-box stores of today is in comparison to the small town "five and dimes" of the 1950s. It has been a sea change of unprecedented magnitude.

In addition, just in the past forty years the old fault lines between the white ethnic groups have virtually disappeared. Intermarriage rates between Protestants, Catholics, and Jews have soared. As we pointed out in chapter 1, there is simply no question to us that the United States is a far more tolerant place that it was fifty years ago.

Why, then, in the midst of affluence and much positive social change are we stuck with political leaders who are at daggers' point while the general population is generally not (Fiorina 2004)? Compared to our political leaders, the public is relatively moderate. We have no easy cure. We wish we did, as we find this trend deeply disturbing. We wish the Sam Rayburns, John Heinzes, Dan Rostenkowskis, Sam Nunns, and so on, would return and bring some sense back into our politics. As citizens, we hope moderation returns before serious cracks in our institutions occur. The great resilience of the American people and their Constitution has prevailed in much worse circumstances. We hope they prevail again.

Notes

Chapter 1

1. October 24, 2004. Quoted at http://www.sfgate.com/cgi-bin/article.cgi?file=/chronicle/archive/2004/10/10/RVG1T9289T1.DTL.

2. Story of August 24, 2004, found at http://www.editorandpublisher.com/eandp/news/article_display.jsp?vnu_content_id=1000592440.

3. Computed from http://www.census.gov/hhes/income/histinc/h01ar.html.

4. We used the least squares unfolding procedure of Poole (1984).

5. On this point, see Snyder (1992).

6. The Census Bureau series does not cover earlier years.

7. A number of commentators date the conservative Republican movement from organizational initiatives, including the formation of think tanks that arose in the early 1970s following the Goldwater candidacy in the 1964 election. See Perlstein (2001) and a *New York Times* opinion article by former New Jersey senator Bill Bradley. See http://www.nytimes.com/2005/03/30/opinion/30bradley.html. Downloaded April 3, 2005.

8. It is difficult to pinpoint the switch from a decline in polarization to a surge. The turning point occurred somewhere between the late 1960s (following the passage of the Great Society program of the Johnson administration and the immigration amendments of 1965) and the mid to late 1970s. The statistical correlations between polarization, income inequality, and immigration are all slightly sensitive to measurement. The polarization measure will change if the sample period used for DW-NOMINATE changes (end the series in 2000 or 2004), if Senate rather than House polarization is used, if a two-dimensional rather than one-dimensional measure is used, etc. Similarly, income inequality will change if one switches from a Gini to various income shares, etc., and the immigration measure will change if one uses percentage non-citizens (chapter 4) rather than percentage foreign born. The substantive tenor of our results is quite robust to these variations.

9. See http://www.ama-assn.org/ama/upload/mm/372/a01report8.rtf. Downloaded December 12, 2004.

10. The Personal Responsibility and Work Opportunity Reconciliation Act of 1996 (PRWORA) restricted Medicaid to permanent residents and a few other special

immigration categories. It also delayed eligibility for five years for new permanent residents. For the details of these changes, see http://www.cms.hhs.gov/immigrants/default.asp.

11. The formal argument has been laid out by Krehbiel (1998) and developed in a policy context by Brady and Volden (1998).

Chapter 2

1. Political polarization has not prevented the political system from remaining competitive. Poole and Rosenthal (1984) noted the dramatic increase in the number of Senate delegations that were split between the two parties. This number grew from fewer than ten in the 1950s to twenty-six in 1978. This number has fallen back to slightly less than twenty over the past decade—well above its average in the 1950s and 1960s (see Brunell and Grofman 1998).

2. For more detailed discussion of the methodological problems of interest group ratings, see Snyder (1992) and Groseclose, Levitt, and Snyder (1999).

3. See Ellenberg (2001) for an elegant, nontechnical discussion of these methods.

4. The most widely used procedures include NOMINATE (Poole 2005), which we use throughout this book; optimal classification Poole (2000); the factor analytic method of Heckman and Snyder (1997); and Bayesian MCMC (Clinton, Jackman, and Rivers 2004).

5. If we were to maximize classification, as Poole (2000) did, the second dimension will always improve classification. Using maximum likelihood techniques as we do in this book, however, classification is not guaranteed to improve as dimensions are added.

6. For each roll call, the Yea vote also has a position on the dimension, as does the Nay vote. (If there were more than one dimension, the legislators and the votes would have positions on each dimension.) See Poole (2005) for a comprehensive exposition of roll call scaling methods.

7. For simplicity, we use classification in our discussion rather than, say, the geometric mean probability of the observed choices. Results are similar (see Poole and Rosenthal 1997). Using three or more dimensions add little to the substantive story. Moreover, improvements to classification for three dimensions or more are very small. Of course, with the large number of observations available to us, these dimensions would be viewed as statistically significant. But they are truly dimensions that only a chi-square can see.

8. There was a conservative GOP uptick, more pronounced in the Senate than in the House, during the New Deal. The few seats in Congress that the Republicans managed to retain represented the most conservative parts of the country at that time.

9. In his speech to the electors of Bristol, British statesman Edmund Burke distinguished between representatives who act as "delegates" by acting only on the expressed wishes of constituents and those who act as trustees, pursuing their own conception of the constituency's interests.

10. In the economic literature on "shirking" politicians, ideology is often measured as the residual from a regression of legislative behavior on district economic interests (e.g., Kalt

and Zupan 1984). Of course, such an interpretation could be valid only if all of the relevant economic interests are included in the model and measured correctly.

11. Let NOM denote a NOMINATE score. This interpretation is valid when β is a consistent estimate of $E(NOM \mid R_i = 1, \mathbf{C}_i) - E(NOM \mid R_i = 0, \mathbf{C}_i)$. Some readers will observe that $E(NOM \mid R_i = 1, \mathbf{C}_i) - E(NOM \mid R_i = 0, \mathbf{C}_i)$ is the "treatment" effect of assigning a Republican (instead of a Democrat) to represent a district with characteristics $\mathbf{C}_i$. For β to be a consistent estimate of the treatment effect, we must assume that the treatment is ignorable (Wooldridge 2002). Let NOM_1 be the NOMINATE score if the district is represented by a Republican and NOM_2 the score if represented by a Democrat. The assumption of ignorabilty of treatment requires that $E(NOM_0 \mid \mathbf{C}, R) = E(NOM_0 \mid \mathbf{C})$ and $E(NOM_1 \mid \mathbf{C}, R) = E(NOM_1 \mid \mathbf{C})$. Wooldridge suggests estimating $\hat{\beta}$ using a "saturated" model including R, $\mathbf{C}$, and interactions of R and $\mathbf{C}$ (in sample mean deviations). The saturated models produced almost identical estimates with the $\gamma = 0$ restricted model, so we do not report them. Another approach to estimating the within-district polarization is the regression discontinuity method proposed by Lee, Moretti, and Butler (2005). This approach compares the ideal point estimates of winners of extremely close elections under the premise that those outcomes reflect almost random selection of the representative's party. This approach produces estimates of within-district polarization slightly smaller than those reported in model B. But like model B, these estimates have grown substantially over time.

12. Because each term directly follows reapportionment, constituency measures derived from the decennial census are more accurate reflections of current conditions in the district. A different selection of congressional terms would not affect our results.

13. The results are essentially unaffected by averaging the NOMINATE scores for districts with more than one representative in a congressional term.

14. For the 2000 census, we compute the percentage of African Americans by adding the number who identify solely as African American and those who chose any multiracial category that included African American.

15. Following the standard designation of the political South by *Congressional Quarterly*, the states are the eleven states of the Confederacy plus Oklahoma and Kentucky. We use this designation throughout the book.

16. In the next chapter, we will see that this nonmonotonic effect of education is apparent in voter choices and partisan identification.

17. In his study of Senate voting, Levitt (1996) finds that constituency plus national party can explain only 50% of the variance.

18. It is plausible that this null finding is due to the linear specification of the African-American percentage. Perhaps there is a threshold effect beyond which the percentage of African Americans moves the representative to the left. Given that majority African-American districts are all represented by African Americans, it would be hard to identify such a threshold with the available data. Nevertheless, it is worth noting that higher percentages of African Americans have no effect on the NOMINATE scores of African-American representatives.

19. A probit analysis predicting the party of the representative from the constituency characteristics supports this claim.

20. The lack of statistical significance for Hispanics may be due to their small numbers in the 93rd and 98th Houses.

21. There is one African-American Republican in our regressions, Gary Franks (CT) in the 103rd House. The coefficient on African American becomes slightly more negative (−0.242 vs. −0.224) when Franks is dropped from the sample.

22. Of the thirty-eight members of the Congressional Black Caucus in the 108th House, only eight had NOMINATE scores to the right of the median Democrat. Almost all are southern, are young, or have relatively small minority populations in their district.

23. Of course, the absolute size of the income gap would increase because of average income growth across all districts even if there were no change in the distribution of income across Republican and Democratic districts. But this effect accounts for only a quarter of the increased gap.

24. The APRE is simply the proportional reduction in error, as defined above, applied to all roll calls on a given issue.

25. The fact that these reforms also decentralized power by strengthening subcommittees is not stressed.

26. See Poole (2005) for a comprehensive discussion of this experiment for Houses 1 to 108.

27. Note that this method, in contrast to regression methods such as Snyder and Groseclose's (2000), does not require a uniform adjustment in the ideal points of all members of a party. Only moderates would need to be disciplined. All that is required is a displacement of the cutpoint.

28. We also find that for many of the estimated cutpoint pairs, the Democratic cutting line is to the left of the Republican cutting line, seemingly inconsistent with party pressure. There is some debate, even among ourselves (see Cox and Poole 2002), about how to interpret this result.

29. Contrary to conventional wisdom, the polarization increases in 1982 and 1992 are much larger than 2002.

30. Indeed, the 1982 and 1992 (but not the 2002) post-apportionment elections still produce larger than average increases in polarization.

31. With respect to this question, our results are somewhat at odds with Cameron, Epstein, and O'Halloran (1996). They argue that white representatives are sufficiently responsive to the size of their African-American constituencies to make the creation of majority—minority districts counterproductive from the perspective of black interests.

32. See Poole (2003).

33. In a recent paper, Carson et al. (2003) find that members representing newly created districts have NOMINATE scores that are more extreme than those from established districts. They did not distinguish between the effects of interregional seat reallocations and the effects of party gerrymandering.

34. These estimates are kernel densities which are essentially smoothed histograms. The bandwidth for these estimates is .025. Counties are weighted by population size so that the figures are not distorted by the Republican advantage in small counties.

35. It is appropriate to look at changes in polarization rather than levels, because of the trends in both polarization series.

Chapter 3

1. That 22% was lower than in recent elections and that Bush obtained no measurable gain from the marriage initiatives did little to slow this storyline.

2. Fiorina argues that the increased partisan differences are as likely to arise as a consequence of elite polarization (as voters better sort themselves into parties) than it is to arise from polarization among the voters.

3. Computed from Green, Palmquist, and Schickler (2002), table 2.3, p. 31. The percentage differences for presidential and midterm election years running from 1972 to 1996 are 25, 30, 32, 36, 34, 35, 36, 34, 36, 29, 38, 48, 50.

4. Frank, "American Psyche," *New York Times Book Review*, November 28, 2004.

5. For example, from comparative political economy, see Acemoglu and Robinson (2005), Alesina and Perotti (1995), Alesina and Rodrick (1993), Benabou (2000), Londregan and Poole (1990), Perotti (1996), and Persson and Tabellini (1994).

6. American Political Science Association (2004).

7. The focus of their work is the stability of individual partisan self-identification, whereas we focus on changes in the demographic correlates of partisan identification. Our main concern is income, but we also find, in addition to the changes in the South, an important shift with regard to gender.

8. In a recent study using a more extended set of occupational class categories, however, Manza and Brooks (1999) find that the class cleavage was stable from 1952 to 1996. Manza and Brooks also provide a nice review of the previous findings.

9. Party identification is measured on a seven-point scale in which the categories are "Strong Democrat, Weak Democrat, Lean Democrat, Independent, Lean Republican, Weak Republican, Strong Republican." This measure is constructed from several questions. Respondents are first asked to choose between Democrat, Independent, and Republican. "Democrats" are then asked if they are Strong or Weak. Ditto for "Republicans." "Independents" are asked if they "lean" to one of the parties. In our analysis of stratification in figure 3.1, we combine the strong and weak Republican categories. In our ordered probit analysis we use all seven categories. We divide the respondents into income quintiles using the Census Bureau's series on the distribution of household income. The details of the computation of our stratification measure are relegated to the appendix.

10. See Romer (1975), Roberts (1977), Meltzer and Richard (1981), Perotti (1996), and Roemer (1999).

11. Romer (1975, 1977), Roberts (1977), and Meltzer and Richard (1981) studied tax preferences when labor supply is considered.

12. Perhaps only gender and age are truly exogenous variables. Having a Republican identity may facilitate networking that increases income. As part of the networking process, Republican identifiers may strategically attend church or change opinions, as evident in George H. W. Bush's shifting from pro-choice to pro-life. Bishop (2004) has recently argued that residence, hence region, is influenced by political beliefs.

Proto-Democrats may find it easier to get high grades from liberal high school teachers. Even race may reflect political preferences, as it is self-identified.

13. Because of the coding of the 1962 NES, the District of Columbia and West Virginia are treated as southern for that year only.

14. Note that the average real income almost never equals exactly one. This is because the real average household income reported by the Census Bureau is used to compute the relative values. The deviations from unity are therefore a consequence of sampling variation within the NES. Figures in table 3.1 for females and blacks are also skewed by response and sampling issues.

15. We also estimated the model both with income effects "dummied" for each year and with each year estimated separately. The separate estimations allow all the coefficients and thresholds to vary over time. The results were substantively identical. As would be expected from inspection of figure 3.2, 1982 and 1998 are least consistent with the general pattern of the results.

16. The estimated growth of the income effect was stunted somewhat by the absence of an income effect in the 1998 NES. We explore this outlier in a subsequent section. If the 1998 election were dropped from the analysis, the trend coefficient would be 0.021 and the income effect for 1992–2002 in model 4 would be 0.175. The dashed line in figure 3.3 reflects the estimates if 1998 is dropped. The deletion of no other election produces such large changes. We discuss the 1998 midterm election in some detail below.

17. The shift to households headed by a single unmarried, separated, or divorced female is extensively documented in Ellwood and Jencks (2004).

18. For a study that links changes in the income distribution across genders to increased divorce rates and changes in the partisanship of women, see Edlund and Pande (2002). Because the NES income variable for female respondents records family income for a respondent from a family and individual income for a respondent from a single-person household, the fall in female income undoubtedly reflects the increased number of females now living in single households.

19. The results are substantively similar when we use other comparison years, such as 1956 and 1996.

20. The regional differences in support for impeachment are smaller than commonly believed. Overall 29% of the respondents supported impeachment and 38% of southern whites did.

21. These are derived from a model where the coefficients of demographic characteristics have linear time trends. Similar results obtain if each year is estimated separately.

22. Glaeser, Ponzetto, and Shapiro (2005) present results that suggest that religion and moral factors were not the source of elite polarization elaborated in our chapter 2. They show in figure 4 that the marginal effect of church attendance was higher in the 1968 and 1972 elections than in those of 1976, 1980, and 1984. Church attendance effects surpass their 1968 levels only in 1988 and 1992. (The figure has no results for 1996 and later.) The onset of polarization, shown in chapter 2, is well before 1988. The source of this polarization is clearly economic rather than religious. While it may be true that a polarized Republican elite succeeded in priming voters to vote more on the basis of religion, the work we report in this chapter shows that the effect of income on voting has increased as well. Moreover, Bartels (2005) argues that economic issues carry more weight with voters than do social ones.

23. It reads, "Would you call yourself a born-again Christian; that is, have you personally had a conversion experience related to Jesus Christ?"

24. Even this difference is somewhat exaggerated after we take into account that the born-again Christians live disproportionately in regions where the cost of living is low.

25. Given that Bartels (2000) finds that partisan identification has become a better predictor of the presidential vote during the period in which the income effect in party identification was increasing, it would have been quite surprising if the income effect in presidential voting had not increased.

26. There are no respondents from Alaska or Hawaii in these studies, and we omit the District of Columbia because of small sample sizes. The remaining sample sizes for each state-quintile combination range from 26 (high-income Wyoming) to 2605 (high-income California).

27. The *age* variable is the median age of residents in the county. The education variables *Some College* and *College Degree* are computed from the proportion of county residents over 24 in those categories. *African-American* is the percentage of self-reported African Americans in the county. Following the 2000 census, we combined all multi-race categories that included an African-American designation. The number of religious congregations is preferable to the number of members and adherents. There is significant variation as to how related membership and adherence are to actual observance and support of religious institutions. The number of congregations better reflected aggregate observance and support. The sample size is smaller when the number of congregations is included because of missing data.

28. Each observation is weighted by county population, and we cluster across counties over time in estimating the standard errors.

29. The full set of results is available at www.voteview.com. The sample size is smaller when demographics are included because of missing data on the number of congregations.

30. See www.census.gov/hhes/www/housing/hus/historic/hist14.html

31. We use a similar approach with data from the Current Population Survey (CPS) in chapter 4.

32. We thank Christine Eibner for sharing these data with us.

Chapter 4

1. Our computations are from the November Current Population Survey. The November CPS family income series includes single adult households but does not combine the incomes of unmarried individuals with the same residence.

2. Welch (1999) finds that inequality has increased much less when one looks within the population that remains in the labor force in two periods or within age cohorts. This also reinforces the main claim of this chapter—that the median voter's incentive to redistribute has not increased. Voters may take into account where they stand in the life cycle when making voting decisions.

3. See chapter 6 for a discussion of these changes in public policy.

4. See http://www.insee.fr/fr/ffc/chifcle_fiche.asp?ref_id=NATTEF02131&tab_id=339, viewed on December 7, 2004. We equate *"étrangers"* to noncitizens. Immigrants, comprising both noncitizens and naturalized (*"acquisition"*) citizens rose slightly from 9.1% to 9.6%. We should point out that France counts citizens of other EU nations as noncitizens even though there is free mobility of labor within the EU. The EU "noncitizens" would have had, until the recent admission of former Soviet bloc nations, a very different skill mix from that of the largely unskilled Latin American, Caribbean, and Asian immigrants who have come to the United States.

5. We thank Patrick Bolton for suggesting this decomposition.

6. Brady (2004, p. 692) presents evidence, like ours drawn from the CPS, that there has been little change in voter turnout by income quintile over the past thirty years. Summarizing the data in terms of the ratio of turnout in the top quintile to the bottom quintile, he finds no trend in midterm elections and an increasing trend in presidential elections. Some of the trend may reflect inaccuracies engendered by how Brady formed quintiles from the categorical data. Brady does not indicate whether he excluded noncitizens in forming the quintiles.

7. From 1972 to 1976 the CPS did not ask directly about citizenship status. These surveys, however, ask respondents who are not registered "why not?"—one of the possible responses is "not a citizen." We make the assumption that all noncitizens are captured by this registration question in this period. This assumption may be reasonably solid, as the percentage of noncitizens grew slowly but steadily from 1972 on.

8. In some National Election Studies, reported turnout was validated by checking to see if the respondent had actually voted. Palfrey and Poole (1987) compared results using reported and validated turnout in models of the effect of information on vote choice. Their results were not highly sensitive to the reported-validated distinction.

9. CPS respondents are interviewed once a month for four months, dropped for eight months, and then re-interviewed once a month for an additional four months. In general it is possible to link information on individuals across months. Because March and November do not fall within a four-month period, we cannot supplement our data with information from the March survey.

10. We used both linear and logarithmic interpolation. The results are highly similar.

11. In particular, the log-normal estimates of the median fall outside the boundary of the category that must (except for sampling error) contain the median as follows: noncitizens: 1976, 1992, 1996, and 2000; nonvoters: 1978, 1986, and 1990; voters: 1972, 1974, 1996, and 2000; all families, 1972, 1974, 1992, and 2000.

12. Results using linear interpolation are highly similar. For a detailed comparison of estimates of the median from the log-normal approximation, linear interpolation, and geometric interpolations, see Rosenthal and Eibner (2005).

13. We believe that the linear interpolation leads to an exaggeration of the all-family 80th centile for 1996, lowering all the ratios. The reason is that the 80th centile for 1996 falls in a very broad income category, $50,000 to $74,999, that is in the right tail of the distribution. Linear interpolation probably imputes too large a value to the income at the 80th centile, leading to a denominator in the ratios that is too large.

14. Again the problem is the centile falling in the $50,000–$74,999 income category. It is also possible that the stock market bubble of the late 1990s sharply increased the income of high-income families.

15. There are only two years, 1996 and 2002, where the percentage of noncitizens decreases from what it was two years earlier. The year 1996, however, was one of record naturalizations, presumably undertaken to benefit the Clinton administration in the 1996 elections. See Department of Homeland Security, (2004, p. 137). The 2002 exception was discussed previously in the main text.

16. Freeman (2004, p. 709) reports a regression similar (but with the dependent variable in log form) to ours, obtaining a positive but insignificant trend and a highly significant presidential-year effect. He then claims that turnout has declined by running a regression where the dependent variable is the natural logarithm of voters as a *proportion of the voting-age population* and the independent variables are trend, presidential year, and the log of the eligible as a proportion of the voting-age population. He views this procedure as a way of dealing with measurement error in the number of eligibles. But the log of the eligible has a t-statistic less than 1.0 in magnitude, which means that adjusted R^2 does not increase from a regression without this variable. It is thus difficult to use this specification to arrive at a firm conclusion of how turnout as a *proportion of the eligible* is changing.

17. Replicating the analysis using the log-normal estimates of the median gives results that are somewhat more favorable to our argument.

18. The self-reports of noncitizenship and ethnicity/race match up quite well with the official yearly statistics on immigrants admitted and naturalizations. See Department of Homeland Security (2004).

19. We begin this analysis in 1974 rather than 1972 because the November CPS did not ask about Hispanic ethnicity in 1972.

20. A private exchange with an academic demographer suggests that overreporting is largely a matter of citizenship claims by unauthorized Mexicans resident in the United States for less than 10 years. The overreport rate is "guesstimated" to be about 20%.

Chapter 5

1. Given that the average household net worth is $35,000, these investments in electoral politics are the equivalent of the typical American spending $525.

2. Steve Forbes is not on his own list. John Kerry's wife, Teresa Heinz Kerry, edged onto the list at $750 million, but her wealth was not a resource for his presidential campaign. Consequently, Kerry had to rely on contributors and his personal fortune of more than $160 million.

3. Corzine dipped further into his fortune to run for governor of New Jersey. Cantwell's story is more cautionary. After spending $10 million to win her seat, she saw her wealth evaporate as the "tech bubble" popped. She'll have to run for reelection the old-fashioned way. See Shaid 2001.

4. http://www.opensecrets.org/bigpicture/millionaires.asp?cycle=2002, downloaded April 27, 2005.

5. Because Senate financial disclosure forms omit the value of primary residences, this estimate is conservative. See Loughlin and Yoon (2003). By comparison, less than one percent of the U.S. population has assets exceeding a million dollars (see Merrill Lynch/ Cap Gemini Ernst & Young (2004)).

6. Section 527 of the Internal Revenue Act provides for organizations that may raise and disburse funds to influence elections. These groups are regulated by and report to the IRS rather than to the Federal Election commission. They may not engage in "express advocacy" for the election or defeat of any federal candidate. Many 527s are affiliated with PACs.

7. http://www.opensecrets.org/527s/527indivs.asp?cycle=2004.

8. Of the members of the Forbes list, only Steven Bing comes close to contributing 2% of his wealth to these groups ($13 million out of $750 million).

9. http://www.opensecrets.org/bigpicture/topindivs.asp?cycle=2002.

10. These figures include only expenditures made by the candidates themselves and do not include independent expenditures made by groups and parties on their behalf.

11. The implications of the increase in real campaign expenditures are open to some dispute. Ansolabehere, de Figueredo, and Snyder (2003) point out that campaign expenditures have not grown as fast as GDP, so campaign expenditures are a falling share of national income. The number of elected offices, however, has not grown on the federal level and is falling at the state and local level, so real spending rather than percentage of GDP seems to be the more appropriate metric.

12. Until the Bipartisan Campaign Finance Reform Act (BCFRA) of 2002, individuals could contribute $1000 to each PAC, and PACs could contribute $5000 per candidate per election (primary and general).

13. Individual contributions are reported to the FEC only if they exceed $200. Therefore the individual contribution totals used in the index are the sum of contributions exceeding $200. The truncation at $200 and the omission of the hundreds of millions of Americans who make zero contributions biases the indices downward. In estimating total contributions by individual, contributors are matched on first name, last name, and state of residence. When this procedure makes an incorrect match (e.g., a common name), the index is inflated a bit, but when it fails to make a match (multiple states of residence—common among the wealthy), the index is underestimated.

14. Other measures of inequality, such as the percentage of contributions made by the top one thousand contributors, show essentially the same pattern.

15. Kroszner and Stratmann (1998) present a particularly insightful discussion of how contributions should flow from interest groups to members.

16. More sophisticated approaches to estimating the ideological behavior of contributors can be found in Poole and Romer (1985) and McCarty and Poole (1999).

17. In this chapter, we use Poole's (1998) "common-space" transformation of NOMINATE so that we can pool contributions to House and Senate members.

18. If a contributor makes N contributions of amounts $d_1, \ldots, d_n$ to candidates with "common-space" adjusted NOMINATE scores $x_1, \ldots, x_n$ (see Poole 1998), then

$$M = \frac{\sum_{i=1}^{n} d_i x_i}{\sum_{i=1}^{n} d_i}$$

and

$$S = \sqrt{\frac{\sum\limits_{i=1}^{n} d_i(x_i - M)^2}{\sum\limits_{i=1}^{n} d_i}}.$$

19. The "unclassified" groups are those for which no interest group designation appears in the FEC master committee file.

20. Including less active political action committees would not alter the basic message of figure 5.4: the inverted U-shaped relationship holds for PACs making as few as eight contributions per cycle.

21. Lowess curves are generated by estimating the relationship between the variables for each narrow band of values in the domain. These local estimates are smoothed by fitting them to a high-order polynomial. These estimates are particularly useful in detecting nonlinearities.

22. Obtaining a value of $S > .577$ is consistent with concentrating contributions on both extremes.

23. This result holds up even when we control for the electoral vulnerability of the incumbent and other relevant factors.

24. One reason why there may be so many individuals with values of S exceeding .577 might be that extremists are more likely to build seniority and power. This scenario would produce bimodal access contributions generating values of S exceeding the random contribution benchmark.

25. Of course, there are other large soft-money contributors who do not give enough hard money to congressional candidates to estimate M. The largest of these is movie producer Steven Bing.

26. This finding is not surprising, however, given S's close relationship to M^2.

27. The results from a Tobit model are very similar. The Heckman model cannot be used because the selection and outcome equations have the same regressors.

28. The fact that M^2 is significant only at the .07 (two-tailed) level is due to its correlation with S. Running the model without S produces a p-value of .001. The joint test of M and M^2 in the full model is also highly significant.

29. See McCarty and Rothenberg (2001) for a formal model of these tradeoffs.

30. See Noah (2004). According to opensecrets.org, the Club for Growth spent more than $13 million, making it the ninth-largest 527 group. This money does not include the more than $4 million raised and spent by its Internet fundraising arm, clubforgrowth.net.

Chapter 6

1. Poole and Rosenthal (1991) provide a more extensive discussion of congressional action on minimum wages through the 1980s.

2. Information found in the Voteview database available at voteview.ucsd.edu.

3. Minimum wage data from U.S. Department of Labor Employment Standards Administration Wage and Hour Division, published April 23, 2005, at http://www.dol.gov/esa/minwage/america.htm. The underlying document was revised in December 2004 to give wages as of January 1, 2005.

4. On the other hand, the Generation Skipping Tax was introduced, an innovation that made estate tax more onerous for very rich families.

5. See http://www.falc.com/flp/flp.htm, downloaded May 17, 2005.

6. Similarly, Medicaid, ostensibly a program to provide medical care for the indigent, now has a large component that provides nursing home care to the elderly. Federal reductions in Medicaid have encountered substantial resistance from governors of both parties.

7. The average level of polarization during postwar divided governments is .64, while the average for unified governments is .55. The difference is statistically significant at the .0246 level (one-tailed test). Such a correlation is predicted by "party balancing" models of voter behavior (e.g., Fiorina 1996, Alesina and Rosenthal 1995, Mebane 2000, Mebane and Sekhon 2002). These theories argue that moderate voters have incentives to split their tickets in order to force polarized parties to bargain towards moderate policies.

8. See Cameron (2000) for the application of bargaining theory to policymaking.

9. See Krehbiel (1998) and Brady and Volden (1998).

10. The most prominent exceptions are budget reconciliation bills, which require only a majority vote. More on this topic below.

11. This formulation embeds a couple of additional assumptions. First, it assumes that the president is generally more extreme than the veto pivots. Second, it assumes that the preferences in the U.S. House are similar enough to those of the Senate that obtaining cloture or an override in the Senate is sufficient to ensure a majority in the House. These are all reasonable approximations.

12. The Byrd Rule, named for Senator Robert Byrd (D-WV), specifies that a point of order may be called on any provision in a reconciliation bill that authorizes discretionary appropriations and provisions increasing entitlement spending or cuts taxes beyond the five (or more)-year window provided for in the reconciliation directive. Because it takes sixty votes to waive the rule, failure to abide by its terms essentially removes the parliamentary protections otherwise afforded reconciliation bills.

13. See Gilmour (1995) and Groseclose and McCarty (2000).

14. The lack of data on trust before the 1970s makes it difficult to evaluate the ability of this hypothesis to explain longer-term trends in polarization.

15. See Mayhew (1991) for the details of his compilation of significant statutes. Figure 6.5 uses both the data published in his original study and his subsequent updates. It also combines Mayhew's series based contemporary judgments with his series based on retrospective judgments.

16. These data are from Petersen (2001) and Clinton and Lapinski (nd).

17. Many political economy models of redistribution predict that there will be more redistribution following increases in pretax and transfer income inequality (e.g., Meltzer

and Richard 1981 and Romer 1975). Our arguments about polarization and gridlock may explain why this redistribution did not happen in the United States.

18. Programs with large middle-class constituencies such as Social Security and Medicare are generally indexed. There are some tax policies, however, such as the Alternative Minimum Tax, where the lack of indexing has negative effects on portions of the upper middle class.

19. One reason states have not indexed the benefits is that the federal block grants are not indexed.

20. Quite similar findings with respect to the adjustment of state fiscal policies are reported by Alt and Lowry (2000).

21. Howell (2003) documents such an effect with respect to the overall issuance of executive orders, and Lewis (2003) finds that presidents are more likely to create agencies by executive order rather than statute when there is inter-branch policy conflict. Moreover, Lewis finds that agencies created by presidential order are often short-lived and underfunded.

22. Such arguments are consistent with the "Separation of Powers" model of judicial decisionmaking. See Ferejohn and Shipan (1990) and Spiller and Gely (1992) for the theory and evidence.

23. See Epstein and O'Halloran (1999).

24. That the September 11 terrorist attacks occurred just eight months into a new administration may not be coincidence.

Chapter 7

1. The president is also, for all intents and purposes, chosen by plurality rule. Although the electoral college can give a result that differs from the popular vote plurality, as was the case in 2000, the presidential election is—barring the knife's edge case that would send the election to the House—a mechanism for aggregating individual votes to choose just one elected individual.

2. See Wittman (1977, 1983) and Calvert (1985).

3. Our argument is consistent with that of Wittman (1983). Such logic is formalized in Groseclose's (2001) extension of Wittman's model.

4. In a proportional representation system, extreme parties that diverge lose votes to moderate parties. As these centrist parties are often pivotal in government formation, the effects of polarization are also lessened. Austen-Smith (2000) presents a model of redistributive politics under proportional representation. The model, however, has no obvious analog under plurality rule. Therefore, he compares his results to the median voter theorem.

5. See chapter 3 for a discussion of our measures of state partisanship by income quintile from the Pew surveys.

6. See Ansolabehere and Stewart (2005).

7. The 2004 National Election Study estimates that 38% of Hispanics voted for George W. Bush, only slightly higher than the 35% of the 2000 election. His African-American vote

went up from 8% to slightly less than 10%. His vote among whites increased more than it did among either of these two groups.

8. Although families with incomes lower than the median for their state can still use chapter 7, they are subject to "credit counseling" and other measures that raise the cost of bankruptcy.

9. Democratic support for AMT reform is somewhat ironic, in that most taxpayers filing under the AMT have family incomes well in excess of $100,000, while the last two Democratic platforms have called for the repeal of tax cuts to families with incomes over $200,000 and tax cuts for those making less than $75,000.

10. The third member of the trio grew up in the 1970s, with gasoline lines and a general sense of malaise.

References

Acemoglu, Daron, and James A. Robinson. 2005. *Economic Origins of Dictatorship and Democracy: Economic and Political Origins.* New York: Cambridge University Press.

Alesina, Alberto. 1988. "Credibility and Policy Convergence in a Two-Party System with Rational Voters." *American Economic Review* 78(4): 796–805.

Alesina, Alberto, Reza Baqir, and William Easterly. 1999. "Public Goods and Ethnic Divisions." *Quarterly Journal of Economics* 114(4): 1243–1284.

Alesina, Alberto, and Edward L. Glaeser. 2004. *Fighting Poverty in the U.S. and Europe.* New York: Oxford University Press.

Alesina, Alberto, and Eliana La Ferrara. 2000. "Participation in Heterogeneous Communities." *Quarterly Journal of Economics* 115(3): 847–904.

Alesina, Alberto, and Eliana La Ferrara. 2002. "Who Trusts Others?" *Journal of Public Economics* 85(2): 207–234.

Alesina, Alberto, and Roberto Perotti. 1995. "Income Distribution, Political Instability, and Investment." *European Economic Review* 40(6): 1203–1228.

Alesina, Alberto, and Dani Rodrick. 1993. "Income Distribution and Economic Growth: A Simple Theory and Some Empirical Evidence." In Alex Cukierman, Zvi Herscovitz, and Leonardo Leiderman, eds. *The Political Economy of Business Cycles and Growth.* Cambridge, MA: MIT Press.

Alesina, Alberto, and Howard Rosenthal. 1995. *Partisan Politics, Divided Government, and the Economy.* New York: Cambridge University Press.

Alesina, Alberto, and Howard Rosenthal. 2000. "Polarized Platforms and Moderate Policies with Checks and Balances." *Journal of Public Economics* 75(1): 1–20.

Alt, James, and Robert Lowry. 2000. "A Dynamic Model of State Budget Outcomes under Divided Partisan Government." *Journal of Politics* 62(4): 1035–1069.

Altonji, Joseph, and David Card. 1989. "The Effects of Immigration on the Labor Market Outcomes of Natives." National Bureau of Economic Research Working Paper No. 3123.

American Political Science Association. 1950. "Toward a More Responsible Two-Party System: A Report of the Committee on Political Parties." *American Political Science Review* 44(3): Part 2, Supplement.

American Political Science Association. 2004. "Inequality and Governance." Report of the Task Force on Inequality and American Democracy.

Ansolabehere, Stephen, John de Figueredo, and James Snyder. 2003. "Why Is There So Little Money in Politics?" *Journal of Economic Perspectives* 17(1): 105–130.

Ansolabehere, Stephen, and Charles Stewart. 2005. "Truth in Numbers." *Boston Review* 30 (February/March).

Atkinson, A. B. 1997. "Bringing Income Distribution in From the Cold." *Economic Journal* 107(441): 297–321.

Austen-Smith, David. 2000. "Redistributing Income under Proportional Representation." *Journal of Political Economy* 108(6): 1235–1269.

Bartels, Larry M. 2000. "Partisanship and Voting Behavior, 1952–1996." *American Journal of Political Science* 44(1): 35–50.

Bartels, Larry M. 2002. "Economic Inequality and Political Representation." Presented at the Annual Meeting of the American Political Science Association, Boston.

Bartels, Larry M. 2004. "Partisan Politics and the U.S. Income Distribution, 1948–2000." Typescript, Princeton University.

Bartels, Larry M. 2005. "What's the Matter with *Whats' the Matter with Kansas*." Paper presented at 2005 American Political Science Association, Washington D.C.

Bean, Frank D., and Stephanie Bell-Rose. 1999. "Introduction" in Bean and Bell-Rose, eds. *Immigration and Opportunity: Race, Ethnicity, and Employment in the United States*. New York: Russell Sage Foundation, 1–28.

Bell, Daniel. 1960. *The End of Ideology: On the Exhaustion of Political Ideas in the Fifties*. Cambridge, MA: Harvard University Press.

Benabou, Roland. 2000. "Unequal Societies: Income Distribution and the Social Contract." *American Economic Review* 90(1): 96–129.

Bishop, Bill. 2004. "The Schism in U.S. Politics Begins at Home." *Austin American-Statesman*, April 4.

Bolton, Patrick, and Gerard Roland. 1997. "The Breakup of Nations." *Quarterly Journal of Economics* 112(4): 1057–1090.

Borjas, George J. 1987. "Immigrants, Minorities, and Labor Market Competition." *Industrial and Labor Relations Review* 40(3): 382–392.

Borjas, George J. 1999. *Heaven's Door: Immigration Policy and the American Economy*. Princeton, NJ: Princeton University Press.

Borjas, George J. 2003. "The Labor Demand Curve *Is* Downward Sloping: Reexamining the Impact of Immigration on the Labor Market." *Quarterly Journal of Economics* 118(4): 1335–1376.

Borjas, George J., Richard B. Freeman, and Lawrence F. Katz. 1997. "How Much Do Immigration and Trade Affect Labor Market Outcomes?" *Brookings Papers on Economic Activity* 1997(1): 1–67.

Bott, Alexander J. 1990. *Handbook of U.S. Election Laws and Practices*. New York: Greenwood Press.

Brady, David W., and Craig Volden. 1998. *Revolving Gridlock: Politics and Policy from Carter to Clinton*. Boulder, CO: Westview Press.

Brady, Henry. 2004. "An Analytical Perspective on Participatory Inequality and Income Inequality." In Kathy Neckerman, ed. *Social Inequality*. New York: Russell Sage Foundation.

Brunell, Thomas L., and Bernard Grofman. 1998. "Explaining Divided Senate Delegations: A Realignment Approach." *American Political Science Review* 92(2): 391–399.

Callander, Steven. 2004. "Electoral Competition in Heterogeneous Districts." Typescript, Northwestern University.

Calvert, Randall L. 1985. "Robustness of the Multidimensional Voting Model: Candidate Motivations, Uncertainty, and Convergence." *American Journal of Political Science* 29(1): 69–95.

Cameron, Charles. 2000. *Veto Bargaining: Presidents and the Politics of Negative Power*. New York: Cambridge University Press.

Cameron, Charles, David Epstein, and Sharyn O'Halloran. 1996. "Do Majority-Minority Districts Maximize Black Substantive Representation in Congress?" *American Political Science Review* 90(4): 794–812.

Carmines, Edward G., and James Stimson. 1989. *Issue Evolution: Race and the Transformation of American Politics*. Princeton, NJ: Princeton University Press.

Carroll, Christopher D. 2002. "Portfolios of the Rich." In Luigi Guiso, M. Haliassos, and Tullio Jappelli, eds. *Household Portfolios*. Cambridge, MA: MIT Press.

Carson, Jamie L., Michael H. Crespin, Charles J. Finocchiaro, and David Rohde. 2003. "Linking Congressional Districts across Time: Redistricting and Party Polarization in Congress." Paper presented at the 2003 Midwest Political Science Association Meetings, Chicago, Illinois.

Clausen, Aage R. 1973. *How Congressmen Decide: A Policy Focus*. New York: St. Martin's Press.

Clinton, Joshua, Simon Jackman, and Douglas Rivers. 2004. "The Statistical Analysis of Roll Call Data." *American Political Science Review* 98(2): 355–370.

Clinton, Joshua, and John Lapinski. Forthcoming. "Measuring Significant Legislation, 1877–1948." In David Brady and Matthew McCubbins, eds. *Process, Party, and Policymaking: Further New Perspectives on the History of Congress*. Palo Alto, CA: Stanford University Press.

Costa, Dora L., and Matthew E. Kahn. 2003a. "Civic Engagement and Community Heterogeneity: An Economist's Perspective." *Perspectives on Politics* 1(1): 103–111.

Costa, Dora L., and Matthew E. Kahn. 2003b. "Understanding the American Decline in Social Capital, 1952–1998." *Kyklos* 56(1): 17–46.

Cox, Gary W., and Jonathan N. Katz. 2002. *Elbridge Gerry's Salamander: The Electoral Consequences of the Reapportionment Revolution*. New York: Cambridge University Press.

Cox, Gary W., and Mathew D. McCubbins. 1993. *Legislative Leviathan: Party Government in the House*. Berkeley: University of California Press.

Cox, Gary W., and Mathew D. McCubbins. 2005. *Setting the Agenda: Responsible Party Government in the U.S. House of Representatives*. New York: Cambridge University Press.

Cox, Gary W., and Keith T. Poole. 2002. "On Measuring Partisanship in Roll-Call Voting: The U.S. House of Representatives, 1877–1999." *American Journal of Political Science* 46(3): 477–489.

Dahl, Robert A. 1961. *Who Governs: Democracy and Power in an American City*. New Haven: Yale University Press.

Department of Homeland Security. 2004. *2003 Yearbook of Immigration Statistics*. Office of Immigration Statistics.

DiMaggio, Paul, John Evans, and Bethany Bryson. 1996. "Have Americans' Social Attitudes Become More Polarized?" *American Journal of Sociology* 102(3): 690–755.

Downs, Anthony. 1957. *An Economic Theory of Democracy*. New York: Harper and Row.

Duca, John V., and Jason L. Saving. 2002. "The Political-Economy of the Mutual Fund Revolution: How Rising Stock-Ownership Rates Affect Congressional Elections." Working paper, Federal Reserve Bank of Dallas.

Duverger, Maurice. 1954. *Political Parties*. New York: Wiley.

Edlund, Lena, and Rohini Pande. 2002. "Why Have Women Become Left-Wing? The Political Gender Gap and the Decline of Marriage." *Quarterly Journal of Economics* 117(3): 917–962.

Ellenberg, Jordan. 2001. "Growing Apart: The Mathematical Evidence for Congress' Growing Polarization." *Slate*. Posted December 26.

Ellwood, David T., and Christopher Jencks. 2004. "The Uneven Spread of Single-Parent Families: What Do We Know? Where Do We Look for Answers?" In Kathryn Neckerman, ed. *Social Inequality*, 3–79. New York: Russell Sage Foundation.

Epstein, David, and Sharyn O'Halloran. 1999. *Delegating Powers: A Transaction Cost Politics Approach to Policy Making under Separate Powers*. New York: Cambridge University Press.

Evans, John H. 2003. "Have Americans' Attitudes Become More Polarized? An Update." *Social Science Quarterly* 84(1): 71–90.

Farhang, Sean. 2003. "The Litigation State: Public Regulation and Private Lawsuits in the American Separation of Powers System." Typescript, Columbia University.

Ferejohn, John, and Charles Shipan. 1990. "Congressional Influence on Bureaucracy." *Journal of Law, Economics, and Organization* 6(1): 1–21.

Fey, Mark. 1997. "Stability and Coordination in Duverger's Law: A Formal Model of Pre-election Polls and Strategic Voting." *American Political Science Review* 91(1): 135–147.

Fiorina, Morris. 1978. *Congress: Keystone of the Washington Establishment*. New Haven: Yale University Press.

Fiorina, Morris. 1996. *Divided Government*. Second Edition. Boston: Allyn and Bacon.

Fiorina, Morris, with Samuel J. Abrams and Jeremy C. Pope. 2004. *Culture War? The Myth of Polarized America*. New York: Longman.

Fiorina 2004

Foley, Duncan K. 1967. "Resource Allocation and the Public Sector." *Yale Economic Essays* 7: 45–98.

Fowler, Linda L. 1982. "How Interest Groups Select Issues for Rating Voting Records of Members of the U.S. Congress." *Legislative Studies Quarterly* 7(3): 401–413.

Frank, Thomas. 2004a. *What's the Matter with Kansas: How Conservatives Won the Heart of America*. Metropolitan Books.

Frank, Thomas. 2004b. "American Psyche." *New York Times Book Review*, November 28.

Freeman, Richard B. 2004. "What, Me Vote?" In Kathryn E. Neckerman, ed. *Social Inequality*, 667–702. New York: Russell Sage Foundation.

Gerber, Elisabeth R., and Rebecca B. Morton. 1998. "Primary Election Systems and Representation." *Journal of Law, Economics, and Organization* 14(2): 304–324.

Gerring, John. 1998. *Party Ideologies in America, 1828–1996*. New York: Cambridge University Press.

Gilens, Martin. 1999. *Why Americans Hate Welfare: Race, Media, and the Politics of Antipoverty Policy*. Chicago: University of Chicago Press.

Gilens, Martin. 2005. "Public Preferences and Public Policy: Democratic Responsiveness and the Heavenly Choir." Paper presented at the Fifth Annual Meeting of the University Working Groups on the Social Dimensions of Inequality, Berkeley, California.

Gilmour, John. 1995. *Strategic Disagreement: Stalemate in American Politics*. Pittsburgh: University of Pittsburgh Press.

Glaeser, Edward L., Giacomo A. M. Ponzetto, Jesse M. Shapiro. 2005. "Strategic Extremism: Why Republicans and Democrats Divide on Religious Values." *Quarterly Journal of Economics* 120(1): 1283–1330.

Glenmary Research Center. 2004. *Religious Congregations and Membership in the United States*.

Goldin, Claudia. 1994. "The Political Economy of Immigration Restriction: The United States, 1890–1921." In Claudia Goldin and Gary Libecap, eds. *The Regulated Economy: A Historical Approach to Political Economy*. Chicago: University of Chicago Press.

Green, Donald, Bradley Palmquist, and Eric Schickler. 2002. *Partisan Hearts and Minds: Political Parties and the Social Identities of Voters*. New Haven: Yale University Press.

Groseclose, Tim. 2001. "A Model of Candidate Location When One Candidate Has a Valence Advantage." *American Journal of Political Science* 45(4): 862–886.

Groseclose, Tim, Steven D. Levitt, and James M. Snyder Jr. 1999. "Comparing Interest Group Scores across Time and Chambers: Adjusted ADA Scores for the U.S. Congress." *American Political Science Review* 93(1): 33–50.

Groseclose, Timothy, and Nolan McCarty. 2000. "The Politics of Blame: Bargaining before an Audience." *American Journal of Political Science* 45(1): 100–119.

Guiso, Luigi, M. Haliassos, and Tullio Jappelli. 2002. *Household Portfolios*. Cambridge, MA: MIT Press.

Hacker, Jacob S. 2004. "Privatizing Risk without Privatizing the Welfare State: The Hidden Politics of Social Policy Retrenchment in the United States." *American Political Science Review* 98(2): 243–260.

Heckman, James, and James Snyder. 1997. "Linear Probability Models of the Demand for Attributes with an Empirical Application to Estimating the Preferences of Legislators." *Rand Journal of Economics* 28: S142–S189.

Hetherington, Marc J. 2004. *Why Trust Matters: Declining Political Trust and the Demise of American Liberalism*. Princeton, NJ: Princeton University Press.

Howell, William. 2003. *Power without Persuasion: The Politics of Direct Presidential Action*. Princeton, NJ: Princeton University Press.

Howell, William, Scott Adler, Charles Cameron, and Charles Riemann. 2000. "Divided Government and the Legislative Productivity of Congress, 1945–1994." *Legislative Studies Quarterly* 25(2): 285–312.

Jacobs, Lawrence R., and Benjamin I. Page. 2005. "Who Influences U.S. Foreign Policy?" *American Political Science Review* 99(1): 107–123.

Kalt, Joseph P., and Mark A. Zupan. 1984. "Capture and Ideology in Politics." *American Economic Review* 74(3): 279–300.

Key, V. O. 1949. *Southern Politics in State and Nation*. New York: A. A. Knopf.

King, David C. 1997. "The Polarization of American Political Parties and Mistrust of Government." In Joseph S. Nye, Philip Zelikow, and David C. King, eds. *Why People Don't Trust Government*. Cambridge, MA: Harvard University Press.

King, David C. 2003. "Congress, Polarization, and Fidelity to the Median Voter." Kennedy School of Government working paper, Harvard University.

Krehbiel, Keith. 1998. *Pivotal Politics: A Theory of U.S. Lawmaking*. Chicago: University of Chicago Press.

Kroszner, Randall S., and Thomas Stratmann. 1998. "Interest-Group Competition and the Organization of Congress: Theory and Evidence from Financial Services' Political Action Committees." *American Economic Review* 88(5): 1163–1187.

Lalonde, Robert J., and Robert W. Topel. 1989. "Labor Market Adjustments to Increased Immigration." In Richard B. Freeman, ed. *Immigration, Trade, and the Labor Market*. Chicago: University of Chicago Press and the National Bureau of Economic Research.

Lee, David S. 1999. "Wage Inequality in the United States during the 1980s: Rising Dispersion or Falling Minimum Wage?" *Quarterly Journal of Economics* 114(3): 977–1023.

Lee, David S., Enrico Moretti, and Matthew J. Butler. 2005. "Do Voters Affect or Elect Policies? Evidence from the U.S. House." *Quarterly Journal of Economics* 119(3): 807–859.

Lerman, Robert. 1999. "U.S. Wage Inequality Trends and Recent Immigration." *American Economic Review: Papers and Proceedings* 89(2): 23–28.

Levitt, Steven D. 1996. "How Do Senators Vote? Disentangling the Role of Voter Preferences, Party Affiliation, and Senator Ideology." *American Economic Review* 86(3): 425–441.

Lewis, David E. 2003. *Presidents and the Politics of Agency Design*. Stanford, CA: Stanford University Press.

Lijphart, Arend. 1997. "Unequal Participation: Democracy's Unresolved Dilemma." *American Political Science Review* 91(1): 1–14.

Londregan, John, and Keith T. Poole. 1990. "Poverty, the Coup Trap, and the Seizure of Executive Power." *World Politics* 62(2): 151–183.

Loughlin, Sean, and Robert Yoon. 2003. "Millionaires Populate U.S. Senate." Accessed at http://www.cnn.com/2003/ALLPOLITICS/06/13/senators.finances/.

Luttmer, Erzo. 2001. "Group Loyalty and the Taste for Redistribution." *Journal of Political Economy* 109(3): 500–528.

Manza, Jeff, and Clem Brooks. 1999. *Social Cleavages and Political Change: Voter Alignments and U.S. Party Coalitions.* New York: Oxford University Press.

Mayhew, David R. 1991. *Divided We Govern: Party Control, Lawmaking, and Investigations, 1946–1990.* New Haven: Yale University Press.

McCarty, Nolan. Forthcoming. "The Policy Consequences of Political Polarization." In Paul Pierson and Theda Skocpol, eds. *The Transformation of American Politics.* Princeton, NJ: Princeton University Press.

McCarty, Nolan, and Keith T. Poole. 1999. "An Empirical Spatial Model of Congressional Campaigns." *Political Analysis* 7(1): 1–30.

McCarty, Nolan, Keith T. Poole, and Howard Rosenthal. 1997. *Income Redistribution and the Realignment of American Politics.* Washington, DC: American Enterprise Institute.

McCarty, Nolan, Keith T. Poole, and Howard Rosenthal. 2001. "The Hunt for Party Discipline in Congress." *American Political Science Review* 95(3): 673–687.

McCarty, Nolan, and Rose Razaghian. 1999. "Advice and Consent: Senate Response to Executive Branch Nominations, 1885–1996." *American Journal of Political Science* 43(3): 1122–1143.

McCarty, Nolan, and Lawrence Rothenberg. 2001. "A Model of Interest Group Alliances with Politicians." Paper presented at the Public Choice Society, New Orleans, Louisiana.

McDonald, Michael P., and Samuel Popkin. 2001. "The Myth of the Vanishing Voter." *American Political Science Review* 95(4): 963–974.

McKelvey, Richard D., and William Zavoina. 1975. "A Statistical Model for the Analysis of Ordinal Level Dependent Variables." *Journal of Mathematical Sociology* 4: 103–120.

Mebane, Walter R. 2000. "Coordination, Moderation, and Institutional Balancing in American Presidential and House Elections." *American Political Science Review* 94(1): 37–57.

Mebane, Walter R., and Jasjeet S. Sekhon. 2002. "Coordination and Policy Moderation at Midterm." *American Political Science Review* 96(1): 141–157.

Meltzer, Allan H., and Scott F. Richard. 1981. "A Rational Theory of the Size of Government." *Journal of Political Economy* 89(5): 914–927.

Merrill Lynch/Cap Gemini Ernst & Young. 2004. *World Wealth Report 2004.* Accessed at http://www.ml.com/index.asp?id=7695_7696_8149_6261_14832_14938.

Micklethwait, John, and Adrian Wooldridge. 2004. *The Right Nation: Conservative Power in America.* New York: Penguin Books.

Myrdal, Gunnar. 1960. *Beyond the Welfare State: Economic Planning and its International Implications*. New Haven: Yale University Press.

Noah, Tim. "Who's Afraid of the Club for Growth?" *Slate*. November 16, 2004.

Palfrey, Thomas R. 1989. "A Mathematical Proof of Duverger's Law." In Peter Ordeshook, ed. *Models of Strategic Choice in Politics*. Ann Arbor: University of Michigan Press.

Palfrey, Thomas R., and Keith T. Poole. 1987. "The Relationship between Information, Ideology, and Voting Behavior." *American Journal of Political Science* 31(3): 511–530.

Perlstein, Rick. 2001. *Before the Storm: Barry Goldwater and the Unmaking of the American Consensus*. New York: Hill and Wang.

Perotti, Roberto. 1996. "Political Equilibrium, Income Distribution, and Growth." *Review of Economic Studies* 60(4): 755–776.

Persson, Torsten, and Guido Tabellini. 1994. "Is Inequality Harmful for Growth? Theory and Evidence." *American Economic Review* 84(3): 600–621.

Petersen, R. Eric. 2001. "Is It Science Yet? Replicating and Validating the *Divided We Govern* List of Important Statutes." Presented at the Annual Meeting of the Midwest Political Science Association, Chicago, Illinois.

Phillips, Kevin. 2002. *Wealth and Democracy: A Political History of the American Rich*. New York: Broadway Books.

Piketty, Thomas, and Emmanuel Saez. 2003. "Income Inequality in the United States, 1913–1998." *Quarterly Journal of Economics* 118(1): 1–39.

Poole, Keith T. 1984. "Least Squares Metric, Unidimensional Unfolding." *Psychometrica* 49: 311–323.

Poole, Keith T. 1998. "Recovering a Basic Space from a Set of Issue Scales." *American Journal of Political Science* 42(3): 954–993.

Poole, Keith T. 2000. "Non-Parametric Unfolding of Binary Choice Data." *Political Analysis* 8(3): 211–237.

Poole, Keith T. 2003. "Changing Minds, Not in Congress!" Typescript, University of California, San Diego.

Poole, Keith T. 2005. *Spatial Models of Parliamentary Voting*. New York: Cambridge University Press.

Poole, Keith T., and R. Steven Daniels. 1985. "Ideology, Party, and Voting in the U.S. Congress, 1959–1980." *American Political Science Review* 79(2): 373–399.

Poole, Keith T., and Thomas Romer. 1985. "Patterns of Political Action Committee Contributions to the 1980 Campaigns for the U.S. House of Representatives." *Public Choice* 47(1): 63–111.

Poole, Keith T., and Thomas Romer. 1993. "Ideology, Shirking, and Representation." *Public Choice* 77(1): 185–196.

Poole, Keith T., and Howard Rosenthal. 1984. "The Polarization of American Politics." *Journal of Politics* 46(4): 1061–1079.

Poole, Keith T., and Howard Rosenthal. 1991. "The Spatial Mapping of Minimum Wage Legislation." In Alberto Alesina and Geoffrey Carliner, eds. *Politics and Economics in the 1980s*. Chicago: University of Chicago Press.

Poole, Keith T., and Howard Rosenthal. 1997. *Congress: A Political-Economic History of Roll Call Voting*. New York: Oxford University Press.

Putnam, Robert. 2000. *Bowling Alone: The Collapse and Revival of American Community*. New York: Simon and Schuster.

Quadagno, Jill S. 1994. *The Color of Welfare: How Racism Undermined the War on Poverty*. Oxford: Oxford University Press.

Roberts, Kevin W. S. 1977. "Voting over Income Tax Schedules." *Journal of Public Economics* 8(3): 329–340.

Roemer, John. 1999. "The Democratic Political Economy of Progressive Income Taxation." *Econometrica* 67(1): 1–19.

Rohde, David W. 1991. *Parties and Leaders in the Post-Reform House*. Chicago: University of Chicago Press.

Romer, Thomas. 1975. "Individual Welfare, Majority Voting, and the Properties of a Linear Income Tax." *Journal of Public Economics* 4(2): 163–185.

Romer, Thomas. 1977. "Majority Voting on Tax Parameters: Some Further Result." *Journal of Public Economics* 7(1): 127–133.

Rosenthal, Howard, and Christine Eibner. 2005. "Immigration and the Median Voter's Incentive to Redistribute Income in the United States." Paper presented at the ASCE meetings, Budapest, Hungary, June 29–July 2.

Shaid, Anthony. 2001. "Sen. Dot-Com." *Boston Globe*, May 21.

Snyder, James. 1992. "Artificial Extremism in Interest Group Ratings." *Legislative Studies Quarterly* 17(3): 319–345.

Snyder, James, and Tim Groseclose. 2000. "Estimating Party Influence in Congressional Roll-Call Voting." *American Journal of Political Science* 44(2): 193–211.

Snyder, James M., and Michael M. Ting. 2002. "An Informational Rationale for Political Parties." *American Journal of Political Science* 46(1): 90–110.

Sorauf, Frank J. 1992. *Inside Campaign Finance: Myths and Realities*. New Haven: Yale University Press.

Spiller, Pablo, and Raphael Gely. 1992. "Congressional Control or Judicial Independence: The Determinants of U.S. Supreme Court Labor-Relations Decisions, 1949–1988." *Rand Journal of Economics* 23(4): 463–492.

Stonecash, Jeffrey M., Mark D. Brewer, and Mack D. Mariani. 2003. *Diverging Parties: Social Change, Realignment, and Political Polarization*. Boulder, CO: Westview Press.

Sundquist, James L. 1981. *The Decline and Resurgence of Congress*. Washington, DC: Brookings Institution.

Uggen, Christopher, and Jeff Manza. 2002. "Democratic Contraction? Political Consequences of Felon Disenfranchisement in the United States." *American Sociological Review* 67(6): 777–803.

Urban Institute. 2005. *Welfare Rules Database.* Accessed at http://www.urban.org/Content/Research/NewFederalism/Data/ANFData.htm.

U.S. Census Bureau. 2005. "Table F–4. Gini Ratios for Families, by Race and Hispanic Origin of Householder: 1947 to 2003." Accessed at http://www.census.gov/hhes/income/histinc/f04.html.

Weingast, Barry R., Kenneth A. Shepsle, and Christopher Johnsen. 1981. "The Political Economy of Benefits and Costs: A Neoclassical Approach to Distributive Politics." *Journal of Political Economy* 89(4): 642–664.

Welch, Finnis. 1999. "In Defense of Inequality." *American Economic Review: Papers and Proceedings* 89(2): 1–17.

Western, Bruce, Josh Guetzkow, and Jake Rosenfeld. 2004. "State-Level Data on Income Inequality, 1963–2002." Accessed at http://www.princeton.edu/~joshg/inequality.htm.

Wittman, Donald. 1977. "Candidates with Policy Preferences: A Dynamic Model." *Journal of Economic Theory* 14(1): 180–189.

Wittman, Donald. 1983. "Candidate Motivation: A Synthesis of Alternatives." *American Political Science Review* 77(1): 142–157.

Wolff, Edward N. 2002. "Recent Trends in Living Standards in the United States." Typescript, New York University.

Wolfinger, Raymond E., and Steven J. Rosenstone. 1980. *Who Votes?* New Haven: Yale University Press.

Woodward, C. Vann. 1951. *Reunion and Reaction: The Compromise of 1877 and the End of Reconstruction.* Boston: Little, Brown.

Wooldridge, Jeffrey M. 2001. *Econometric Analysis of Cross Section and Panel Data.* Cambridge, MA: MIT Press.

Index